This book is dedicated to Cyrus Emerson

and

Beston J. & Ethel Emerson

the Applegate Trail of 1846

A Documentary Guide to the Original Southern Emigrant Route to Oregon
by William Emerson

Figure 1 Goose Lake at sunset

the Applegate Trail of 1846

A Documentary Guide to the Original Southern Emigrant Route to Oregon

by William Emerson

EMBER ENTERPRISES, PUBLISHERS
P.O. BOX 1343 ASHLAND, OR 97520-0045 USA

Cataloging-in-Publication Data
Emerson, William
The Applegate Trail of 1846: A Documentary Guide to the Original
Southern Emigrant Route to Oregon
1, Applegate Trail. 2, Emigration and immigration. 3, Pioneers.
4, Oregon History --To 1859. 5, Oregon Trail.
6, California Trail. 7, Indians of North America-History.
8, Frontier and pioneer life.
9, Overland journeys to the Pacific. I. Title.
F880.E53 979.5 EME 96-084925
Library of Congress Catalog Card Number: 96-084925
ISBN 1-889082-00-7

Published and Printed
in
the United States of America

First edition
Published by Ember Enterprises
P. O. Box 1343
Ashland, Oregon 97520

Text Editing Consultant: William Ashworth

Cover: Designed by William Emerson

Cover Base Map Base Map and Base Map for Location of Native American Tribes and
Bands along the existing pack trail in Oregon: *Atlas to Accompany the Official Records of the Union and Confederate Armies.* Washington: Government Printing Office. 1891-1895. Plate 162. Military Departments, December 31, 1860.

Geography Base Map: provided by the Oregon Department of Environmental Quality

All other Base Maps: United States Geological Survey

Photograph of Goose Lake in 1926: Provided by George R. Burrell

All other photographs were taken by the author.

Book Design and all Illustrations by the Author

TABLE OF CONTENTS

Foreword

William Emerson has rendered readers a great service by providing the first truly comprehensive, objective and well organized overview of the southern emigrant route into Oregon, now officially designated as the Applegate Trail. As the title suggests this exhaustively researched work concentrates on the Applegate Trail of 1846, but in many respects Emerson's scope is really much broader: The first chapter, for example, admirably sets the stage for what follows by discussing a wide array of historic forces and colorful individuals. Because the author is familiar with numerous primary and secondary sources prior to 1846, he ably discusses the convergence of native Oregonians, Hudson's Bay Company and free American trappers as well as later explorers and settlers prior to 1846. The trail, called by many names throughout its history, served various needs at different points in time as Emerson shows us not only in words but through a visually enriched text containing twelve illustrations, and some fifty photographs, and maps. The incorporation of well chosen quotations from a plethora of primary sources including diaries, recollections and reminiscences throughout the book leave the reader informed as well as entertained. Leading the

way through complex controversies as arduous as the trail itself is no easy task. Emerson proves himself a trustworthy guide as he replaces myths concerning the trail, its blazers, and earliest emigrant sojourners with documentation that is admirably detailed in copious footnotes and an excellent appendix. To further aid the reader in visualizing the nature of the time and its attendant difficulties a glossary of wagon terms is provided. The Appendix boasts the most complete list of adult emigrants using the 1846 trail ever compiled, a real service to scholars, searchers and genealogists. These innovations, along with an exceptionally thorough and chronologically structured text, make *THE APPLEGATE TRAIL OF 1846* an indispensable volume for any student or scholar interested in the history of the overland experience in America's west. I heartily recommend it.

Shannon Applegate
Yoncalla, Oregon

Introduction

This book describes all the events that happened on the first wagon train to take the new southern route to Oregon. This trail was established in 1846 as a cutoff from the Oregon Trail to avoid the dangers of rafting the rapids on the Columbia River. Additionally, it provided an alternate route for American emigrants to enter Oregon in case there was a war with Britain. "The Applegate Trail" used the

established California Trail from the Oregon Trail near Fort Hall, Idaho through Utah and Nevada to a cutoff on the Humboldt River. From the "cut-off," the first wagon train of 90 to 100 wagons traveled northwest through Nevada, California and into southern Oregon toward the Willamette Valley.

One purpose for writing this book was to bring the thrills, joys, tragedies and adventures that happened on this first train, together, as one narrative. I have combined writings, diaries, recollections and reminiscences as close as possible to the order they happened, to make this story more true to life and true to history.

Fortunately, this first "Applegate Trail" wagon train was before most troubles between the settlers and the Native Americans had started. When the emigrants traveled on this new southern route to Oregon there had been little communication between the pioneer emigrants and the Native Americans. The new settlers avoided contact with the Indians. The Native Americans were curious. In most regions of travel, the local tribe's people seemed to think of the cattle as fair game. Most had never seen a covered wagon. Language was a barrier. If they could have communicated, they would have understood each other more.

Read about the events as they happened, and imagine what the American (Indians) who lived in these areas must have thought. Then imagine what the emigrants must have thought. They shared misunderstanding and fear of each other. Both were strangers to each other.

Another difference of this era was the way men viewed women. Most of the women who wrote journals and diaries mentioned what the men did. The men who wrote journals did not mention what the women did. Husbands hardly mentioned the first name of their wives. For example, I never did find out what J. Quinn Thornton's wife's name was. He always referred to her as Mrs. Thornton. Tolbert Carter was a teamster for a woman who was a widow. The wagon they traveled with was her wagon, but he never mentioned her first or last name.

The women did all the washing by hand. They took care of the children, churned butter, picked wild edibles and cooked the meals. They would keep the wagon cleaned, the bedding changed, and there was usually a table cloth on whatever makeshift table they ate on.

The men would drive the teams and corral the wagons at night. They would herd, feed and care for the livestock and keep the wagons in working order. They would yoke the oxen every day and feed them every evening. The men protected the camp from the wolves. They usually built a fire and pitched the tent if there was one.

The men would hunt game and the women would cook it and clean up the dishes after dinner. The children helped both their parents. When it came to caring for the children, women's work was never done. Women did as much work if not more, than men. Women's work was not believed to be as important as men's. The truth was, they needed each other and relied on each other. All the work was necessary.

The trail was more a man's world because it was a rough life. It was harder on the women and children. The wagon was the only thing that made life on the trail bearable for a woman. Single men would travel by horse with a couple of pack mules. Men did not care much about domestic things. They adapted to the dust and dirt easier. They did have some of the dirtiest jobs.

I hope this will make the reading more understanding, acceptable and enjoyable. This was over 150 years ago and many modern conveniences we take for granted today had not even been imagined. This is a documentary. When things are mentioned that add more of a human element to the story, they are not just thrown in. They actually happened. I hope you enjoy reading this historical documentary, half as much as I enjoyed writing it.

William Emerson, 1996

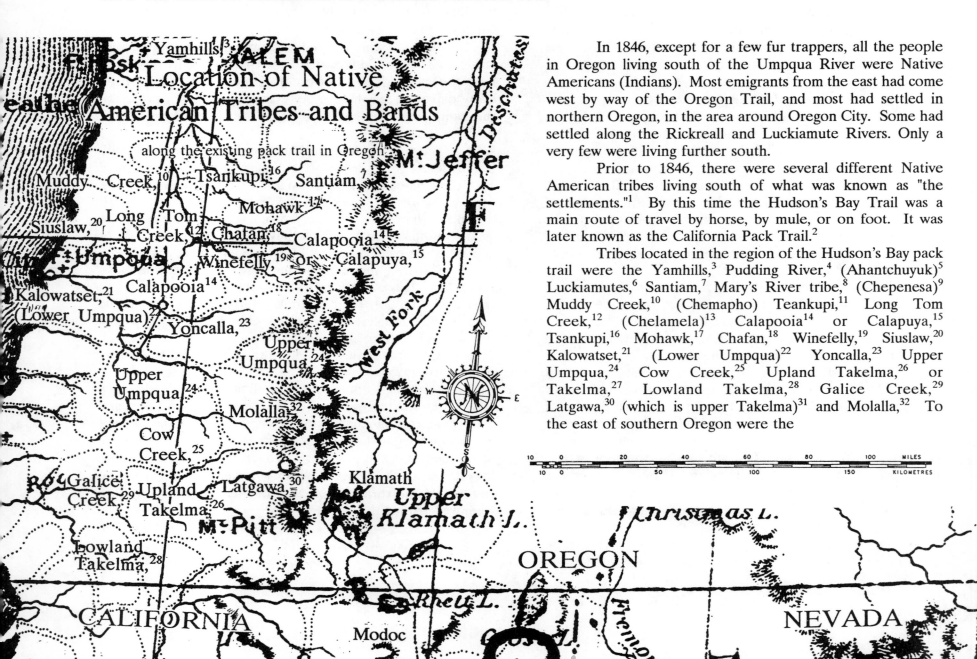

Location of Native American Tribes and Bands along the existing pack trail in Oregon

In 1846, except for a few fur trappers, all the people in Oregon living south of the Umpqua River were Native Americans (Indians). Most emigrants from the east had come west by way of the Oregon Trail, and most had settled in northern Oregon, in the area around Oregon City. Some had settled along the Rickreall and Luckiamute Rivers. Only a very few were living further south.

Prior to 1846, there were several different Native American tribes living south of what was known as "the settlements."[1] By this time the Hudson's Bay Trail was a main route of travel by horse, by mule, or on foot. It was later known as the California Pack Trail.[2]

Tribes located in the region of the Hudson's Bay pack trail were the Yamhills,[3] Pudding River,[4] (Ahantchuyuk)[5] Luckiamutes,[6] Santiam,[7] Mary's River tribe,[8] (Chepenesa)[9] Muddy Creek,[10] (Chemapho) Teankupi,[11] Long Tom Creek,[12] (Chelamela)[13] Calapooia[14] or Calapuya,[15] Tsankupi,[16] Mohawk,[17] Chafan,[18] Winefelly,[19] Siuslaw,[20] Kalowatset,[21] (Lower Umpqua)[22] Yoncalla,[23] Upper Umpqua,[24] Cow Creek,[25] Upland Takelma,[26] or Takelma,[27] Lowland Takelma,[28] Galice Creek,[29] Latgawa,[30] (which is upper Takelma)[31] and Molalla,[32] To the east of southern Oregon were the

Klamath and Modoc tribes.[33]

The North Umpqua or Upper Umpqua Native American Indians lived in the area of present day Roseburg. They had a winter camp at what is today the town of Winchester. In the 1840s the chief's name was "Captain."[34] Every spring Captain and his tribe would camp in the mountains at a place called "Cap's Illahee."[35] Native Americans from the Klamath, Modoc, Kalapuya and Umpqua tribes would meet to trade, gamble, and race ponies in the meadow at this retreat.[36] The Umpquas traded salmon and camas. The Klamaths and the Modocs brought basketry, obsidian, roots and seeds. Tribes from the coast would bring shells and seal bone.[37] "Cap's Illahee" was located along the North Umpqua River about forty-five miles east of Winchester close to the North Umpqua Hot Springs.[38] Today the meadow where the Indians used to race their ponies is part of a cattle ranch.[39]

Further south in the area of the Takelmas were the Dagelmas[40] which meant "living along the river,"[41] and the Latgawas which meant "living in the Uplands."[42] In the 1840's the Degelmas were known as the "Rogue river [sic] Indians."[43] The Latgawas were known as the "Table Rock band [sic]."[44] This is in reference to those Indians who lived on the Table Rocks and other high elevations such as Grizzly Peak and the area around Bear Creek. Grizzly Peak was called "Lath'kawkh"[45] by the Native American Indians. Bear Creek was called "Si-ku-ptat." The Table Rocks were called "Ha'o-phakh" and had religious significance to these Americans.[46]

In 1823, the Northwest Fur Company merged with The Hudson's Bay Company.[47] In 1824,[48] Doctor John McLoughlin, chief factor of the Hudson's Bay Company west of the Rocky Mountains,[49] moved to Oregon to become chief factor of the Columbia District of the Hudson's Bay Company.[50] As chief factor his first order was to build a new fort on the Columbia River over one hundred miles from the Pacific Ocean,[51] just north of the present day city of Portland.[52] The new fort was named Fort Vancouver after Captain George Vancouver, an early British navigator.[53] After Fort Vancouver was built the existing old Fort George was torn down.[54] Within a few years, the Hudson's Bay Company under the direction of McLoughlin, monopolized the trade in all areas south of the settlements in the Willamette Valley.[55]

In September of 1826, Peter Skene Ogden left Fort Vancouver on an expedition and traveled east to the main Falls of the Columbia River where he met John McLoughlin's stepson,[56] Thomas McKay.[57] With McKay, Ogden led a brigade of fur trappers on an expedition down the Deschutes and Crooked Rivers to Hanley Lake.[58] From Hanley Lake, Ogden and his party traveled to the Klamath region.[59]

While in southern Oregon, Ogden and his brigade crossed the Siskiyou Mountains and explored the Rogue River Valley.[60] He was the "first Euro-American land-based explorer" to reach the Rogue River and travel as far north as the South Umpqua River.[61] Peter Ogden and his party passed the south side of Goose Lake to return to Fort Vancouver by way of the Snake River.[62]

In the spring of 1828,[63] Jedediah Smith led a party of trappers north along the California coast.[64] Jedediah Smith was one of the three partners of the Rocky Mountain Fur Company of St. Louis.[65] He and his men worked their way up the coast, crossing a river and entering Oregon. This river is now known as Smith River.[66] Continuing north on the Oregon coast, they crossed the Rogue River, the Coquille

River and the Coos River.[67] They made camp at the Umpqua River and its north branch. Jedediah Smith, Richard Leyland,[68] and an Indian acting as their guide, traveled by canoe up the Umpqua River[69] to decide the course for the day.[70]

While Smith was gone, a breakdown in communication at his encampment caused a fight with one of the Indian Tribes.[71] Arthur Black escaped and managed to make it to the coast and up the coast to Fort Vancouver.[72] John Turner fought off the Indians with a "brand from the fire at which he was cooking."[73] Jedediah Smith and Leyland[74] returned to the disaster. Both men and Turner escaped and made it to the ocean. They followed the Oregon coast north to near present day Tillamook and were helped to Fort Vancouver by Tillamook Indians.[75]

At Fort Vancouver, John McLoughlin was preparing a fur trapping expedition led by Alexander Roderick[76] Mcleod to the same area the men had just fled. Michel LaFramboise was immediately sent out to do what he could.[77] LaFramboise[78] had good relationships with all the Umpqua Tribes. He claimed a Umpqua woman to be his wife in several different villages.[79]

Almost a month later, Jedediah Smith accompanied McLeod toward the Umpqua River. They met LaFramboise near Champoeg on his way back to Fort Vancouver.[80] There was no sign of the rest of Jedediah Smith's men, and the furs had been dispersed throughout the country.[81] After McLeod's communication with the Umpqua chief, most of Jedediah's furs, belongings and about thirty-five horses were returned.[82] They found the massacred remains of the men near the ocean at the entrance of the north branch of the Umpqua River, a second river on the Oregon coast known today as Smith River.[83]

In January of 1829, Alexander McLeod was sent out by McLoughlin[84] on the expedition he had planned. These plans included McLeod going to California. Thomas McKay, who had earlier assisted Ogden, was employed as a guide from the Umpqua River to the Rogue River.[85] John Turner was a California guide.[86] After reaching the Umpqua River, Mcleod followed the route Ogden had discovered through the Umpqua and Rogue River Valleys.[87] He traveled over the Siskiyou Mountains and eventually arrived at the Sacramento Valley in the summer of 1829.[88]

Later the same year, Alexander "Roderick" McLeod was killed in the Siskiyous on his return trip to Oregon. Aside from aiding in the progress of forming the Oregon-California Trail, he is credited with naming the Siskiyou Mountains. McCloud's River was later named after him.[89]

Through different expeditions and explorations by different trappers and explorers, the Hudson's Bay Company had explored and traveled the entire route of the new Hudson's Bay pack trail from Fort Vancouver to California.[90] They kept this route a "closely guarded secret" because they feared other trappers might make competition for them.[91]

In 1829, Fort Vancouver was rebuilt at a new location closer to the river and about one mile west of the old fort.[92] The new fort consisted of thirty buildings including John McLoughlin's mansion. It was enclosed by a twenty-five foot high fir log wall with "great double-ribbed, riveted gates" to form the entrance.[93]

By 1832,[94] the Hudson's Bay Company had established a fur post north of the Yoncalla Valley,[95] on Calapooya Creek near its junction with the Umpqua River.[96] It was later known as "Umpqua, old fort."[97]

By 1836,[98] the Hudson's Bay Company had built a second Fort Umpqua. This small fort was on the Elk River.[99] It was located on one hundred acres near present day Elkton, Oregon,[100] and had four log buildings, a barn, and a store house all enclosed by a twelve foot high log wall.[101] The men from the Hudson's Bay Company established good relations with the Native Americans and used the pack trail extensively from Fort Umpqua to Fort Vancouver.[102]

In 1834, Ewing Young and Hall Jackson Kelley, along with over sixteen men, decided to use this trail to transport about one hundred and thirty horses and mules from San Jose to the Columbia River.[103] John Turner was a member of this party.[104] He had returned to California from Fort Vancouver, on an expedition led by Michel LaFramboise in 1832-1833.[105]

Young started with seven men and about fifty horses.[106] Hall J. Kelley was a Massachusetts schoolteacher who persuaded Young to guide him to Oregon.[107] Before leaving California, fourteen men with seventy-seven horses and mules had joined. Kelly later referred to some of these men as "marauders."[108] Some of them had been sailors, but had become deserters.[109]

At a camp after crossing the Joaquin River,[110] three of the "marauders"[111] went back to an Indian village they had passed on the river, and "ravished [sic]" the women while the men were away. The next day, the Indians showed up to question Young's party.[112] After the Indians left, two of the party followed them. Kelley said he heard shots and the men returned with the chief's bow and quiver.[113]

They now noticed signs of Indians following them. Days later, while they were camped on the Sacramento River across from an Indian village, seven horses were killed in camp. Kelley believed it was revenge from the Indians further south. Young and his men believed it was the Indians across the river.[114] While they were discussing who it was, seven men from the village across the river showed up with gifts. Young's men jumped to conclusions and killed these Indians.[115]

After much difficulty, Young and his party reached the Rogue River. Some men, including Kelley, had malaria. They camped on an island on the river to keep the horses from running off. While they were camping, two Indians came across to visit. Ewing Young thought if these men reported the condition of the men and the amount of horses they had with them, the Indians would attack. Fearing the worst, he decided to kill the two men.[116] After discovering the bodies of their friends,[117] the "Indians of the Rogue"[118] started revenging their deaths from that time on.[119]

In the Umpqua Valley, Kelley was too sick to travel. The Hudson's Bay brigade traveling north,[120] led by Michel La Framboise,[121] caught up with Kelley and helped him to Fort Vancouver.[122]

Young's troubles were not over. The Hudson's Bay Schooner, "Cadboro," had arrived from Monterey with a letter from Governor Jose' Figueroa, of Mexican California, to Chief Factor John McLoughlin of Fort Vancouver. The letter accused Young of being a horse thief.[123]

When Kelley arrived he was allowed to stay in a cabin to recuperate, but was not allowed in the fort.[124] Young arrived at the French-Canadian settlement where he had friends and found out John McLoughlin refused to help him in any way. He was furious to find out he had been branded a thief.[125] Young had planned to return to California the following spring.[126] Meanwhile, he and his men settled in the Chehalem Valley,[127] near present day Newberg.[128]

They became the only settlers, including the missionaries, who did not rely on the Hudson's Bay Company for survival.[129]

In 1835, a party of eight trappers from Sacramento traveled north on the trail toward the Columbia River. They camped on the Rogue River[130] near the mouth of Foots Creek below Rocky Point.[131] They fought with the Native Americans of the Rogue Valley. Four out of the eight survived[132] and managed to make it to the settlement in the Willamette Valley.[133] Their names were John Turner, George Gay,[134] Dr. William J. Bailey[135] and a Mr. Woodworth.[136]

In 1836, Ewing Young was still angry about the accusations against him.[137] The French settlers and the missionaries established communication with Young and his men against McLoughlin's wishes.[138] Governor Figueroa of Mexican California eventually sent a letter exonerating Young of the accusations after learning the real thieves had merely traveled with Young and Kelley.[139]

Young bought a caldron used for pickling salmon, and started to build a still.[140] This concerned the missionary, Jason Lee, and others. A meeting was called of the Oregon Temperance Society.[141] Young admitted he was building the still out of financial necessity.[142]

William A. Slacum was a visitor to the Columbia River as a representative of President Andrew Jackson.[143] He observed that one thing there was a lack of, was cattle.[144]

In January 1837, a meeting was held at the Methodist Mission, and an agreement was made to form the Willamette Cattle Company.[145] Ewing Young was chosen to be the leader of the venture.[146] Philip Leget Edwards from the mission, was made treasurer. Young, Edwards, and a group of men including John Turner[147] sailed aboard a brig[148] Slacum had chartered,[149] called the "Lorit."[150] They traveled south to the California coast to purchase 700 to 800 head of cattle.[151]

They bought 729 head of[152] "wide horned, slimed [sic] flanked stock"[153] and forty horses.[154] Most of the cattle were the wildest type possible. The drive started at the San Jose Mission,[155] traveled up the California Pack Trail,[156] through the Siskiyous and into Oregon on the Hudson's Bay pack trail.[157] This time eleven men took part in the drive.[158]

While they were camped in Shasta Valley, Edwards overheard several of the men mutter something about hoping they could kill an Indian. Some friendly Indians came into their camp. George Gay, one of Turner's friends, killed one of them.[159] Ewing Young reprimanded the man for having shot the Indian without cause.[160] Pierre Depot was the only man who agreed with Young and Edwards.[161] He felt the Indian should not have been shot.

They reached the Rogue River in early September. They were cautious because of the experience of two years before.[162] Indians were all around as they herded the cattle through the Siskiyou Pass.[163] Later, the Native Americans ambushed the cattle drivers. They killed one of the cattle[164] and put two arrows in Young's horse,[165] killing it.[166] Young and the cattlemen succeeded in reaching the Willamette Valley about the middle of October, with 630 head of cattle and a loss of three men.[167] Cattle driving the pack trail was abandoned for a few years.[168]

That same year, Jacob P. Lease drove 450 sheep north to the Willamette Valley on the Hudson's Bay pack trail.[169] Lease had a trading post in Yerba Buena. Today, Yerba Buena is known as San Francisco. Ewing Young was an old friend of Lease. He had seen Lease when he was in California.[170]

In 1841, the first emigrants to use the Hudson's Bay pack trail traveled south under the command of Lieutenant George F. Emmons. He had four commissioned officers and thirty-four men.[171] Joe Meek was their guide for the first part of the expedition.[172]

This overland expedition consisted mainly of the survivors of the "Peacock," a vessel wrecked at the mouth of the Columbia on a coastal exploration by Lieutenant Charles Wilkes of the U. S. Navy.[173] They stopped at Fort Umpqua (Elkton) and J. D. Dana,[174] a geologist, and several emigrants with their families traveled with them to California.[175] They had no trouble with the Indian people in the Rogue Valley. Lieutenant Emmons attributed this success to "using strict military discipline, and allowing no Indians in his camp."[176]

Cattle drives began again from California in 1842.[177] A significantly large one took place in 1843. There were 250 head of cattle, 600 horses and mules, and 900 head of sheep driven from Sacramento to the Willamette Valley.[178] Tribes people watched from afar, but their main attackers on this drive were thousands of insects.[179] Most of the Hudson's Bay pack trail consisted of Native American trade routes that were already established.[180] Different tribes used these trails constantly.[181] One can only imagine the enormous disruption of everyday life that occurred when hundreds of animals were driven through a small trail at one time.

In the spring of 1843,[182] Lansford W. Hastings[183] persuaded a group of 1842 emigrants to leave Oregon.[184] He took this discontented group of twenty-five persons, with Stephen H. Meek as their guide, from Oregon to California by way of the Hudson's Bay and California Pack Trail. Meek had traveled with Thomas McKay's expedition to California.[185]

South of the Rogue River the Hastings' party met a group coming north on the trail. After camping together, two-thirds of Hastings' party decided to return to the Willamette Valley.[186]

Meanwhile, a branch of the Oregon Trail was established to California. The California Trail began in 1841 when the Bidwell-Bartleson wagon company took the first wagons from Idaho through to the Sacramento Valley.[187] They left the Oregon Trail just past Soda Springs in Idaho, then down Bear River and west across the desert. Unfortunately they had to abandon their wagons to complete the journey. They traveled with pack animals across the mountains and followed the Humboldt River, eventually arriving in California.[188]

The route of the California Trail was changed by the Chiles-Walker Party in 1843 when they took Raft River out of Fort Hall, then followed Goose Creek and Thousand Springs to the Humboldt River.[189] The Humboldt River was known at the time as Mary's River.[190] Some emigrants and explorers referred to the Humboldt River as Ogden's River, named after Peter Skene Ogden.[191] Ogden called it the "Unknown River."[192] It was named the Humboldt River by General John Charles Fremont in 1845, after Alexander von Humboldt, a German geographer.[193] This was the same route the Applegate exploring party would eventually use to lead the first wagon companies to the new southern route to Oregon.[194] Levi Scott called it "the emigrant road to California."[195] Lindsay Applegate called it "the California route."[196] It went southeast 750 miles from Fort Hall

- 13 -

COAST RANGE

CASCADE RANGE

WILLAMETTE VALLEY

DESCHUTES-UMATILLA PLATEAU

BLUE MOUNTAIN

HIGH LAVA PLAINS

BASIN AND RANGE

KLAMATH MOUNTAINS

Calapooya Mountains

Rogue River Valley

Siskiyou Mountains

Nestucca R.
Yamhill R.
Siletz
Yaquina R.
Marys R.
Alsea
Willamette R.
Pudding R.
Molalla R.
Clackamas R.
Sandy
White
Warm Springs R.
Santiam R.
N. Santiam R.
S. Santiam R.
Santiam
Calapooia R.
McKenzie
M. Fork
N. Fork
M. Fork Willamette
Fork Willamette
Sharps Cr.
Salt
Waldo Lake
Wickiup Res.
L. Deschutes
Deschutes
Siuslaw
Coos
Umpqua
Calapooya
N.
Umpqua
S. Umpqua
M. Fork
E. Fork
Coquille
Sixes R.
Rogue
S. Fork
Ro
Evans
Bear
Applegate
Chetco
Pistol R.
Illinois
Little Butte Cr.
Dry Cr.
Williamson
Crater Lake
Sprague
Upper Klamath Lake
Sycan
Klamath
Lost R.
Goose

Thirtymile Cr.
John
Trout Cr.
Crooked
Bear Cr.
Mountain Cr.
Canyon
Malheur
S. Fork John Day
N. Fork Malheur
Silvies
Harney Lake
Silver
Summer Lake
Silver Lake
Lake Abert
Hart Lake
Crump Lake

Geography

Geography Base Map: provided by the Oregon Department of Environmental Quality

0   50
miles

through Idaho, Utah, Nevada, and into California.[197]

The Oregon Trail was becoming known as "an immigrant's road to Oregon."[198] A few had used this route before 1843.[199] A party led by Thomas Fitzpatrick first traveled the trail in 1812 going east[200] and again west on the return trip to Oregon through the South Pass in 1813.[201] This route developed into a regular pack trail.

In 1843, it became the Oregon Trail.[202] This was the year of the Great Migration.[203] Eight hundred and seventy-five[204] to nearly 1,000 people went on the first wagon train to Oregon.[205] Peter H. Burnett was elected captain and J. W. Nesmith was orderly sergeant.[206] Captain John Gantt was chosen to guide the train to Fort Hall.[207] After eight days on the trail, Burnett resigned, and William Martin was chosen to take his place.[208]

The train was soon divided into two more manageable trains. The first half was called "the 'light column'."[209] The last half of the wagon train was known as the "Cow Column."[210] Within the first week Jesse Applegate was named captain of this last half of the wagon train.[211] The emigrants were able to stock up on supplies at Fort Laramie, but for a high price.[212]

Doctor Marcus Whitman can take credit for leading the emigrants from Fort Hall to Grande Ronde,[213] although from Salmon Falls he had gone ahead with a small party and left notes behind to direct the wagons.[214] After reaching the Blue River, heavy timber blocked their way, and forty men took five days to clear a path for the wagons to follow.[215]

At Fort Walla Walla the emigrants were advised by Whitman and Archibald McKinlay to leave their wagons until spring.[216] Many emigrants retained their wagons, and traveled by land to The Dalles.[217] The John Day and Deschutes Rivers were their main obstacles.[218] From The Dalles, they traveled by raft down the Columbia River to the Cascades.[219] A few traveled through the Cascade Mountains by a cattle trail.[220]

Some emigrants abandoned their wagons and left their cattle at Fort Walla Walla.[221] They were told by McKinlay they could receive cattle in the Willamette Valley in trade for cattle they left behind.[222] They built rafts and floated downstream, past The Dalles, and through the rapids to the Willamette Valley.[223]

Like many emigrants, the Applegates traveled on this wagon train with their families. Along with the Jesse Applegate family, there were the Lindsay and the Charles Applegate families.[224] Toward the end of this 2,000-mile journey,[225] they decided to leave their wagons and take to the rapids of the Columbia River.[226] One of their Mackinaw boats,[227] carrying both Jesse and Lindsay Applegate's sons, overturned and both their sons[228] and Alexander McClellan,[229] the seventy-year-old driver, were drowned in the Columbia.[230]

When the Applegates arrived at The Dalles, they were met by a friend, Robert Shortess, who had a canoe loaded with provisions for the Applegate families. These provisions were soon consumed by seventy people, who had just taken the rapids of the Columbia River.[231]

Applegate mentions that later at the mission, they received one Spanish cow for two emigrant oxen they had left.[232] All three families settled in Polk County[233] near the LaCreole River,[234] later known as the Rickreall River.

Prior to 1846, most of the emigrants had come to Oregon by way of the Oregon Trail. Most emigrants who settled in Oregon were living above the Luckiamute River. There was only a small number of settlers living further south. By 1834, John Work had a small cabin near present day Scottsburg.[235] Fort Umpqua, near present day Elkton, was built in 1836.[236]   There was a McFuller who lived about seven miles north of present day Corvallis.[237]   In 1845 A. C. Avery built the first cabin on Mary's River at what is known today as Corvallis.[238]   By the summer of 1846 Eugene Skinner had partially built a cabin on what is known today as Skinner Butte at the north end of present day Eugene.[239]

From the settlements, the rich fertile soil of the Willamette Valley opened wide and fairly level as far south as Eugene Skinner's cabin (Eugene).[240]   The valley narrowed and continued south with the coastal mountain range closing in to the west and the Cascades forming a formidable barrier to the east.[241]   Here the Calapooya Mountain Range formed a natural barrier between the north and the south.[242]   The Calapooya Mountains extended southeast[243] to meet the Cascade Range.[244]   South of the Calapooya Range were the North Umpqua River and the South Umpqua River.[245]

At the south end of the Cascades were the Siskiyou Mountains[246] forming a natural boundary east and west between the Oregon territory and California.[247]   They ran from the coast to the Cascades.[248]   Just north of the Siskiyou Mountains was the Rogue River Valley,[249] and the Rogue River also running east and west.[250]   This area south of the Calapooya Mountains was a very difficult country to explore.   It was full of hills and mountains covered with heavy timber.[251]

East of the Cascades was the Great Klamath Basin. Peter Skene Ogden had visited this area in 1826 and 1827.[252]   At the south end of the basin there were several large lakes.   They are known today as Upper Klamath Lake, Lower Klamath Lake, Tule Lake, Goose Lake and Clear Lake.

Further east was the Nevada desert.   Northern Nevada was entirely desert with small mountains, canyons, alkali lakes, sage brush and hot springs.[253]

On the Oregon Trail in 1845, a man named Elijah[254] White believed he had found a shorter route to the Willamette Valley.[255]   The route was a cut-off of the Oregon Trail.   It started at Fort Hall, Idaho.[256]   The new trail crossed the Malheur[257] Mountains between Owyhee and the South Fork of the Malheur River.[258]   Losing his way,[259] Stephen Meek led about 200 wagons[260] through Crane Prairie, past Lake Malheur[261] and far to the south.[262]   The people Meek was leading refused to continue in the same direction and turned north over a ridge between the John Day and Deschutes Rivers.[263]   The train was rescued on the Crooked River by a party led by Moses "Black" Harris.[264]   This trail has since been called the "Meek Cut-off."[265]

Two weeks ahead of the Meek party, Samuel Barlow and his wagon party started crossing the Cascade Mountains by traveling south of Mount Hood from The Dalles to Oregon City.[266]   Other members of this party were Joel Palmer and William H. Rector.[267]   This alternate route was proposed to eliminate the danger of rafting the Columbia River.[268]   Unfortunately, these dangers were replaced with other obstacles: "...thick forest, fallen logs crossed and recrossed upon each other, rocks, creeks, canons [sic] or barriers of some kind."[269]   They managed to get about five miles from the summit of the Cascade Mountains with their wagons.[270]   Leaving their wagons after much hardship and many setbacks, they made it to Oregon City by Christmas 1845.[271]

By cutting through thick forests, canyons and creeks, they managed to bring the wagons down in the spring of 1846.[272]   Samuel Barlow was authorized by the Oregon Legislature to construct a road across the Cascades.[273]   The road was to be paid for by collecting a toll.[274]   This trail was later called the Barlow Road.[275]   The Barlow Road could only be used in the summer months because of the heavy winter snows.[276]

Another reason for finding an alternate route to the Willamette Valley was the concern that war might break out between United States and Britain.[277] If this happened, there would be no way to bring emigrants or troops from the south to the settlements.[278]

Peter Skene Ogden succeeded Dr. McLoughlin as chief officer of the Hudson's Bay Company in 1845. He was acting chief when Oregon became a territory of the United States.[279] McLoughlin resigned and moved to Oregon City.[280]

Figure 1 Looking south near Elk Creek.

The emigration of 1846 was expected to be unusually large.[281] The settlers in the Willamette Valley raised money and commissioned Levi Scott to explore a new route through the Cascade Mountains.[282] He and fourteen other mountain men volunteered to go south to find a new trail.[283]

They left May 15, 1846, with General Cornelius Gilliam as their leader.[284] They crossed over the Calapooya Mountains and got as far south as the Umpqua Valley. The Calapooya Mountains were one of the most formidable obstacles to cross. Here General Gilliam decided to return to the Willamette Valley.[285] Soon after, around Elk Creek, three others made up their minds to return.[286]

The rest continued two more days and arrived at Calapooya Creek in the Umpqua Valley, near present day Oakland. One mountain man was Moses "Black" Harris. He had taken over as leader, but was not sure which direction to go. After going 150 miles south of the settlements, they all decided to turn back.[287]

Levi Scott stopped at a place about six or eight miles north of Mary's River and decided to settle there. He told the others that if another company decided to explore a new road further, he would leave in a moment's notice and join the expedition.[288]

NOTES   Chapter 1

1.a) *History of the Pacific Northwest: Oregon and Washington.* (Portland, OR: North Pacific History Co., 1889), Vol. I, p. 370.
b) Hubert Howe Bancroft, *The Works of Hubert Howe Bancroft* (San Francisco, CA: The History Company, 1886), Vol. XXIX, p. 565.

2. Norman Dennis Schlesser, *Bastion of Empire, the Hudson's Bay Company's Fort Umpqua: Being a Narrative of the Early Explorations and the Fur Trade in Douglas County* (Oakland, OR: Oakland Printing Co., c.1973), p. 16. [California Pack Trail was also known as the Oregon-California Trail. (Mildred Brook Hoover, Hero Eugene Rensch and Ethel Grace Rensch, *Historic Spots in California*, (Stanford, CA: Stanford University Press, 1966), p. 501.) It was known to some as the Siskiyou Trail. (Lindsay Applegate, "The Applegate Trail," *Overland Journal* (Independence, MO: Oregon-California Trails Association), Vol. 2, No. 1, (Spring, 1993), p. 21.)]

3.a) *Indians of the Rogue Valley* (Medford, OR: Jackson County Extension Office of Oregon State University, 1980), p. 4.
b) Samuel Newton Dicken, *The Making of Oregon: a Study in Historical Geography* (Portland, OR: Oregon Historical Society, 1979), p. 42.

c) Jeff Zucker, *Oregon Indians: Culture, History & Current Affairs* (Portland, OR: Western Imprints, the Press of the Oregon Historical Society, 1983), p. 9.

4.a) *Indians of the Rogue Valley*, p. 4.
b) Dicken, *Making of Oregon*, p. 42.

5. *Indians of the Rogue Valley*, p. 4.

6.a) Zucker, *Oregon Indians*, p. 9.
b) *Indians of the Rogue Valley*, p. 4.
c) Dicken, *Making of Oregon*, p. 42.

7.a) Zucker, *Oregon Indians*, p. 9.
b) *Indians of the Rogue Valley*, p. 4.
c) Dicken, *Making of Oregon*, p. 42.

8.a) *Indians of the Rogue Valley*, p. 4.
b) Dicken, *Making of Oregon*, p. 42.

9.a) *Indians of the Rogue Valley*, p. 4.
b) Zucker, *Oregon Indians*, p. 9.

10. *Indians of the Rogue Valley*, p. 4.

11. Ibid., p. 4.

12.a) *Indians of the Rogue Valley*, p. 4.
b) Dicken, *Making of Oregon*, p. 42.

13. *Indians of the Rogue Valley*, p. 4.

14. Ibid., p. 7.

15. Dicken, *Making of Oregon*, p. 42.

16. *Indians of the Rogue Valley*, p. 4.

17. Ibid., p. 4.

18. Ibid.

19. Ibid.

20.a) *Indians of the Rogue Valley*, p. 4.
b) Dicken, *Making of Oregon*, p. 42.
c) Zucker, *Oregon Indians*, p. 9.

21. *Indians of the Rogue Valley*, p. 4.

22.a) *Indians of the Rogue Valley*, p. 4.
b) Dicken, *Making of Oregon*, p. 42.
c) Zucker, *Oregon Indians*, p. 9.

23.a) *Indians of the Rogue Valley*, p. 4.
b) Dicken, *Making of Oregon*, p. 42.
c) Zucker, *Oregon Indians*, p. 9.

24.a) Zucker, *Oregon Indians*, p. 9.
b) *Indians of the Rogue Valley*, p. 4.

c) Dicken, *Making of Oregon*, p. 42.

25.a) Zucker, *Oregon Indians*, p. 9.
b) *Indians of the Rogue Valley*, p. 4.

26.a) Dicken, *Making of Oregon*, p. 42.
b) *Indians of the Rogue Valley*, p. 4.

27. Zucker, *Oregon Indians*, p. 9.

28. Dicken, *Making of Oregon*, p. 42.

29.a) Zucker, *Oregon Indians*, p. 9.
b) *Indians of the Rogue Valley*, p. 4.

30. *Indians of the Rogue Valley*, p. 4.

31. Ibid., p. 4.

32.a) Zucker, *Oregon Indians*, p. 4.
b) Dicken, *Making of Oregon*, p. 42.

33.a) *Indians of the Rogue Valley*, p. 4.
b) Dicken, *Making of Oregon*, p. 42.
c) Zucker, *Oregon Indians*, p. 9.
d) Robert H. Ruby, *Indians of the Pacific Northwest: a History* (Norman, OK: University of Oklahoma Press, 1981), p. 39.

34. Lavola J. Barker, *Land of the North Umpquas: Peaceful Indians of the West* (Grants Pass, OR: Te-Cum-Tom Publications, 1973), p. 25.

35. Ibdi., p. 25, 29.

36. Ibid., p. 25.

37. Zucker, *Oregon Indians*, p. 42, 44.

38. Barker, *North Umpquas*, p. 29.

39. Ibid., p. 36.

40. Kay Atwood, '"As Long as the World Goes On': The Table Rocks and the Takelma," *Oregon Historical Quarterly*, Vol. 95, No. 4 (Portland, OR: Oregon Historical Quarterly, 1994-95), p. 518.

41. IBid.

42. Ibid.

43. *Hist. of the Pac. N. W.*, Vol. I, p. 372.

44. Atwood, "Takelma," Vol. 95, p. 519.

45. Ibid.

46. Ibid.

47. Jack Sutton, *The Pictorial History of Southern Oregon and Northern California* (Grants Pass, OR: The Grants Pass Bulletin, 1959), p. 20.

48.a) *Hist. of the Pac. N. W.*, Vol. I, p. 175.
b) Alberta Brooks Fogdall, *Royal Family of the Columbia: and His Family* (Fairfield, WA: Ye Galleon Press, 1978), p. 15.
c) Schlesser, *Fort Umpqua*, p. 14.

49. *Hist. of the Pac. N. W.*, Vol. I, p. 174.

50.a) Schlesser, *Fort Umpqua*, p. 14.
b) Fogdall, *John McLoughlin*, p. 15.

51. Philip Hammon Parrish, *Before the Covered Wagon* (Portland, OR: Binfords & Mort., c.1931), p. 230.

52. *Hist. of the Pac. N. W.*, Vol. I, p. 174.

53. Fogdall, *John McLoughlin*, pp. 60, 265.

54. Dale Lowell Morgan, *Jedediah Smith and the Opening of the West* (Indianapolis, IN: Bobbs-Merrill, 1953), p. 270.

55. *Hist. of the Pac. N. W.*, Vol. I, p. 175.

56.a) Archie Fred Binns, *Peter Skene Ogden: Fur Trader* (Portland, OR: Binfords & Mort, 1967), p. 157.
b) Fogdall, *John McLoughlin*, p. XXVII, 229.

57. Binns, *Peter Skene Ogden*, p. 190.

58.a) Claude W. Nichols, *The South Road: its Development and Significance* (Master's Thesis, University of Oregon, 1953), p. 28.
b) Jeffrey M. LaLande, *First Over the Siskiyous: a Commentary on Peter Skene Ogdon's 1826-1827 Journey Through the Oregon-California Borderlands* (Portland, OR: Oregon Historical Society Press, 1987), p. XXX.

59. LaLande, *First Over the Siskiyous*, p. 3. ["Clair-metis" (Klamath) is a French word meaning "clouds" or "a light mist." The Klamath Tribes pronounced it "Tlamath." Fremont used this spelling. (T. C. Elliott, "The Peter Skene Ogden Journals," *Oregon Historical Quarterly*, Vol. 11, No. 4 (Portland, OR: Oregon Historical Society, 1923), p. 202.)]

60.a) LaLande, *First Over the Siskiyous*, p. 44.
b) Elliott, "Ogden Journals," *Vol. 11, No. 4*, p. 203.
c) Schlesser, *Fort Umpqua*, p. 15.
d) Binns, *Peter Skene Ogden*, p. 200.

61. LaLande, *First Over the Siskiyous*, p. 96. [Before Jeff LaLande's book, "First Over The Siskiyous," credit for crossing the Siskiyou Mountians had gone to Alexander McLeod (LaLande, *First Over the Siskiyous*, p. 128.) Credit for reaching the Rogue River first had already been given to *Peter Skeen Ogden* by *Archie Binns*, in Peter Skene Ogden: Fur Trader, Portland, 1967, page 200 (a) Binns, *Peter Skene Ogden*, p. 200.; b) Elliott, "Ogden Journals," *Vol. 11, No. 4, p. 203, 217.)]

62. IBid., p. XXIV.

63.a) Howard McKinley Corning, *Dictionary of Oregon History: Compiled From the Research Files of the Former Oregon Writer's Project with Much Added Material* (Portland, OR: Binfords & Mort, 1989), p. 227.
b) Ralph J. Roske, *Everyman's Eden: A History of California* (New York, NY: The MacMillan Company, 1968), p. 172.

64.a) Morgan, *Jedediah Smith*, p. 264.
b) Alice B. Maloney, "Camp Sites of Jedediah Smith on the Oregon Coast," *Oregon Historical Quarterly*, Vol. 41, No. 3 (Portland, OR: Oregon Historical Society, 1940), p. 305.

65. a) Corning, *History*, p. 227.
b) Charles Henry Carey, *A General History of Oregon Prior to 1861* (Portland, OR: Metropolitan Press, 1935), Vol. 1, p. 163.
c) *Hist. of the Pac. N. W.*, Vol. I, p. 369.

66. Maloney, "Camp Sites," p. 305.

67. Morgan, *Jedediah Smith*, p. 265, 266.

68. Maloney, "Camp Sites," p. 320. [or Leland (Morgan, *Jedediah Smith*, p. 267.)]

69. Morgan, *Jedediah Smith*, p. 267.

70. Carey, *History*, Vol. 1, p. 166.

71. Morgan, *Jedediah Smith*, p. 268.

72. Parrish, *Before the Covered Wagon*, p. 320.

73.a) Maloney, "Camp Sites," p. 320.
b) Parrish, *Before the Covered Wagon*, p. 243.

74. Maloney, "Camp Sites," p. 321. [or Leland a) Morgan, *Jedediah Smith*, p. 269.; b) Carey, *History*, Vol.1, p. 167.)]

75. Morgan, *Jedediah Smith*, p. 269.

76. a) Alice B. Maloney, "Hudson's Bay Company in California," *Oregon Historical Quarterly*, Vol. 37, No. 1 (Portland, OR: Oregon Historical Society, 1936), p. 11.
b) Maloney, "Camp Sites," p. 322. [or Roderic (Morgan, *Jedediah Smith*, p. 274.)]

77. Morgan, *Jedediah Smith*, p. 274.

78. Maloney, "Camp Sites," p. 319. [or Laframboise (Morgan, *Jedediah Smith*, p. 274.)]

79. Ibid., p. 319.

80. Morgan, *Jedediah Smith*, p. 274. [Champoeg was the site of the first warehouse of the Hudson's Bay Company on the Willamette River, between present day Newberg and Butteville. (Lewis A. McArther, *Oregon Geographic Names* (Portland, OR: Oregon Historical Society Press, 1992), p. 165.)]

81. Ibid.

82. Ibid., p. 277.

83. Ibid., p. 278.

84. Nichols, *South Road*, p. 34.

85.a) LaLande, *First Over the Siskiyous*, p. 126, 128.
b) Fogdall, *John McLoughlin*, p. 233.

86. Maloney, "Camp Sites," p. 322.

87. Fogdall, *John McLoughlin*, p. 128.

88.a) Maloney, "Hudson's Bay Company," p. 11.
b) Nichols, *South Road*, p. 34.

89. Maloney, "Hudson's Bay Company," p. 11.

90. Nichols, *South Road*, p. 36.

91. Ibid.

92.a) Fogdall, *John McLoughlin*, p. 60.
b) LaLande, *First Over the Siskiyous*, p. XXIV.

93. Corning, *History*, p. 90.

94.a) Corning, *History*, p. 90.
b) Jack Sutton, *Pictorial History*, p. 22.

95. Corning, *History*, p. 90.

96.a) Schlesser, *Fort Umpqua*, p. 15.
b) Leslie M. Scott, "John Work's Journey From Vancouver to Umpqua River, and Return, in 1834," *Oregon Historical Quarterly*, Vol. 24, No. 3 (Portland, OR: Oregon Historical Society, 1923), p. 259.

97.a) Scott, "John Work's Journey," p. 257.

98.a) Schlesser, *Fort Umpqua*, p. 19.
b) Corning, *History*, p. 90.

99.a) Bancroft, *Works*, Vol. XXIX, p. 565.
b) Nichols, *South Road*, p. 37.
c) Schlesser, *Fort Umpqua*, p. 16.

100.a) *Hist. of the Pac. N. W.*, Vol. I, p. 371.
b) Sutton, *Pictorial History*, p. 22.

101. Sutton, Pictorial History, p. 22.

102. Nichols, *South Road*, p. 24.

103.a) *Hist. of the Pac. N. W.*, Vol. I, p. 370.
b) Bancroft, *Works*, Vol. XXIX, p. 90.
c) Carey, *History*, Vol. 1, p. 260.
d) Corning, *History*, p. 277.

104. Kenneth L. Holmes, *Ewing Young Master Trapper* (Portland, OR: Binfords & Mort, for the Peter Binford Foundation, 1967), p. 97.

105. Maloney, "Camp Sites," p. 322.

106. Holmes, *Ewing Young*, p. 97.

107.a) Holmes, *Ewing Young*, p. 94, 96.
b) Sutton, *Pictorial History*, p. 23.
c) Parrish, *Before the Covered Wagon*, p. 261.
b) Corning, *History*, p. 90.

108. Holmes, *Ewing Young*, p. 97.

109. Ibid., p. 98.

110. Ibid., p. 99. [In his writing Kelly spells this river "Jaquin river." This is probably the present day San Joaquin River.]

111. Ibid., p. 97.

112. Ibid., p. 99.

113. Ibid., p. 100.

114. Ibid.

115. Ibid., p. 102.

116. Ibid.

117. Ibid., p. 103.

118. *Hist. of the Pac. N. W.*, Vol. I, p. 370.

119. Holmes, *Ewing Young*, p. 103.

120. Ibid.

121. Parrish, *Before the Covered Wagon*, p. 261. [or Laframboise (Holmes, *Ewing Young*, p. 103.)]

122.a) Holmes, *Ewing Young*, p. 103.
b) Bancroft, *Works*, Vol. XXIX, p. 90.

123.a) Holmes, *Ewing Young*, p. 106.
b) Bancroft, *Works*, Vol. XXIX, p. 91.
c) Parrish, *Before the Covered Wagon*, p. 262.

124.a) Holmes, *Ewing Young*, p. 107.
b) Carey, *History*, Vol. 1, p. 261.

125.a) Holmes, *Ewing Young*, p. 108.
b) Bancroft, *Works*, Vol. XXIX, p. 93.

c) Parrish, *Before the Covered Wagon*, p. 263.

126. Holmes, *Ewing Young*, p. 96.

127.a) Holmes, *Ewing Young*, p. 110.
b) Bancroft, *Works*, Vol. XXIX, p. 92.

128. Lewis A. McArther, *Oregon Geographic Names* (Portland, OR: Oregon Historical Society Press, 1992), p. 170.

129. Holmes, *Ewing Young*, p. 111.

130.a) *Hist. of the Pac. N. W.*, Vol. I, p. 370.
b) Bancroft, *Works*, Vol. XXIX, p. 95.

131. *Hist. of the Pac. N. W.*, Vol. I, p. 370.

132.a) Ibid.
b) Bancroft, *Works*, Vol. XXIX, p. 95.

133. *Hist. of the Pac. N. W.*, Vol. I, p. 370.

134.a) Ibid.
b) Bancroft, *Works*, Vol. XXIX, p. 96.

135.a) Holmes, *Ewing Young*, p. 120, 132.
b) Bancroft, *Works*, Vol. XXIX, p. 96.

136.a) *Hist. of the Pac. N. W.*, Vol.I, p. 370.
b) Nichols, *South Road*, p. 47.

137. Holmes, *Ewing Young*, p. 113.

138. Ibid., p. 114, 115.

139. Bancroft, *Works*, Vol. XXIX, p. 97.

140.a) Holmes, *Ewing Young*, p. 116.
b) Bancroft, *Works*, Vol. XXIX, p. 98.

141.a) Holmes, *Ewing Young*, p. 117.
b) Bancroft, *Works*, Vol. XXIX, p. 98.
c) Carey, *History*, Vol. 1, p. 264.

142. Holmes, *Ewing Young*, p. 118.

143.a) Holmes, *Ewing Young*, p. 117.
b) Sutton, *Pictorial History*, p. 23.

c) Carey, *History*, Vol. 1, p. 262.

144.a) Holmes, *Ewing Young*, p. 119.
b) Oscar O. Winther, "Commercial Routes From 1792 to 1843 by Sea and Overland," *Oregon Historical Quarterly*, Vol. 42, No. 3 (Portland, OR: Oregon Historical Society, 1941), p. 240.
c) Sutton, *Pictorial History*, p. 23.
d) Carey, *History*, Vol. 1, p. 265.

145.a) Holmes, *Ewing Young*, p. 120.
b) Winther, "Commercial Routes," p. 240.
c) Corning, *History*, p. 266, 277.

146.a) Maloney, "Hudson's Bay Company," p. 14.
b) Winther, "Commercial Routes," p. 241.
c) Sutton, *Pictorial History*, p. 23.

147.a) Nichols, *South Road*, p. 47.
b) Maloney, "Camp Sites," p. 323.

148.a) Sutton, *Pictorial History*, p. 23.
b) Holmes, *Ewing Young*, p. 120.
c) Bancroft, *Works*, Vol. XXIX, p. 100.
d) Corning, *History*, p. 266.

149.a) Bancroft, *Works*, Vol. XXIX, p. 100.
b) Carey, *History*, Vol. 1, p. 262.

150.a) Sutton, *Pictorial History*, p. 23.
b) Holmes, *Ewing Young*, p. 120.
c) Bancroft, *Works*, Vol. XXIX, p. 100.

151. Holmes, *Ewing Young*, p. 120, 123.

152. *Hist. of the Pac. N. W.*, Vol. I, p. 370.

153.a) Holmes, *Ewing Young*, p. 134.
b) Winther, "Commercial Routes," p. 241.

154. Winther, "Commercial Routes," p. 241.

155. Parrish, *Before the Covered Wagon*, p. 128.

156.a) *Hist. of the Pac. N. W.*, Vol. I, p. 370.
b) Holmes, *Ewing Young*, p. 131.

157. Holmes, *Ewing Young*, p. 131.

158. *Hist. of the Pac. N. W.*, Vol. I, p. 370.

159. Holmes, *Ewing Young*, p. 132.

160.a) Holmes, *Ewing Young*, p. 133.
b) Nichols, *South Road*, p. 48.

161. Holmes, *Ewing Young*, p. 133.

162. Nichols, *South Road*, p. 48.

163. Holmes, *Ewing Young*, p. 133.

164.a) *Hist. of the Pac. N. W.*, Vol. I, p. 370.
b) Holmes, *Ewing Young*, p. 133.

165. Nichols, *South Road*, p. 48.

166. Holmes, *Ewing Young*, p. 133.

167.a) *Hist. of the Pac. N. W.*, Vol. I, p. 371.
b) Holmes, *Ewing Young*, p. 134.
c) Sutton, *Pictorial History*, p. 24.

168. *Hist. of the Pac. N. W.*, Vol. I, p. 371.

169. Nichols, *South Road*, p. 50.

170. Holmes, *Ewing Young*, p. 125.

171.a) *Hist. of the Pac. N. W.*, Vol. I, p. 371.
b) Sutton, *Pictorial History*, p. 25.

172. Carey, *History*, Vol. 1, p. 380.

173.a) Ibid.
b) Bancroft, *Works*, Vol. XXIX, p.249.

174. *Hist. of the Pac. N. W.*, Vol. I, p. 371.

175. Carey, *History*, Vol. 1, p. 380.

176. *Hist. of the Pac. N. W.*, Vol. I, p. 371.

177. Ibid.

178. Nichols, *South Road*, p. 52.

179. Ibid., p. 53.

180.a) Shannon Applegate, *Skookum: an Oregon Pioneer Family's History and Lore* (New York, NY: Beech Tree Books, 1988, p. 59.
b) Barker, *North Umpquas*, p. 7, 25.
c) Ruby, p. 107.
d) Zucker, *Oregon Indians*, p. 42.

181.a) Zucker, *Oregon Indians*, p. 42.
b) Barker, *North Umpquas*, p. 25.

182.a) Bancroft, *Works*, Vol. XXIX, p. 266.
b) Winther, "Commercial Routes," p. 242.
c) Carey, *History*, Vol. 1, p. 325.

183. Corning, *History*, p. 108.

184. Carey, *History*, Vol. 1, p. 325. [There was not a wagon road yet, so they must have traveled by mule or horse.]

185. Nichols, *South Road*, p. 59.

186.a) Bancroft, *Works*, Vol. XXIX, p. 266.
b) Winther, "Commercial Routes," p. 242.
c) Nichols, *South Road*, p. 60.

187. Thomas H. Hunt, *Ghost Trails to California* (American West Publishing Company, 1974), p. 64.

188. Ibid., p. 65.

189. Ibid.

190.a) Devere & Helen Helfrich, "Applegate Trail," *Klamath Echoes*, Vol. 9, (Klamath Falls, OR: Klamath County Historical Society, 1971), p. 17.
b) Binns, *Peter Skene Ogden*, p. 229.

191.a) Jesse Applegate, *Applegate's Way Bill* (Oregon City, OR: The Oregon Spectator, 1848), p.2.
b) Jessy Quinn Thornton, *Oregon and California in 1848* (New York, NY: Arno Press, 1973 c1849), Vol. 1, p. 177, 181.

192. Binns, *Peter Skene Ogden*, p. 229.

193. Ibid., p. 230.

194.a) Levi Scott, *From Independence to Independence* (Sitka, AL: unpublished manuscript by James Layton Collins, 1967), p. 127.
b) Lindsay Applegate, "Notes and Reminiscences of Laying Out and Establishing the Old Emigrant Road into Southern Oregon," *Oregon Historical Quarterly*, Vol. 22, No. 1 (Portland, OR: Oregon Historical Society, March, 1921), p. 37.

195. Scott, *Independence*, p. 127.

195. Applegate, "Old Emigrant Road," p. 37.

197. Hunt, *Ghost Trails*, p. 64.

198. Winther, "Commercial Routes," p. 238.

199. Sutton, *Pictorial History*, p. 25.

200. Corning, *History*, p. 186.

201. Carey, *History*, Vol. 1, p. 248.

202.a) Joseph Schafer, Ph D., *Jessie Applegate Pioneer and State Builder* (Eugene, OR: The University of Oregon Bulletin, 1912), p. 9.
b) "The Applegate Trail: 1846-1883 The Southern Route," *The Trail Marker*, Vol. 5, No. 1 (Summer 1994), p. 1.

203.a) Sutton, Pictorial History, p. 25.
b) Schafer, *Jessie Applegate*, p. 9.

204.a) Winther, "Commercial Routes," p. 238.
b) Sutton, *Pictorial History*, p. 27.

205. Schafer, *Jessie Applegate*, p. 9.

206.a) Carey, *History*, Vol. 1, p. 392.
b) Bancroft, *Works*, Vol. XXIX, p. 395.

207. Carey, *History*, Vol. 1, p. 392.

208.a) Bancroft, *Works*, Vol. XXIX, p. 396.
b) Carey, *History*, Vol. 1, p. 392.

209. Ibid.

210.a) Wilford H. Brown, ed., *This Was a Man* (North Hollywood, CA: Camas Press, 1971), p. 17, 67.
b) Maude Applegate Rucker, *The Oregon Trail and Some of its Blazers* (New York, NY: W. Neale, 1930), p. 71.
c) Carey, *History*, Vol. 1, p. 392.

211.a) Brown, ed., *Man*, p. 17.
b) Carey, *History*, Vol. 1, p. 392.

212. Carey, *History*, Vol. 1, p. 393.

213. Ibid., p. 316.

214. Bancroft, *Works*, Vol. XXIX, p. 401.

215.a) Ibid., p. 402.
b) Carey, *History*, Vol. 1, p. 394.

216. Bancroft, *Works*, Vol. XXIX, p. 405.

217.a) Ibid., p. 408.
b) Carey, *History*, Vol. 1, p. 394.

218. Bancroft, *Works*, Vol. XXIX, p. 408.

219.a) Carey, *History*, Vol. 1, p. 394.
b) Bancroft, *Works*, Vol. XXIX, p. 409.

220. Carey, *History*, Vol. 1, p. 394.

221.a) Ibid.
b) Bancroft, *Works*, Vol. XXIX, p. 407.

222. Bancroft, Works, Vol. XXIX, p. 406.

223. Winther, "Commercial Routes," p. 238.

224. Brown, ed., *Man*, p. 17.

225.a) Ibid.
b) Corning, *History*, p. 186.

226. Brown, ed., *Man*, p. 18.

227.a) Applegate, *Skookum*, p. 37.

b) Ferol Egan, *Fremont: Explorer for a Restless Nation* (Garden City, NY: Doubleday & Company, Inc., 1977), p. 168.

228.a) Brown, ed., *Man*, p. 18.
b) Applegate, *Skookum*, p. 50.

229. Applegate, *Skookum*, p. 51.

230.a) Brown, ed., *Man*, p. 18.
b) Applegate, *Skookum*, p. 50.
c) Egan, *Fremont*, p. 170.

231. Bancroft, *Works*, Vol. XXIX, p. 410.

232.Ibid., p. 406.

233. Corning, *History*, p. 9, 10.

234. A. E. Garrison, *Life and Labours of Rev. A. E. Garrison* (Monmouth, OR: Published by the Garrison Clan, 1943) (Portland, OR: Oregon Historical Society, Mss #1009), p. 45.

235. Nichols, *South Road*, p. 37.

236.a) *Hist. of the Pac. N. W.*, Vol. I, p. 370.
b) Sutton, *Pictorial History*, p. 22.
c) Barker, *North Umpquas*, p. 11.

237. A. H. Garrison, "Reminiscences of Abraham Henry Garrison - Over the Oregon Trail in 1846," *Overland Journal* (Independence, MO: Oregon - California Trails Association), Vol. 2, No. 2, (Summer, 1993), p. 30.

238.a) Fred Lockley, *Conversations With Pioneer Women* (Eugene, OR: Rainy Day Press, 1981), p. 89.
b) Tolbert Carter, *Pioneer Days* (Portland, OR: Transactions of the Oregon Pioneers Association, 1906), p. 89.
c) Scott, *Independence*, p. 166.
d) Corning, *History*, p. 15.

239.a) Carter, *Pioneer Days*, p. 86.
b) Dale Lowell Morgon, *Overland in 1846: Diaries and Letters of the California-Oregon Trail*

(Georgetown, CA: Talisman Press, 1963), Vol.1, p. 196.
c) Lucia Moore, *The Story of Eugene* (New York, NY: Stratford House, 1949), p. 13.
d) Corning, *History*, p. 225.

240. Moore, *Eugene*, p. 2. [Also U.S.G.S. maps.]

241.a) Schlesser, *Fort Umpqua*, p. 7.
b) *Hist. of the Pac. N. W.*, Vol. I, p. 368.

242. *Hist. of the Pac. N. W.*, Vol. I, p. 368.

243. Schlesser, *Fort Umpqua*, p. 7.

244.a) *Hist. of the Pac. N. W.*, Vol. I, p. 368.
b) Scott, *Independence*, p. 94.
c) Schlesser, *Fort Umpqua*, p. 7.

245. *Hist. of the Pac. N. W.*, Vol. I, p. 368.

246.a) LaLande, *First Over the Siskiyous*, p. 128.
b) Nichols, *South Road*, p. 10.

247.a) Applegate, "The Applegate Trail," p. 21.
b) Scott, *Independence*, p. 101.
c) LaLande, *First Over the Siskiyous*, p. 129.

248. McArthur, *Or. Geog. Names*, p. 771.

249.a) Applegate, "Old Emigrant Road," p. 2.
b) Corning, *History*, p. 317.
c) *Hist. of the Pac. N. W.*, Vol. I, p. 369.

250. *Hist. of the Pac. N. W.*, Vol. I, p. 369. [The Umpqua River also had its own Umpqua Valley. (a) Schlesser, *Fort Umpqua*, p.7. b) Scott, *Independence*, p. 94.; c) *Hist. of the Pac. N. W.*, Vol.I, p. 369.

251.a) Ibid.
b) Scott, *Independence*, p. 94.

252. LaLande, *First Over the Siskiyous*, p. 122.

253. Sessions S. Wheeler, *The Nevada Desert* (Caldwell, ID: The Caxton Printers, Ltd., 1971)

254. Bancroft, *Works*, Vol. XXIX, p. 253.

255.a) Corning, *History*, p. 164.
b) Bancroft, *Works*, Vol. XXIX, p. 512.

256. Carey, *History*, Vol. 1, p. 396.

257. Bancroft, *Works*, Vol. XXIX, p. 512.

258. Corning, *History*, p. 164.

259. Carey, *History*, Vol. 1, p. 396.

260.a) Corning, *History*, p. 164.
b) Carey, *History*, Vol. 1, p. 396.

261. Corning, *History*, p. 164.

262. Bancroft, *Works*, Vol. XXIX, p. 512. [Steven Meek's brother, Joseph Meek, was the first territorial sheriff of the newly formed provisional government at Champoeg in the Willamette Valley. (a) Sutton, *Pictorial History*, p. 26.; b) Corning, *History*, p. 50, 164.

263. Bancroft, *Works*, Vol. XXIX, p. 513.

264.a) Corning, *History*, p. 164.
b) Bancroft, *Works*, Vol. XXIX, p. 515.

265. Corning, *History*, p. 164.

266.a) Carey, *History*, Vol. 2, p. 724.
b) *Hist. of the Pac. N. W.*, Vol. II, p.203.

267. Carey, *History*, Vol. 1, p. 397.

268.a) Morgan, *Overland in 1846*, Vol. 1, p. 72.
a) *Hist. of the Pac. N. W.*, Vol. II, p. 205.

269. *Hist. of the Pac. N. W.*, Vol. II, p. 205.

270. Ibid., p. 203.
b) Morgan, *Overland in 1846*, Vol. 1, p. 72.

271.a) *Hist. of the Pac. N. W.*, Vol. II, p. 204.
b) Carey, *History*, Vol. 1, p. 397.

272. *Hist. of the Pac. N. W.*, Vol. II, p. 205.

273. Morgan, *Overland in 1846*, Vol. 1, p. 71.

274.a) Carey, *History*, Vol. 2, p. 724.
b) Sutton, *Pictorial History*, p. 28.

275.a) *Hist. of the Pac. N. W.*, Vol. II, p. 205.
b) Morgan, *Overland in 1846*, Vol. 1, p. 90.
c) Sutton, *Pictorial History*, p. 28.
d) McArthur, *Geographic Names*, p. 44.
e) Carey, *History*, Vol. 2, p. 724.

276. Sutton, *Pictorial History*, p. 28.

277.a) William James Ghent, *The Road to Oregon: A Chronicle of the Great Emigrant Trail* (New York, NY: Green and Co., 1929), p. 86, 87.
b) Bancroft, *Works*, Vol. XXIX, p. 543.

278.a) Bancroft, *Works*, Vol.XXIX, p. 543.
b) Emerson Hough, *54-40 or Fight* (New York, NY: A. L. Burt Company, 1909), p. 239.

279. Corning, *History*, p. 178.

280. Fogdall, *John McLoughlin*, p. 271.

281.a) *Hist. of the Pac. N. W.*, Vol. I, p. 371.
b) Brown, ed., *Man*, p. 21.

282.a) Bancroft, *Works*, Vol. XXIX, p. 543.
b) Scott, *Independence*, p. 91.

283. Scott, *Independence*, p. 91.

284. Ibid., p. 100.

285. Ibid., p. 102.

286. Ibid., p. 103.

287. Ibid.

288. Ibid., p. 104. [According to Bancroft, the leader of this first expedition had been Levi Scott.] Bancroft, *Works*, Vol. XXIX, p. 544.

Ch. 2 EXPLORING and BLAZING the NEW SOUTHERN ROUTE TO OREGON

From LaCreole near Present Day Dallas, in Oregon to Fort Hall: Oregon, California, Nevada, Utah and Idaho

Toward the end of the first week of June, 1846, a party of emigrants guided by John Turner left LaCreole Creek.[1] Turner had been in trouble with the Indians in the Rogue River Valley on previous expeditions.[2] There were eighty people in this party.[3] They were on their way to California by way of the Hudson's Bay pack trail.

Jesse and Lindsay Applegate, along with others, had promoted the idea of finding a south wagon road to the Willamette Valley.[4] When the first expedition failed to find a new route, and those men returned,[5] a new company was formed by Jesse Applegate.[6] There were fifteen men: Levi Scott, Jesse Applegate, Moses Harris, David Goff, Robert Smith, William Sportsman, William G. Parker, John M. Scott, Benjamin F. Burch,[7] John Owens,[8] Lindsay Applegate,[9] John Jones,[10] Samuel H. Goodhue,[11] Henry Bogus[12] and Bennett Osborne.[13]

On the morning of June 20, 1846, they left from LaCreole, near present day Dallas, Oregon, to explore a new southern route to Oregon.[14] Each man provided his own saddle horse, pack horse,[15] arms, ammunition, blankets and provisions.[16] "They left with a firm determination never to retrace their steps - never to abandon the noble and philanthropic enterprise until they shall have found a good wagon road, if such thing be possible." (*Oregon Spectator*, July 9, 1846).[17]

Before leaving, they met with Peter Skene Ogden, the new chief factor for the Hudson's Bay Company.[18] He had been through this portion of the country.[19] He told the exploring party there was a desert area called the Klamath Basin on the other side of the Cascade Mountains. When he was there, he and his men had hiked up to the mountains and filled their sacks with snow for water to cross the desert.

Ogden gave Jesse Applegate a map of the Oregon Territory to help find their way.[20] The southeast portion of the country they were to cross was marked "unexplored region" on the map.[21]

After meeting Levi Scott near Corvallis, the exploring party traveled south down the Willamette Valley. They crossed the Calapooya Mountains and entered the Umpqua Valley by following the California Pack Trail.[22] In the Umpqua Valley an old Indian showed them the way to the foot trail that crossed over the Calapooya Mountains.[23] They crossed the North Umpqua River and the South Umpqua River.

Coming up the South Umpqua the explorers met a party of eight or ten emigrants coming north from California.[24] These emigrants had been attacked by Indians. One of them was wounded by an arrow and one cow was killed. This happened on a creek now known as Cow Creek.[25]

That evening the exploring party arrived at the Umpqua Canyon.[26] After camping for the night, the men entered the canyon the next morning. They traveled four or five miles through the canyon and crossed Canyon Creek several times. "...the little trail we were following turned up the side of the ridge where the woods were more open, and wound its way to the top of the mountain."[27] The trail turned up the right side of the canyon.[28]

Figure 1 The Umpqua Valley

After camping through the night, Jesse Applegate, W. G. Parker, B.F. Burch, and Levi Scott went back to explore the canyon. This time they entered from the south and followed it to where they had been the day before. After exploring the canyon, they decided a road could be made for wagons to travel through the canyon.[29] There were some steep places and the canyon was very thick with brush. There were also logs and boulders that would have to be moved.[30]

That evening as they camped they heard Indians near the horses and saw tracks very close the next day. "Whenever the trail passed through the cuts we dismounted and led our horses, having our guns in hand ready at any moment to use them in self-defense, for we had adopted this rule, never to be the aggressor."[31]

The exploring party traveled down Cow Creek and crossed it. They passed over a range of hills and crossed Grave Creek. They traveled down wooded broken country to Jump Off Joe.[32] Crossing Jump Off Joe Creek, they saw a small party of Indians. They went toward them to ask directions. The Indians fled when they saw these strange men.[33]

When they came to the Rogue River there was an Indian Village on the creek at the crossing.[34] They spent the night in a prairie north of the river, and proceeded to the village the next morning. Most of the native people hid out while a few of them helped the explorers cross with a canoe. The men stood guard on the north side while one man in the canoe crossed with some packs. Next they drove the horses across, then their packs with one man crossing each time.[35] They gave the Indians who helped a tent and some tobacco for their troubles.[36]

The exploring party traveled along the south side of the Rogue River.[37] As they traveled along the Rogue River there were Indians about on the north shore.[38] This was just south of the Table Rocks. They eventually traveled southeast along the south side of Bear Creek.[39]

They later found that the party of emigrants that headed south two weeks before had had trouble with the Indians. These emigrants had a few horses stolen.[40] This was the party of emigrants led by John Turner.[41]

The exploring party encountered no ill fate and continued on down the Rogue River Valley.[42] "All day long we traveled over rich black soil covered with rank grass, clover, and pea vine, and at night encamped near the other party on the stream now known as Emigrant Creek, near the foot of the Siskiyou Mountains."[43]

That evening south of the present site of Ashland they caught up with the party of emigrants. This party consisted of Canadians, French, and French-Canadians. The emigrants told the exploring party there was a way into the Siskiyou Mountains by traveling along a creek later known as Emigrant Creek.[44] This other party continued traveling on the California Pack Trail south to the Siskiyou Mountains.[45]

The exploring party traveled southeast along Emigrant Creek, east along Tyler Creek, and entered the Cascade Mountains through what is known today as the Greensprings. They crossed Keene Creek near the summit of the Siskiyou Ridge, camped at Round Prairie and traveled along a stream after crossing present day Jenny Creek. Jesse Applegate and Levi Scott found a beaver in the stream. Levi Scott shot the beaver and afterward they called it Beaver Creek.[46]

The explorers had taken a natural course and traveled toward the south. When they came to the Klamath River they decided to travel north and try to find a place to cross. They traveled a considerable distance without finding a possible route, so they turned and traveled south and again found nothing.[47]

After finding a suitable camp, four of the men, including Levi Scott, took off toward higher ridges to survey the area. Six or eight miles from camp, on the top of a high butte in Long Prairie, they saw Klamath River and beyond. They saw through the forests to the open country below. This gave them a good view of a possible route.[48] This was July 4, 1846. "It was an exciting moment...." said Lindsay Applegate,

> ...after the many days spent in dense forests and among the mountains, and the whole party broke forth in cheer after cheer. An Indian who had not observed us until the shouting began, broke away from the river bank near us and ran to the hills a quarter of a mile distant. An antelope could scarcely have made better time, for we continued shouting as he ran and his speed seemed to increase until he was lost from our view among the pines."[49]
> (Lindsay Applegate, 1877)

The exploring party crossed the Klamath River. They traveled along the river and along Lower Klamath Lake. They saw signal fires off in the distance. The Indians knew they had arrived.[50]

Traveling along Lower Klamath Lake, the explorers journeyed from the Oregon Territory to what is today California and camped on Hot Creek. This was the same location Colonel Fremont had been at a few months before while traveling north.[51] He had lost three of his men.[52] The explorers found evidence on the ground that looked like a burial site.[53]

The next day they traveled northeast in the direction of Tule Lake. Here they saw a group of Indians. The Indians ran about in every direction.[54] The men felt the Indians must have thought they were here to avenge the deaths of the men of Fremont's party.[55]

> On every line of travel from the Atlantic to the Pacific, there has been great loss of life from a failure to exercise a proper degree of caution, and too often have reckless and foolhardy men who have, through the want of proper care, become embroiled in difficulties with the Indians, gained the reputation of being Indian fighters and heroes, while the men who were able to conduct parties in safety through the country of warlike savages, escaped the world's notice.
> (Lindsay Applegate, 1877)[56]

Figure 2 Klamath River and beyond

The explorers rode up to a wigwam that appeared to be an Indian village and found a very old Indian woman. She offered them a fish she had in her hands. They looked at the fish and rode on, leaving her with it. A short distance after meeting the older woman, they confronted two Indian men carrying packs. The Indians saw them, dropped their packs and fled. Inspecting the packs, the exploring party found the Indian men were carrying seeds and roots.[57] As they left the packs and rode on, they saw more signal fires in all directions.[58]

After camping on the west side of the lake, they ascended a rocky ridge to decide which direction to take. The ridge was made of lava formations with many caves, cracks and crevices that could cause their horses to slip. After determining they would travel east around the south end of the lake, they decided to retrace their steps to descend the ridge. The men became separated among the rocks. When they got to the bottom, David Goff was missing. They traveled a little further north and camped to wait for him.[59]

As they camped, a horseman came riding toward them. The men soon discovered the horseman was David Goff. He had found some mountain sheep and was pursuing them when he lost his way.[60] Indians were in canoes on the lake shore, but he was left unharmed.[61]

On the east side of Lower Klamath Lake the exploring party came upon what is now known as Lost River. They followed up Lost River to find a place to cross.[62] They saw an Indian family across the river and used sign language to ask for directions. The family was surprised and a little fearful of these men. The Indian family came toward the shore making peaceful signs. The spokesman for the group showed them immediately that by going upstream they would find a place to cross. He motioned by showing the height on his ankle how deep the ford would be.[63]

About a mile north they found a crossing known later as Stone Bridge. The water was 6 to 15 inches deep.[64] Just before these road hunters crossed Lost River they were again in Oregon. (U.S.G.S. maps)

Passing Tule Lake, the exploring party traveled east in the direction of a butte which they used as a guide post. They followed along what is today approximately the state line, passing north of Clear River Marsh,[65] through a country covered with juniper trees.[66] Clear River Marsh is known today as Clear Lake.[67] They were traveling east, but they were no longer following Ogden's map. The men could no longer decipher the route traveled by Ogden.[68]

As they camped, the men were disappointed with Captain Jesse Applegate's decisions of direction. This was mainly because they found no water. He decided to resign his post. They did not really want him to. Levi Scott proposed they choose two men to act as counselors. Jesse Applegate agreed to this. The two men chosen were Levi Scott and David Goff.[69]

Traveling southeast, the exploring party camped that evening at a good spring. The water was warm.[70] They named the spring Goff's Spring[71] Goff's Spring is known today as Pot Hole Springs.[72]

Traveling east from Goff's Spring they came upon an Indian near a patch of willows. He was startled when he saw them. He handed them a ground hog he had in his hand. They looked at the ground hog and then handed it back to him with a piece of tobacco. He looked at the piece of tobacco and then looked at the men. They made a sign to him that he was free to go. He walked away. The further he

Figure 3 Lower Klamath Lake

walked, the faster he walked until he was out of sight.[73]

The next day the men came to a large Lake.[74] They saw wild geese on this shallow lake and named the lake Goose Lake.[75] After traveling around the south side of the lake, they climbed a ridge and entered a valley, now known as Surprise Valley.[76] They were surprised to find plenty of water and grass in this valley.[77]

From here they entered a more desert country.[78] They traveled east across the desert and came to "...a sheer wall of solid granite, varying in height from twenty or thirty to several hundred feet, and entirely impassable."[79] It was probably Hays Canyon Range. (U.S.G.S. Maps) They separated into two groups to decide which way to go.[80] The party that traveled south found an opening in this range. They gathered the others and proceeded forward.[81] They came to Upper High Rock Canyon where the valley narrowed, and the grade descended into a gorge that led into High Rock Canyon.[82]

The road hunters exited High Rock Canyon and came to present day High Rock Lake and Mud Meadows. There

Figure 4 They saw wild geese on this shallow lake and named the lake Goose Lake.

were springs here.[83]   They camped for the night at one of the springs.

 The next day they entered present day Black Rock Desert between two mountain ridges.[84]   In the distance They saw smoke rising in the air.[85]   They continued south[86] about 20 miles and came to present day Black Rock.   The smoke they saw was steam coming from "an immense boiling springs"[87] at Black Rock.   "The cliffs, at the extremity of the ridge, were formed of immense mass of black volcanic rock and all about were vast piles of cinders, resembling those from a blacksmith's forge." (Lindsay Applegate, 1877)[88]

 The road hunters thought by this time they should have found Ogden's River.   From Black Rock they could see an immense desert before them in many directions.[89]   They could not agree on which direction to take to look for the river.   One thing they could agree on was to separate.[90] Jesse Applegate, Lindsay Applegate, Bob Smith, Henry Bogus, William Sportsman, and "Black" Harris went toward the southeast.[91]   Levi Scott, David Goff, Benjamin F. Burch, William G. Parker, John Owens, Bennett Osborne, Samuel H. Goodhue, John Jones and John M. Scott went south.[92]

 After Scott's party traveled about 20 miles, they came upon some willows.   When they approached the willows, an Indian sprang up, saw the men and took off running.   He had made a camp fire and had been roasting a badger.   There was an excellent spring here and they camped for the night.[93]

> We did not molest the poor, frightened Indian's property, but left everything just as we found it.   He might have remained and enjoyed his badger feast and our company in perfect safety if he had only known it.[94]

 From here Scott and his party traveled southeast.[95] Twelve miles further they found another spring in this "vast, sandy desert."[96]   They traveled south the next day and came across Indian tracks.   The men followed the tracks assuming they would probably lead them to water.   The tracks headed in an easterly direction.[97]   They reached the summit of a mountain by sunset.   In the distance they could see a stretch of greenery. This was a welcome sight.   With dry throats, they only managed to reach the foot of another mountain by dark. The green they saw was still in the distance.[98]

 As they camped that night, John Jones did not tie his horse.   He insisted that his horse would not run off.   By morning it was gone.   He went searching for his horse while the others went searching for water toward the green in the distance.[99]

Meanwhile, Jesse Applegate's group traveled southeast about fifteen miles and found jack rabbit tracks.[100] They followed the rabbit tracks about five more miles and found holes in the ground. It was a spring animals were using for water. It was not a good spring, but it was water.[101] From that time on, this spring was known as Rabbit Hole Springs.[102]

That morning Applegate and his men saw clouds of smoke to the east. They continued in a southeasterly direction.[103] Traveling along a ridge they saw more rabbit tracks. They followed the tracks and eventually came to another spring. It took the rest of the day and into the night to gather enough water for the men and their horses.[104]

The next morning the Applegate party continued along the ridge four or five miles and came to a large spring, but they found this to be so full of alkali, "...we could only use it in making coffee."[105]

There was nothing but a vast desert in front of them. The heat was getting to them. The alkaline water had not helped their thirst. They thought they saw a lake in the distance, but after a while it proved to be a mirage, "...one of those optical illusions so often experienced on the desert."[106] A while later they saw willows. They rode in the direction of the willows and found they were lava rocks.[107]

Applegate and his men traveled eastward for another day in search of water and the river. From the top of some rocks they saw a green spot in the desert. It appeared to be five or six miles away. Robert Smith was suffering from a severe headache and decided to rest a while. The others traveled on to find the spot of green.[108]

After four or five miles Applegate and his men saw a man on horseback approaching. They found that it was John Jones. Jones' horse had found water, he had found his horse and was riding toward them. Seeing the Humboldt River they immediately made a "stampede" to reach the water.[109]

At length both parties met up on the Humboldt River.[110] Bogus and Sportsman filled a container with water and took it back to Bob Smith who had managed to make it a little further toward the river.[111] They had found the Humboldt River and their horses could only drink from the steep bank.[112] It was about eight feet wide, but full which was refreshing to them.[113]

As the exploring party traveled northeast following the river it became wider with a very shallow stream. There were a lot of tules along the bank. This accounted for the green they kept seeing.[114]

Following along the Humboldt River the men saw a blackened "mass of loose sand and ashes"[115] which was burnt "peat bogs" from a fire that had stretched for miles. This was the cause of the smoke they had seen earlier. The river was about 30 feet wide, but sluggish and filled with alkali.[116]

The explorers traveled three more days up the river. The river bottom eventually widened out into a meadow and in the distance to the west there was a ridge with a pass through it. They set up camp and the next day Levi Scott and William Parker left to explore a route for the wagons to take to Black Rock.[117]

Three days later Jesse Applegate, Moses Harris, Henry Bogus, David Goff, and John Owens left for Fort Hall to secure supplies and to persuade the emigrants coming from the east to take the new road. It was July 25.[118] The rest of the expedition stayed behind to recoup themselves and their horses. Those who remained continued to travel slowly up the river to be closer to the emigrants as they came from the east.[119]

Figure 5 Black Rock

On the way to Fort Hall, Bogus rode off toward St. Louis to try to catch up with a friend of his. His friend was the son of Captain Grant, Commander of Fort Hall. Bogus had heard that Grant's son had started for Canada by way of St. Louis.[120] Bogus was never heard from again.[121]

By the time Jesse Applegate and the three men with him had arrived at Fort Hall, many emigrants had already traveled through. They were either on their way to Oregon by way of the Oregon Trail or on their way to California by way of the California Trail. This was probably around August 7.

On August 8, Jesse Applegate had gone west of Fort Hall and caught up with emigrants who had made about eight miles and persuaded them to backtrack and take his new route.[122] At Fort Hall he mailed a letter to the *Western Expositor* in Independence, Missouri. It was an open letter to future Oregon emigrants:

Fort Hall, August 10, 1846[123]
Gentlemen:

The undersigned are happy to inform you that a southern route to the Willamette, has just been explored, and a portion of the emigrants of the present year are now on the road. Owing to the unavoidable delay, the exploring party did not arrive at the fork of the road until some of the front companies of emigrants were passed, perhaps eighty or one hundred wagons.

The new route follows the road to California about 320 miles from this place, and enters the Oregon Territory by the way of the Clamet [sic] Lake, passes through the splendid valley of the Rogue and Umpqua rivers, and enters the valley of the Willamette near its south eastern extremity.

The advantages gained to the emigrant by this route is of greatest importance--the distance is considerably shortened, the grass and water plenty, the sterile regions and dangerous crossings of the Snake and Columbia Rivers avoided as well as the Cascade Mountain[sic]--he may reach his place of destination with his wagons and property in time to build a cabin and sow wheat before the rainy season. This road has been explored, and will be opened at the expense of the citizens of Oregon, and nothing whatever is demanded of the emigrants....

Editors of Missouri, Illinois, and Iowa, friendly to the prosperity of Oregon will please insert the foregoing communication.

Jesse Applegate.[124]

NOTES   Chapter 2

1.a) Nichols, *South Road*, p. 64.
b) Bancroft, *Works*, Vol. XXIX, p. 545.

2.a) Lambert Florin, *Western Wagon Wheels: a Pictorial Memorial to the Wheels That Won the West* Seattle, WA: Superior Pub. Co., 1970), pp. 35, 44, 47.

3.a) Nichols, *South Road*, p. 64.
b) Bancroft, *Works*, Vol. XXIX, p. 545.

4. Bancroft, *Works*, Vol. XXIX, p. 544.

5. Nichols, *South Road*, p. 76.

6. Scott, *Independence*, p. 96.

7.a) Applegate, "Old Emigrant Road," pp. 14, 43.
b) Applegate, "Applegate Trail," pp. 5, 18.
c) Morgan, *Overland in 1846*, Vol. 2, p. 638.
d) Scott, *Independence*, p. 104.

e) *Hist. of the Pac. N. W.*, Vol. I, p. 371.

f) Bancroft, *Works*, Vol. XXIX, p. 544.

g) Alice Applegate Sargent, "A Sketch of the Rogue River Valley and Southern Oregon History," *Oregon Historical Quarterly*, Vol. 22, No. 1, (Portland, OR: Oregon Historical Society, March, 1921), p. 2.

h) Mildred Baker Burchard, "Scott's and Applegate's Old South Road," *Oregon Historical Quarterly*, Vol. 41, No. 4 (Portland, OR: Oregon Historical Society, December, 1942), p. 406.

i) Buena Cobb Stone, "Southern Route into Oregon: Notes and a New Map," *Oregon Historical Quarterly* Vol. 57, No. 2 (Salem, OR: Statesman Publishing Co., June, 1946), p. 138.

8.a) Applegate, "Old Emigrant Road," pp. 14, 43.

b) Applegate, "Applegate Trail," pp. 5, 18.

c) Scott, *Independence*, p. 104.

d) *Hist. of the Pac. N. W.*, Vol. I, p. 371.

e) Bancroft, *Works*, Vol. XXIX, p. 544.

f) Sargent, "Sketch of the Rogue River Valley," p. 2.

g) Burchard, "South Road," p. 406.

h) Stone, "Southern Route," p. 138.

9.a) Applegate, "Old Emigrant Road," pp. 14, 43.

b) Applegate, "Applegate Trail," pp. 5, 18.

c) Morgon, *Overland in 1846*, Vol. 1, p. 638.

d) Scott, *Independence*, p. 104.

e) *Hist. of the Pac. N. W.*, Vol. I, p. 371.

f) Bancroft, *Works*, Vol. XXIX, p. 544.

g) Burchard, "South Road," p. 406.

h) Stone, "Southern Route," p. 138.

10.a) Applegate, "Old Emigrant Road," pp. 14, 43.

b) Applegate, "Applegate Trail," pp. 5, 18.

c) Morgon, *Overland in 1846*, Vol. 1, p. 638.

d) *Hist. of the Pac. N. W.*, Vol. I, p. 371.

e) Bancroft, *Works*, Vol. XXIX, p. 544.

f) Sargent, "Sketch of the Rogue River Valley," p. 2.

g) Burchard, "South Road," p. 406.

h) Stone, "Southern Route," p. 138.

11.a) Applegate, "Old Emigrant Road," p. 14.

b) Applegate, "Applegate Trail," p. 5.

c) Morgan, *Overland in 1846*, Vol. 1, p. 638.

d) Scott, *Independence*, p. 104.

e) *Hist. of the Pac. N. W.*, Vol. I, p. 371.

f) Bancroft, *Works*, Vol. XXIX, p. 544.

g) Sargent, "Sketch of the Rogue River Valley," p. 2.

h) Burchard, "South Road," p. 406.

i) Stone, "Southern Route," p. 138.

12.a) Scott, *Independence*, p. 104.

b) *Hist. of the Pac. N. W.*, Vol. I, p. 371.

c) Bancroft, *Works*, Vol. XXIX, p. 544.

d) W. A. Moxley, Papers, *The Scott-Applegate, or Southern Route to Oregon*, (Portland, OR: Oregon Historical Society Mss #855, 1950), p. 1.

13.a) Applegate, "Applegate Trail," p. 5.

b) Morgan, *Overland in 1846*, Vol. 1, p. 638.

c) *Hist. of the Pac. N. W.*, Vol. I, p. 371.

d) Moxley, OHS Mss #855, p. 1.

14.a) Applegate, "Old Emigrant Road," p. 15.

b) Bancroft, *Works*, Vol. XXIX, p. 544.

c) Burchard, "South Road," p. 406. [This was about two weeks after the party of emigrants headed by John Turner left for California.]

15. Sargent, "Sketch of the Rogue River Valley," p. 2.

16. Applegate, "Applegate Trail," p. 2.

17. Nichols, *South Road*, p. 72.

18. Corning, *History*, p. 178.

19.a) LaLande, *First Over the Siskiyous*, p. 46.

b) Helfrich, "Applegate Trail," (1971), Vol. 9, p. 2.

20.a) Scott, *Independence*, p. 104.

b) Helfrich, "Applegate Trail," (1971), Vol. 9, p. 2.

21. Applegate, "Old Emigrant Road," p. 15.

22.a) Scott, *Independence*, p. 105.

b) Applegate, "Old Emigrant Road," p. 15.

c) Bancroft, *Works*, Vol. XXIX, p. 545.

23.a) Applegate, "Old Emigrant Road," p. 16.

b) Burchard, "South Road," p. 406.

24.a) Scott, *Independence*, p. 105.

b) Applegate, "Old Emigrant Road," p. 17.

25. Scott, *Independence*, p. 106.

26.a) Applegate, "Old Emigrant Road," p. 16.

b) Scott, *Independence*, p. 105.

c) Applegate, "Applegate Trail," p. 20.

27. Applegate, "Old Emigrant Road," p. 16.

28. Scott, *Independence*, p. 106.

29.a) Applegate, "Old Emigrant Road," p. 17.

b) Scott, *Independence*, p. 106.

30. Scott, *Independence*, p. 106.

31. Applegate, "Old Emigrant Road," p. 17.

32. Scott, *Independence*, p. 107. [A few years before the Applegate Trail, Joe McLoughlin, John McLoughlin's son, escaped a party of pursuing Indians by jumping off a bluff into a thicket of bushes at a creek and managed to get safely back to his camp. The creek was named Jump Off Joe Creek.] Scott, *Independence*, p. 107.

33. Ibid.

34.a) Ibid., p. 108.

b) Applegate, "Old Emigrant Road," p. 18.

35. Scott, *Independence*, p. 108.

36. Ibid., p. 109.

37.a) Scott, *Independence*, p. 109.
Applegate, "Old Emigrant Road," p. 19.

38. Applegate, "Old Emigrant Road," p. 19.

39.a) Scott, *Independence*, p. 109.

Applegate, "Old Emigrant Road," p. 19.

40. Applegate, "Old Emigrant Road," p. 19.

41. Nichols, *South Road*, p. 64.

42. Applegate, "Old Emigrant Road," p. 19.

43. Ibid.

44. Scott, *Independence*, p. 109.

45. Applegate, "Old Emigrant Road," p. 19.

46. Scott, *Independence*, p. 109.

47. Ibid.

48. Ibid., p. 110.

49.a) Applegate, "Old Emigrant Road," p. 21.

b) Bancroft, *Works*, Vol. XXIX, p. 546.

50.a) Devere & Helen Helfrich, "Applegate Trail II: 'West of the Cascades'," *Klamath Echoes*, Vol. 14, (Klamath Falls, OR: Klamath County Historical Society, 1976), p. 21.

b) Bancroft, *Works*, Vol. XXIX, p. 546.

51. a) Bancroft, *Works*, Vol. XXIX, p. 546.

b) "News and Comment: Monuments and Memorials," *Oregon Historical Quarterly* Vol. 31, No. 3 (Portland, OR: Oregon Historical Society, 1930), p. 407.

52. "News and Comment: Monuments and Memorials," *Oregon Historical Quarterly* Vol. 32, No. 2 (Portland, OR: Oregon Historical Society, 1931), p. 185.

53.a) Applegate, "Old Emigrant Road," p. 21.

b) Bancroft, *Works*, Vol. XXIX, p. 547.

54. Scott, *Independence*, p. 110.

55.a) Applegate, "Applegate Trail," p. 8.

b) Applegate, "Old Emigrant Road," p. 22.

c) Bancroft, *Works*, Vol. XXIX, p. 547.

56. Applegate, "Old Emigrant Road," p. 22.

57. Scott, *Independence*, p. 111.

58.a) Ibid.
b) Bancroft, *Works*, Vol. XXIX, p. 546.

59. Applegate, "Old Emigrant Road," p. 23.

60. Ibid.

61. Applegate, "Old Emigrant Road," p. 24. [Reference to David Goff is according to Lindsay Applegate. Bancroft, however, tells the story referring to the person as Levi Scott. (Bancroft, *Works*, Vol. XXIX, p. 548.) Levi Scott does not mention this incident at all. (Scott, *Independence*, p. 112.)]

62.a) Applegate, "Old Emigrant Road," p. 24.
b) Bancroft, *Works*, Vol. XXIX, p. 548.
c) Scott, *Independence*, p. 112.

63.a) Scott, *Independence*, p. 112.
b) Applegate, "Old Emigrant Road," p. 24.

64.a) Scott, *Independence*, p. 113.
b) Applegate, "Old Emigrant Road," p. 24.

65. Applegate, "Old Emigrant Road," p. 25.

66. Scott, *Independence*, p. 113.

67. Applegate, "Old Emigrant Road," p. 25. [Jesse Applegate referred to it as Shallow Lake in his 1848 Way Bill (Applegate, *Way Bill*, p. 3.)]

68. Scott, *Independence*, p. 114.

69. Ibid.

70. Helfrich, "Applegate Trail," (1971), Vol. 9, p. 80.

71. Scott, *Independence*, p. 115.

72. Helfrich, "Applegate Trail," (1971), Vol. 9, p. 80.

73. Scott, *Independence*, p. 115.

74.a) Applegate, "Old Emigrant Road," p. 26.
b) Bancroft, *Works*, Vol. XXIX, p. 549.
c) *Hist. of the Pac. N. W.*, Vol. I, p. 373.
d) Scott, *Independence*, p. 115.

75. Scott, *Independence*, p. 115.

76.a) Applegate, "Old Emigrant Road," p. 26.
b) Scott, *Independence*, p. 116.
c) Bancroft, *Works*, Vol. XXIX, p. 549.
d) William S. Brown, *California Northeast: The Bloody Ground* (Oakland, CA: Biobooks, 1951), p. 11.

77.a) Applegate, "Old Emigrant Road," p. 27.
b) Bancroft, *Works*, Vol. XXIX, p. 549.
c) Nichols, *South Road*, p. 77.

78. Applegate, "Old Emigrant Road," p. 27.

79.a) Bancroft, *Works*, Vol. XXIX, p. 549.
b) Applegate, "Old Emigrant Road," p. 28.

80. Ibid.

81.a) Applegate, "Old Emigrant Road," p. 28.
b) Bancroft, *Works*, Vol. XXIX, p. 549.

82. Scott, *Independence*, p. 116.

83.a) Applegate, "Old Emigrant Road," p. 30.
b) Bancroft, *Works*, Vol. XXIX, p. 550.

84. Bancroft, *Works*, Vol. XXIX, p. 550.

85. Applegate, "Old Emigrant Road," p. 31.

86. Scott, *Independence*, p. 116.

87. Applegate, "Old Emigrant Road," p. 31.

88. Ibid.

89. Scott, *Independence*, p. 117.

90.a) Ibid.
b) Applegate, "Old Emigrant Road," p. 31.

91. Scott, *Independence*, p. 117.

92. Ibid.

93. Scott, *Independence*, p. 118.

94. Ibid.

95. Ibid.

96. Ibid., p. 119.

97. Ibid.

98. Ibid., p. 120.

99. Ibid., p. 121.

100. Applegate, "Old Emigrant Road," p. 31.

101. Scott, *Independence*, p. 123.

102.a) Scott, *Independence*, p. 123.
b) Applegate, "Old Emigrant Road," p. 32.

103. Applegate, "Old Emigrant Road," p. 32.

104. Ibid., p. 33.

105. Applegate, "Old Emigrant Road," p. 32.

106. Ibid., p. 33.

107. Ibid., p. 33, 34.

108. Ibid., p. 34.

109. Ibid., p. 35.

110.a) Ibid.
b) Scott, *Independence*, p. 125.

111. Scott, *Independence*, p. 125.

112. Ibid., p. 121.

113. Ibid., p. 122.

114. Ibid.

115. Ibid., p. 121.

116. Applegate, "Old Emigrant Road," p. 35.

117. Ibid., p. 36.

118. Ibid., p. 37.

119. Ibid.

120. Ibid., p. 39. [This was probably Johnnie Grant, Junior. (Frank C. Robertson, *Fort Hall: Gateway to the Oregon Country* (New York: NY, Hastings House, Publishers, 1963), p.284.)]

121. Applegate, "Old Emigrant Road," p. 39.

122. Burchard, "South Road," p. 411.

123. Morgan, *Overland in 1846*, Vol. 2, pp. 637, 766.

124. Ibid., pp. 637, 638. [*New York Tribune*, October 24, 1846]

CHAPTER 3. The CALIFORNIA TRAIL

From Fort Hall to Mary's River (the Humboldt River) to the new cutoff: Idaho, Utah, and Nevada

While Jesse Applegate and three others were at Fort Hall, Levi Scott and William G. Parker explored the new route. They left the rest of the men camped at the approximate location of the new cut-off. (This was the new Oregon cut-off they would be taking from the existing California Trail on the Humboldt River.) They rode northeast toward Black Rock. Their principal concern was the lack of water. There were sixty sandy, sage brush desert miles to go through.

After riding about fifteen miles they found one spring.[1] The second day they found a second spring. It was approximately twenty-five miles from the first and surrounded by rabbit holes.[2] Finding a spring within the path they would need to travel relieved their concern for water. From there they could see it was another twenty miles to Black Rock. Rather than continue, they turned back. When they were near the first spring they had discovered, they saw an antelope. Thinking of food and their lack of provisions, Parker dismounted, leaving his horse with Scott.[3]

When he got within range he fired a single shot. The animal fell "dead in its tracks."[4] From that time on this spring gained the name Antelope Springs.[5]

When they arrived back at camp about ten or eleven o'clock that evening,[6] the camp was deserted. They fired some shots in the air to get a response. The sound of a gunshot was immediately returned. They rode further up the river in the direction of the returned gunshot and found the men had moved their camp while they were gone.[7]

On August 7, back on the Oregon Trail, a Harrison Linville company arrived at the cut-off to the California Trail.[8] This company was led by a mountain man named Medders Vanderpool.[9]

That same day Virgil and Pherne Pringle and their family of five[10] passed Fort Hall.[11] Out of Fort Hall the Oregon Trail followed the Snake River past American Falls.[12] Today this part of the Snake River is covered by American Falls Reservoir.[13] Just past American Falls, Virgil Pringle met Jesse Applegate.[14] After hearing about the new trail the Pringles decided to take it.

The next day, August 10, they continued down the Snake River to the fork in the road at Raft River crossing[15] and turned left onto the California Trail that led them to the new route to Oregon. The California Trail followed along Raft River, then down Cassia Creek[16] and past the City of Rocks, now a National Park reserve.[17] After the City of Rocks the trail cut through the Snake River Mountains,[18] over present day Granite Pass. From here it followed Goose Creek for about a mile, left Idaho, and continued down the creek a distance of about four miles through a corner of Utah.[19] In Utah, Pringle and other emigrants camped at Goose Creek.[20] They worked their way to Thousand Springs Creek in Hot Springs Valley.[21] This creek eventually took them to the Humboldt River.[22]

On Tuesday, August 11, Jesse Applegate started back to the road party with supplies and some young energetic men who would join the road party.[23] Levi Scott was concerned about there being enough extra men to go ahead to help build the road. The road party continued to move slowly up the river while waiting for the others to return. After they had moved to Thousand Springs Valley, two of the men who had gone to Fort Hall returned with fourteen more wagons. Medders Vanderpool was the captain of these wagons. "Black" Harris was a friend of Vanderpool.[24] He had heard Vanderpool was leading a wagon train down the Snake River, so he intercepted the wagons at Goose Creek and convinced the company to try the new route. Harris had given the Vanderpool train the impression that they could go right into Oregon without any difficulty. These wagons, along with Harrison Linville's company, were the beginning of the wagon train.[25]

The next day seven more wagons arrived with a note from Jesse Applegate. The note said to go ahead and start down the trail. He would catch up in a couple of days with provisions and enough additional men to help open the road.[26]

They pushed on ahead to help improve the new road. David Goff and Levi Scott were the two original exploring party members who were to remain with the wagon train to help guide them to Oregon.[27] Before the road party left, they warned the emigrants that they should travel in companies of not less than twenty wagons each.[28] The emigrants on their way to the new Applegate cut-off and those traveling to California were all sharing the California Trail. The emigrants felt safer traveling in numbers. One of their concerns was the Indians in the area. These Indians were called Digger Indians.[29] They were probably called Digger by the pioneers because they gathered roots for their winter food supply.[30]

On August 13, a young man named Robey traveling with the main wagon train died of consumption. He had been going west for his health. He was buried along the trail.[31]

Also on August 13, Jesse Applegate met up with the Dunbar Wagon Train.[32] This was near Raft River.[33] This company of wagons consisted of Mr. and Mrs. J. Quinn Thornton, the James Smith family, the Henry Smith family, Rev. J. A. Cornwall and his family, Albert Alderman, and several others.[34] Applegate managed to secure two more men from this company to be part of the road crew. Their names were William Kirquendall and Charles Putnam.[35] A few days later Applegate caught up with the small train. He had only brought five or six more men.[36] One of them was Levi Scott's son William. They had not seen each other in two years.[37] According to Lindsay Applegate's journal and other sources, the other young men who came to help were Thomas Powers, Joseph Burke, Powell, Perrin, Alfred Stewart, Shaw, Carnahan,[38] Charles Putnam and William Kirquendall.[39] Some of these men were sons of emigrants on the wagon train.[40] One member of the exploring party brought his mother. She was traveling in a horse drawn carriage. John Owens and his father had come to Oregon a year or so before. John had come this way to bring his mother back to be with his dad. She planned to travel ahead with the road working party and her son John.[41] Applegate added, "A Bannock Indian from about the head of Snake River also joined us."[42] The road workers pushed ahead with Jesse Applegate to join the other road builders in opening the new road.[43]

Soon more wagons joined the train. In a short time there were about seventy-five wagons in the lead wagon companies.[44] Somewhere between Hot Springs Valley and the Humboldt River, Sutton Burns died,[45] leaving a wife and three children.[46]

Another emigrant family traveling with one of the first two trains was Rev. Abraham Elison Garrison and his wife Margaret, along with their sons Abraham Henry[47] and

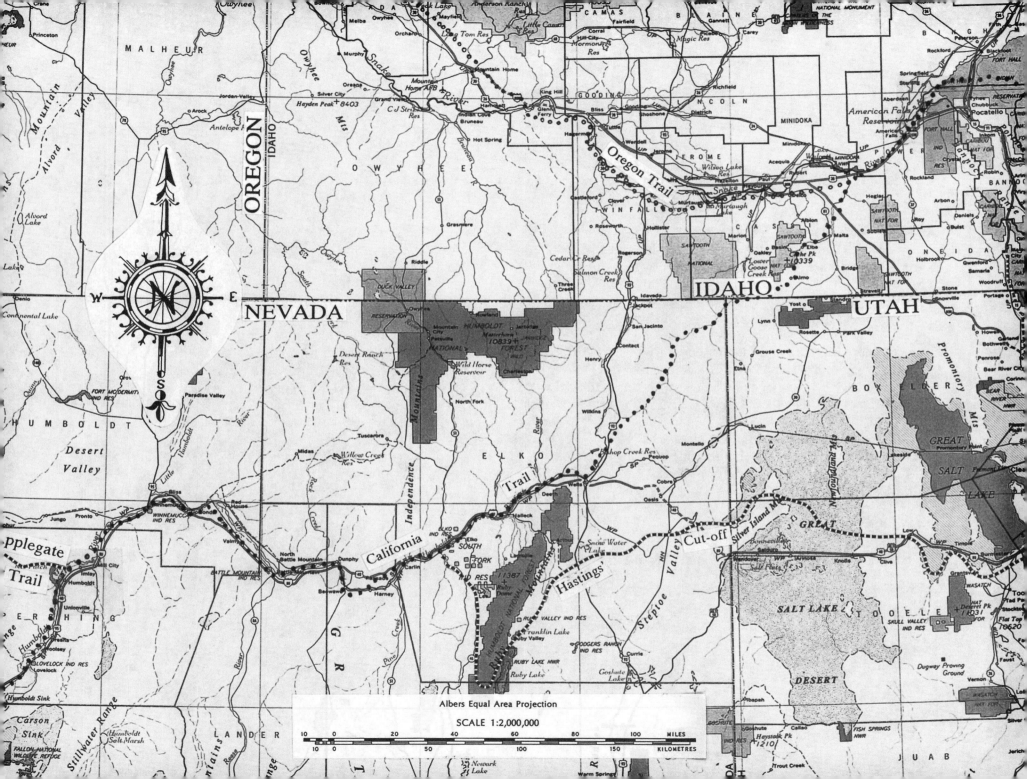

David.[48]   The Garrisons called one of their wagons, "the family wagon."[49]   It was not drawn by oxen.   Rev. A. E. Garrison would sit in it to drive instead of walking alongside.[50]   Rev. A. E. Garrison had been sick and confined to the wagon bed before reaching Fort Hall.   When they reached Fort Hall Garrison could sit in the wagon and drive.

Traveling with the Garrisons was a man named Martin Hoover and a hired hand named David Tanner.[51]   At this time Martin Hoover took sick.[52]   He had been with Garrison since crossing the North Platte River on the Oregon Trail.[53] After not getting along with the wagon group he was with, he asked Garrison if he could travel with them until he found something else.   He had proved to be a better hand than Garrison's hired hand so Garrison kept him on.[54]

Now the emigrants were on the Humboldt River.[55] The Humboldt River was called Mary's River by Levi Scott, Virgil Pringle and others.[56]   Jesse Applegate referred to it as Ogden's river in his Way Bill[57] because he thought this was the river that Ogden called Mary's River.   They followed the Humboldt for over 200 miles.[58]

While on the Oregon Trail the Thorntons had been traveling with the Donner family.   They had also camped together on Little Sandy[59] before reaching Fort Bridger.[60] Fort Bridger was on the Oregon Trail, 172 miles before Fort Hall.[61]   At Fort Bridger the Hastings Cut-off went south below the Great Salt Lake and came across Utah and Nevada to go around the Ruby Mountains, where it came out at the south fork of the Humboldt River and met with the California Trail.[62]

At Fort Bridger the Donners were persuaded to take the Hastings Cut-off.   This was supposed to be a shorter route but ended up being a longer route.[63]   At first Tamsen Donner felt uneasy about this decision. She tried to persuade her husband not to take this new unestablished route, but on July 20th, on the lower Sandy, the Donner Party decided to take what was supposed to be an easier and shorter route.[64] About sixty miles down the Humboldt River on the South Fork is the location where the Hastings Cut-off comes in from the south to join the California Trail.[65]   This is where the Donners would have come out ahead of the Applegate Party. As it was, the Donners did not reach the California Trail until around the first part of October.[66]   This eventually caused the Donners to be late in arriving at the California Sierras, where they met with tragedy at what is now known as Donner Lake.[67]

Along the Humboldt thirty-two miles from the Hastings Cut-off was Gravelly Ford.[68]   This was another location made famous by the Donner saga.[69]   Allegedly at this location on October 5, 1846[70] a man named James F. Reed was banished from the Donner wagon train for killing a man named John Snyder in self-defense.[71]   This has since been determined to have happened at Iron Point.[72]

Just past Gravelly Ford, along the Humboldt River between present day Beowawe and present day Dunphy, it was noted in the diary of a California bound emigrant named Nicholas Carriger on August 26, 1846 that three men in the Vanderpool Company were sick and not expected to live.[73]

Traveling on the Humboldt River, Martin Hoover was still sick and confined to Garrison's wagon.[74]   He was getting worse every day.   He was so sick that he needed to be carried from the tent to the wagon.[75]

On the California Trail before the Applegate Trail intersection, William E. Taylor was with a lead wagon going to California.   According to his diary, he had been visited by a large party of Indians at Big Meadows with no ill fate.[76]

About the time Levi Scott and the lead wagons reached Big Meadows, John Owens and another man came riding up. They had come for reinforcements. They said the Indians had shot one horse and taken another. They wanted help to get the horse back.[77] Levi Scott and five volunteers rode about four miles up the trail with John Owen and his friend to the scene. They found a party of about fifty Indians on the other side of the river. Leading the others, Levi Scott approached the Indians slowly until he was close enough to make signs. One man named Dan Toole was on foot. Three Indians came running toward them, one on each side and one in the middle. The Indians stopped and then started shouting at the men. They were making the sign to go away.[78] Scott tried to sign to them about the horses but they kept making the sign to go away. Scott realized he was getting nowhere. He decided to return without the horses. He told the men to leave slowly. Scott did not want to give the impression they were retreating out of fear. The men did not listen to his advice. Instead they turned their horses around and rode off. Levi Scott, John Owens and Dan Toole were all that remained. Scott and Owens continued to retreat slowly and cover Dan Toole. Assuming the gesture of the other men to be an act of defeat the Indians started shooting arrows at the three who remained. The other men waited a little downstream and Dan Toole jumped on the back of one of their larger horses. The other men stopped long enough to fire off a shot and then rode off again.[79] Scott and Owens were left alone to defend themselves. They dismounted and fired a few shots back at the Indian braves. The Indians kept advancing and shooting their arrows. Scott and Owens decided to get back on their horses to get some distance between themselves and their pursuers. Just as Scott saddled up he was struck in the leg by an arrow. His horse was also struck.[80]

They rode as fast as possible for about a quarter of a mile, dismounted, and reloaded their rifles. When they finished loading, they remounted and turned toward the war party. The Indians stopped running toward them. The fight was over and the men rode slowly away.[81]

By the time the two men returned to camp the story of the Indians had been exaggerated to include five hundred braves. They assumed Scott and Owens were dead. Scott did his best to calm everyone's fears. The wounds he and his horse suffered healed in about a week. He left a note on the top of a willow branch stuck in the ground beside the trail, warning all approaching wagons of the events that had occurred.[82]

Thornton told of a skirmish that also happened at Big Meadows. Because Levi Scott was leading all the wagons, this had to have taken place after the Scott and Owen incident. An Indian was shot in one of the wagon camps during one of their stops. He was shot by Mr. Lovelin with a shotgun owned by Jesse Boone, "a great-grandson of the celebrated Indian fighter, Daniel Boone, of Kentucky."[83] There were other Indians that were shot among the willows. Mr. Whately and Mr. Sallee were also wounded. Mr. Sallee did not live.[84] He was buried a few miles past the Applegate cut-off. Mr. Whately was the captain of six wagons.[85] This had happened before Thornton had even reached the Humboldt River.[86]

1. Scott, *Independence*, p. 128.

2. Ibid., p. 128. [This was the same spring Jesse Applegate's exploring party had found traveling east to explore the location of Ogden's river. (Applegate, "Old Emigrant Road," p. 32.)]

3. Ibid., p. 128.

4. Ibid.

5. Ibid.

6. Ibid.

7. Ibid., p. 129.

8. Morgon, *Overland in 1846*, Vol. 1, p. 392.

9.a) Bancroft, *Works*, Vol. XXIX, p. 559.
b) Scott, *Independence*, p. 130.
c) J. A. C. Leland, "Pioneer Days on Grave Creek Seen Again in Memory." *Grants Pass (Oregon) Daily Courier*, January 23, 1934, p. 2.

10. Tabitha Brown, "A Brimfield Heroine," *Oregon Historical Quarterly*, Vol. 39, No. 2 (Portland, OR: Oregon Hiatorical Society, June, 1904), p. 200.

11. Morgan, *Overland in 1846*, Vol.1, p. 178.

12. Ibid., p. 179.

13. Gregory M. Franzwa, *Maps of the Oregon Trail* (Gerald, MO: The Patrice Press, 1982), p. 185.

14. Morgan, *Overland in 1846*, Vol. 1, p. 179.

15. Franzwa, *Maps*, p. 189.

16. Devere Helfrich, *Emigrant Trails West: a Guide to Trail Markers Placed by Trails West, Inc. Along The California, Applegate, Lassen and Nobles' Emigrant Trails in Idaho, Nevada, and California* (Reno, NV: Trails West, 1984),p. 36.

17.a) Bancroft, *Works*, Vol. XXIX, p. 559.
b) Walter E. Meacham, *Applegate Trail* (Portland, OR: printed by James, Kerns & Abbott, 1947), p. 10.

18. Morgan, *Overland in 1846*, Vol. 1, p. 179.

19. Helfrich, *Trails West*, p. 37.

20.a) Morgan, *Overland in 1846*, Vol. 1, p. 179.
b) Meacham, *Applegate Trail*, p. 10.

21.a) *Morgan, Overland in 1846*, Vol. 1, p. 180.
b) Applegate, "Old Emigrant Road," p. 39.
c) Applegate, *Way Bill*, p. 2.

22. Applegate, "Old Emigrant Road," p. 38.

23. Helfrich, "Applegate Trail," (1971), Vol. 9, p. 6.

24. Scott, *Independence*, p. 130.

25. Ibid., p. 130.

26. Ibid.

27. Meacham, *Applegate Trail*, p. 10.

28. Bancroft, *Works*, Vol. XXIX, p. 559.

29. Meacham, *Applegate Trail*, p. 10.

30. Helfrich, "Applegate Trail," (1971), Vol. 9, p. 6.

31.a) Meacham, *Applegate Trail*, p. 10.
b) Brown, ed., *Man*, p. 96.

32.a) Thornton, *Or. and Ca. in 1848*, Vol. 1, p. 165.
b) Narcissa Cornwall, *Cornwall Family, Papers: Capt. Dunbar's Co. 1846, The Applegate Route From Ft. Hall* (Portland, OR: Oregon Historic Society, Mss #1509), p. 35.

33. Helfrich, "Applegate Trail," (1971), Vol. 9, p. 6.

34. Cornwall, *Capt. Dunbar's Co. 1846*, OHS Mss #1509, p. 35.

35. Thornton, *Or. and Ca. in 1848*, Vol. 1, p. 165.

36. Scott, *Independence*, p. 130.

37. Ibid., p. 131.

38.a) Applegate, "Old Emigrant Road," p. 39.
b) Helfrich, "Applegate Trail," (1971), Vol. 9, p. 7.

39. Thornton, *Or. and Ca. in 1848*, Vol. 1, p. 165.

40.a) Applegate, "Old Emigrant Road," p. 39.
b) Helfrich, "Applegate Trail," (1971), Vol. 9, p. 7.

41. Scott, *Independence*, p. 136.

42.a) Applegate, "Old Emigrant Road," p. 39.
b) Helfrich, "Applegate Trail," (1971), Vol. 9, p. 7.

43. Scott, *Independence*, p. 136.

44. Ibid., p. 131.

45. Bancroft, *Works*, Vol. XXIX, p. 559.

46. Meacham, *Applegate Trail*, p. 10.

47. Garrison, "Reminiscences," p. 10.

48. Garrison, *Life and Labours*, OHS Mss #1009, p. 29.

49. Garrison, "Reminiscences," p. 23.

50. IBid., p. 23.

51.a) Garrison, *Life and Labours*, OHS Mss #1009, p. 26.
b) Scott, *Independence*, p. 149.

52. Garrison, *Life and Labours*, OHS Mss #1009, p. 27.

53. Ibid., p. 26.

54. Ibid., p. 26, 27.

55. Morgan, *Overland in 1846*, Vol. 1, p. 180.

56.a) Ibid., p. 180.
b) Scott, *Independence*, p. 127.

57. Applegate, *Way Bill*, p. 2.

58. Meacham, *Applegate Trail*, p. 10.

59. Thornton, *Or. and Ca. in 1848*, Vol. 1, p. 140, 141.

60. Ibid., p. 142.

61. Morgan, *Overland in 1846*, Vol. 1, pp. 177, 178.

62. Thornton, *Or. and Ca. in 1848*, Vol. 1, p. 142.

63. Morgan, *Overland in 1846*, Vol. 1, p. 177, 178.

64.a) Meacham, *Applegate Trail*, p. 7.
b) C. F. McGlashan, *History of the Donner Party: a Tragedy of the Sierra* (Stanford, CA: Stanford University Press, 1947), p. 31.

65. Adrietta Applegate Hixon, *On to Oregon* (Fairfield, WA: Ye Galleon Press, 1973), p. 86.

66. McGlashan, *Donner Party*, p. 44.

67. Bancroft, *Works*, Vol. XXIX, p. 557.

68. Helfrich, *Trails West*, p. 41.

69. McGlashan, *Donner Party*, p. 41.

70. Ibid., p. 44.

71. Ibid., p. 47.

72. Harold Curran, *Fearful Crossing: The Central Overland Trail Through Nevada* (Reno, NV: Great Basin Press, 1982), p. 34.

73. Helfrich, "Applegate Trail," (1971), Vol. 9, p. 7.

74. Garrison, *Life and Labours*, OHS Mss #1009, p. 27.

75. Ibid., p. 28.

76. Helfrich, "Applegate Trail," (1971), Vol. 9, p. 7.

77. Scott, *Independence*, p. 136.

78. Ibid., p. 137.

79. Ibid., p. 138.

80. Ibid., p. 139.

81. Ibid.

82. Ibid., p. 140.

83. Thornton, *Or. and Ca. in 1848*, Vol. 1, p. 171.

84. Ibid.

85. Helfrich, "Applegate Trail," (1971), Vol. 9, p. 8.

86. Thornton, *Or. and Ca. in 1848*, Vol. 1, p. 167.

Chapter 4. The CUT-OFF

The new southern route to Oregon
The Applegate Trail from the Mary's River to California: Nevada

The California Trail followed along the Humboldt River. Those taking the new southern route to Oregon used this route until turning right and going northwest, leaving the Humboldt River and following the path marked for them.[1] There were about thirteen hundred people who went to Oregon in 1846 and approximately three hundred who went to California.[2] All these people tried to travel at the same time to take advantage of the weather and good grazing for the livestock.[3]

There were about ninety to a hundred wagons that took the Applegate Trail to Oregon.[4] Those emigrants going to California that day said farewell to their friends taking the Applegate's new cut-off and continued traveling south along the Humboldt River. The emigrants going to Oregon turned right just past the Humboldt Sink and pulled into camp to wait for the others.[5] David Goff decided to remain at the cut-off until all the wagons had found their way. He was afraid that some of them might miss the turn.[6] Virgil K. Pringle reached the new Applegate cut-off Saturday, September 5th.[7]

These emigrants were now leaving the existing trail to forge a new one. They were leaving the dry desert and entering a more desolate dry desert. They were leaving a river that was fairly dry and heading for a few hot springs along the way, using as little water as possible to get through.[8] They had followed the Humboldt River for over two hundred miles.[9]

The first stop after leaving the cut-off was Antelope Springs.[10] Today it is known as Willow Springs. At first, it was known as Diamond Spring.[11] One can only speculate why it was called Diamond, although it was a gem to find a spring at the beginning of the desert. Rev. Garrison, who had been further back on the trail, caught up with the foremost wagons somewhere on the desert.[12]

They continued crossing the desert early the next morning.[13] The next spring was Rabbit Hole Springs.[14] It was about seventeen miles from Antelope Springs. Knowing Rabbit Hole Springs was weak, Scott sent Rev. Garrison ahead that afternoon to dam up some water at the spring.[15] While Garrison was enlarging the spring to get more water[16] and digging a barrier to stop the water from running off, his son David came to tell him that Martin Hoover had just died[17]

The train of emigrants continued nonstop all day across the dry, dusty desert with its sharp cutting sand blowing in their eyes and causing their throats to be even drier. They reached Rabbit Hole Spring that evening.[18] Martin Hoover was buried at sunset.[19] Margaret Garrison did not find out Hoover had died until the wagons were stopped, because she was riding in the other wagon.[20] After dinner they pushed on to take advantage of the cooler night.[21] That evening Mrs. Garrison asked her son Henry to take a bucket and try to get some milk. Henry drove a cow ahead to milk it before the rest of the loose stock caught up. He did this with five or six cows before finding enough milk. After the eight or ten children on the train had enough milk there was still a little left for the mothers to get a little relief from thirst.[22]

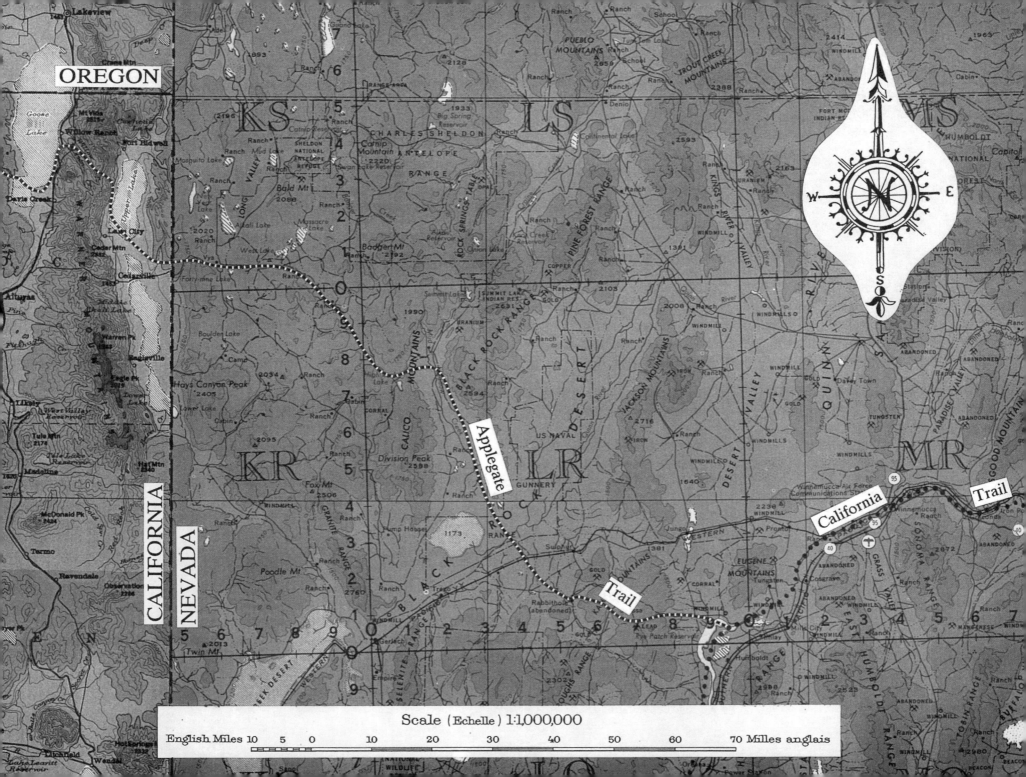

There was a chill in the air as the cold winds picked up after dark.[23] During the night while traveling along in the desert Mrs. Garrison became ill. She lost the use of her legs and one arm.[24] Garrison was barely well himself. The wagons pushed on to Black Rock.[25] There were about twenty miles left from Rabbit Hole Springs across the Black Rock Desert to Black Rock which had another hot spring (U.S.G.S. maps). The first wagons reached Black Rock as the sun was rising.[26] The last of the wagons of the foremost wagon train arrived at Black Rock by 10 o'clock that morning[27] Here they found Boiling Springs.[28] They stayed at Boiling Springs a couple of days to rest and revive their teams and themselves.[29] While at Boiling Springs the men tried to retrieve the cattle that had run off[30] The women used the hot spring to do their laundry without having to boil water.[31]

Another family traveling on the first wagon train to cross the Applegate Trail was the Robert and Rhoda Henderson family with their two daughters, Lucy Anne[32] and Salita Jane.[33] Salita was also known as Lettie.[34] At one of their camps about three days from Black Rock the girls were playing and they found a bag hanging on a nail on the sideboard of the wagon. They each decided to taste its contents and did not like what they tasted. They put it back. Then Lettie drank the whole bottle. Not knowing what it was she went to the camp fire where her mother was cooking and decided to lie down. She went to sleep and never woke up. When supper was ready their mother called the children to dinner and noticed that she was sleeping and decided not to disturb her. When she tried to wake her later, she found that she had died. The bag she had drunk from contained a bottle of laudanum. It was too late to save her. Her father took black walnut boards that had been used for a table and made a coffin.[35] When they reached Black Rock Lucy Anne's mother, Rhoda Henderson, gave birth to a little girl. They named her Olive.[36]

The day after reaching the cut-off, the Pringle family and the wagons they were traveling with arrived at Antelope Springs. It was about four o'clock that afternoon. Pringle said it was fifteen miles. They managed to get a little water for themselves and their famished teams. They stopped only long enough to eat and continued to the next spring.[37]

The Pringles arrived at Rabbit Hole Springs at about four o'clock in the morning. It was about ten miles.[38] There was less water at Rabbit Hole Springs than there was at Antelope Springs.[39] They rested until about nine o'clock that morning then pushed on toward Black Rock.[40]

Some of the first settlers tried driving the trail during the day, which caused their stock to be weakened even more.[41] After traveling all day in the hot dry sun, they reached the spring just past Black Rock at around eight in the evening. "The road good and level and generally firm. The mountains barren and dark looking rocks."[42] (Virgil Pringle, September 7, 1846) Two steers belonging to the Collins family had died.[43]

There were many miles between some groups of wagons.[44] Some were far to the rear. Many of them simply did not take the cut-off until later because they left on the Oregon Trail later. One of the last emigrants to turn right at the cut-off was J. Quinn Thornton. According to his diary, they did not arrive at the cut-off until September 15th, two weeks behind the rest of the wagons.[45] When Thornton finally arrived he was surprised to find that David Goff was still waiting at the forks in the road to make sure they did not

Figure 1 They rested until about nine o'clock that morning, then pushed on toward Black Rock.

Figure 2 ...Thornton went back to the spring and worked all day and into the night collecting water....

up...."[47] After the Thorntons had replenished their supply of water from the spring and were leaving, they "saw a dense cloud of dust rolling up in the distance behind."[48] They were not sure whether it was Indians leaving a smoke signal or the company of Brown and Allen. They knew Brown and Allen were not far behind.[49]

Traveling through the first part of the desert between the springs Thornton writes, "The earth appeared to be as destitute of moisture, as if a drop of rain or dew had never fallen upon it from the brazen heavens above."[50] That night they camped about three-fourths of a mile from Rabbit Hole Springs.[51]

The Thorntons did not find any water until moving on the next morning.[52] This is the only time that I have found a reference to Thornton actually using his spade. He never referred to using his spade to do any clearing of the roads, since he was one of the last travelers in the forty-six wagon train. Instead he did use it to remove earth to collect more water around the spring he had

miss the cut-off. Thornton and the emigrants he was with took so long getting there that they had already started thinking they might have passed the cut-off.[46]

Now Thornton was heading into the Black Rock Desert. Thornton referred to it "as the River of Death dried

_____

Figure 3 High Rock Canyon

just found. That morning everyone retired to their tents to escape the heat while Thornton went back to the spring and worked all day and into the night collecting water to fill his keg until two o'clock in the morning.

The Thorntons again resumed their journey early the next morning.[53] "The earth was iron and the heavens brass. Everything was parched and arid...."[54] They stopped just before sunset, resting their cattle, then continued their journey as the sun set. As Thornton was crossing the Black Rock Desert he looked out across the horizon. "Nothing presented itself to the eye, but a broad expanse of a uniform dead-level plane, which conveyed to the mind the idea that it had been a muddy and sandy bottom of a former lake....and having its muddy bottom jetted into cones by the force of the fire of perdition."[55]

After reaching Black Rock he stayed one day and one night to rest his team. He said of Black Rock, "The tops of these high bluffs or hills appeared to be covered with volcanic scoria, or a substance resembling the slag formed in iron furnaces."[56] He remained another two days and two nights at the "Great Boiling Springs" at Black Rock.[57]

Some emigrants never found the springs. They had made it all the way to Black Rock for as much as three days and two nights without water. Mr. Crump got help from Mr. David Butterfield because he had lost oxen on the way.[58]

After Black Rock there were another twenty-five miles to go before the end of Black Rock Desert. There was one more spring, Double Hot Springs.[59] It was about five miles past Black Rock (U.S.G.S. maps). There were hot and cold springs there.[60] There was another 20 miles through Black Rock Desert to reach Mud Meadow. Applegate called Mud Meadow "Salt Valley" in his 1848 Way Bill.[61] Mud Meadow is now known as Soldier Meadow[62] Virgil Pringle called it a "heavy pulling road."[63]

From here they descended Fly Canyon. This Canyon sloped downward about 45 degrees. It was typical for the emigrants to lock their wagon wheels and hold the wagons back by ropes when descending a steep slope. One wagon going down Fly Canyon flipped over onto the team.[64]

After descending Fly Canyon they passed High Rock Lake to enter High Rock Canyon.[65] The entrance was known as The Devil's Gate.[66] This is not to be mistaken for The Devil's Gate on the Oregon Trail in Wyoming, but they are similar.[67] There were plenty of springs in the area.[68] The road was narrow but good. It varied from 15 to 20 feet wide and the rocks went almost straight up towering 60 to 80 feet high in some places.[69] It was barely wide enough in some places for a wagon.[70] "The High Rock Canion [sic] is a great natural curiosity, a good road, handsome little meadows and excellent water enclosed by beetling cliffs, rising in places hundreds of feet perpendicular." Jesse Applegate, 1848.[71] There was a cave about two miles inside the canyon that most emigrants found to be "a curiosity."[72] The cave was on the right-hand side. There were also springs on the north slopes. A small stream bed ran through the canyon and there were more springs on the left about two miles in.[73]

From High Rock Canyon there was the Upper High Rock Canyon.[74] The Upper High Rock Canyon sloped gradually upward so the walls of the canyon were lower.[75] Now the emigrants were beginning to see trees for the first time since they entered the desert.[76]

As Levi Scott was guiding the Vanderpool wagon company on the new trail, there were also other small companies traveling with them. Together, this group of wagon companies was called the foremost company.[77] The Rev. A. E. Garrison had been chosen captain of the small company of wagons he was with.[78] He and his family had also joined the foremost wagons.[79]

Pringle was still in the second group of wagon companies.[80] It was September 14 and he had just traveled through the High Rock Canyon. It had been a very dusty road and there was more dust to follow, but he had found an open grassy flat area for his team to graze. At this point he could see the lead wagon train ahead. He noted there were twenty-nine wagons.[81] They were about six hours ahead of the wagons the Pringles were with.[82]

The wagons in Thornton's vicinity were Mr. Caldwell, Crump, Baker, Butterfield, Bosworth, Morin, Putnam, Newton, Lovelin, Boone, and Dodd. Dodd was with Stokes. Their wagons had recently caught up with Mr. Hall, Croizen, and Whately. "Whately was suffering much from a wound received in a battle with the Indians on Ogden's River."[83] (Thornton 1846)

After leaving Upper High Rock Canyon the foremost company probably camped at Emigrant Springs near Painted Point. The emigrants were traveling northwest. They passed Massacre Spring, Massacre Creek, and Massacre Lake. They were not called that at the time. It is not known why so many features in the area are named Massacre. There is a mass grave in the area, but there are no known records of any massacres having happened there.[84] There had been a fire in the area. Unfortunately it had burned most of the good grazing for the livestock. All that was left was a tough, wiry, small bulrush type of grass.[85] It was just too tough to burn, and the oxen did not like it.

They passed through Painted Point crossing Long Valley at Forty Nine Lake.[86] This is just south of present day Vya, Nevada.[87] Next they crossed "Little Mountain Pass."[88] Today it is known as '49 Summit.[89]

Figure 4 They passed through Painted Point crossing Long Valley....

NOTES   Chapter 4

1. Bancroft, *Works*, Vol. XXIX, p. 558.

2. Ghent, *Road*, p. 86.

3. Helfrich, "Applegate Trail," (1971), Vol. 9, p. 8.

4. Ibid.

5. Garrison, "Reminiscences," p. 23.

6. a) Bancroft, *Works*, Vol. XXIX, pp. 558, 559.
b) Helfrich, "Applegate Trail," (1971), Vol. 9, p. 8.

7. Morgan, *Overland in 1846*, Vol. 1, p. 181.

8. Garrison, *Life and Labours*, OHS Mss #1009, p. 27.

9. Meacham, *Applegate Trail*, p. 10.

10. a) Hixon, *On to Oregon*, p. 83.
b) Helfrich, "Applegate Trail II," (1976), Vol. 14, p. 17.
c) Nichols, *South Road*, p. 87.

11. Bancroft, *Works*, Vol. XXIX, p. 558.

12. a) Garrison, "Reminiscences," p. 24.
b) Garrison, *Life and Labours*, OHS Mss #1109, p. 29.

13. Helfrich, "Applegate Trail," (1971), Vol. 9, p. 17.

14. Helfrich, "Applegate Trail," (1971), Vol. 9, p. 17. [The hole in this spring surrounded by rabbit tracks helped in choosing the name.]

15. a) Garrison, *Life and Labours*, OHS Mss #1009, p. 29.
b) Helfrich, "Applegate Trail," (1971), Vol. 9, p. 20.

16. Bancroft, *Works*, Vol. XXIX, p. 558.

17. Garrison, *Life and Labours*, OHS Mss #1009, p. 29.

18. Scott, *Independence*, p. 140.

19. Garrison, *Life and Labours*, OHS Mss #1009, p. 30.

20. Garrison, *Life and Labours*, OHS Mss #1009, pp. 10, 30. [Margaret Garrison was Rev. Garrison's wife.]

21. Ibid., p. 30.

22. Garrison, "Reminiscences," p. 24

23. a) Garrison, *Life and Labours*, OHS Mss #1009, p. 30.
b) Garrison, "Reminiscences," p. 24.

24. Garrison, *Life and Labours*, OHS Mss #1009, p. 30.

25. Scott, *Independence*, p. 141.

26. Ibid.

27. Garrison, *Life and Labours*, OHS Mss #1009, p. 30.

28. a) Helfrich, "Applegate Trail," (1971), Vol. 9, pp. 26, 27. b) Garrison, *Life and Labours*, OHS Mss #1009, p. 31.

29. Scott, *Independence*, p. 141.

30. Ibid.

31. Garrison, "Reminiscences," p. 24.

32. Lockley, *Pioneer Women*, p. 81.

33. Ibid., p. 86.

34. Ibid., pp. 84, 86.

35. Ibid., p. 84.

36. Ibid., p. 85.

37. Morgan, *Overland in 1846*, Vol. 1, p. 181.

38. Ibid.

39. a) Ibid.
b) Helfrich, "Applegate Trail," (1971), Vol. 9, p. 20.

40. Morgan, *Overland in 1846*, Vol. 1, p. 181.

41. a) Ibid.
b) Thornton, *Or. and Ca. in 1848*, Vol. 1, p. 177.

42. Morgan, *Overland in 1846*, Vol. 1, p. 181.

43. Ibid.

44. Helfrich, "Applegate Trail," (1971), Vol. 9, p. 7.

45. a) Thornton, *Or. and Ca. in 1848*, Vol. 1, p. 170.
b) Helfrich, "Applegate Trail," (1971), Vol. 9, p. 2.

46. Thornton, *Or. and Ca. in 1848*, Vol. 1, p. 172.

47. Ibid., p. 179.

48. Ibid., p. 177.

49. Ibid.

50. Ibid., p. 178.

51. Ibid.

52. Ibid.

53. Ibid.

54. Ibid., p. 179.

55. Ibid.

56. Ibid., p. 184.

57. Ibid., p. 186.

58. Ibid., p. 180.

59. Helfrich, "Applegate Trail," (1971), Vol. 9, p. 27.

60. Morgon, *Overland in 1846*, Vol. 1, p. 181.

61. a) Applegate, *Way Bill*, p. 3.
b) Morgan, *Overland in 1846*, Vol. 1, p. 393.

62. a) Morgan, *Overland in 1846*, Vol. 1, p. 181.
b) Helfrich, "Applegate Trail," (1971), Vol. 9, p. 26.

63. Morgan, *Overland in 1846*, Vol. 1, p. 181.

64. Garrison, "Reminiscences," p. 32.

65. a) Morgan, *Overland in 1846*, Vol. 1, pp. 182, 392.
b) Helfrich, "Applegate Trail," (1971), Vol. 9, pp. 36, 48.

66. Helfrich, "Applegate Trail," (1971), Vol. 9, p. 46.

67. Ibid., p. 52.

68. Morgan, *Overland in 1846*, Vol. 1, p. 182.

69. Morgan, *Overland in 1846*, Vol. 1, p. 47.

70. Ibid., p. 49.

71. Applegate, *Way Bill*, p. 3.

72. Helfrich, "Applegate Trail," (1971), Vol. 9, p. 52.

73. Ibid.

74. Ibid., p. 46.

75. Ibid., p. 52, 54.

76. Ibid., p. 54.

77. Morgan, *Overland in 1846*, Vol. 1, p. 183.

78. Garrison, "Reminiscences," p. 23.

79. a) Garrison, *Life and Labours*, OHS Mss #1009, p. 29.
b) Garrison, "Reminiscences," p. 24.

80. a) Garrison, "Reminiscences," p. 24.
b) Morgan, *Overland in 1846*, Vol. 1, p. 182.

81. Morgan, *Overland in 1846*, Vol. 1, pp. 182, 393.

82. Ibid., p. 182, 183.

83. Thornton, *Or. and Ca. in 1848*, Vol. 1, p. 188.

84. Helfrich, "Applegate Trail," (1971), Vol. 9, p. 57.

85. Scott, *Independence*, p. 142.

86. Helfrich, "Applegate Trail," (1971), Vol. 9, p. 58.

87. Helfrich, *Trails West*, p. 47. [There are many references to '49 in this area. They are referring to the '49 Gold Rush days, which happened three years later.]

88. a) Applegate, *Way Bill*, p. 3.
b) Helfrich, *Trails West*, p. 135.
c) Helfrich, "Applegate Trail," (1971), Vol. 9, p. 58.

89. a) Applegate, "Applegate Trail," p. 22.

b) Helfrich, "Applegate Trail," (1971), Vol. 9, p. 58.
c) Helfrich, *Trails West*, p. 135.

Ch. 5 The APPLEGATE TRAIL in CALIFORNIA

The new Oregon Trail through California also including Lost River in Oregon: California

As the emigrants crossed Sand Creek they had just crossed the border from Nevada to California.[1] The country south from the present day Oregon and Idaho border was all called California in 1846 This border was the Mexican border.[2] It follows the 42nd parallel (U.S.G.S. map). Oregon, Washington, Idaho as well as Montana were all known as the Territory of Oregon[3] "The emigrants who started for the disputed territory of Oregon were eventually to learn that while on their way the treaty had been signed which made it a part of the United States."[4] (W. J. Ghent, 1929)

The first area in California was Surprise Valley.[5] (U.S.G.S. map) This Valley was named "Surprise" by the emigrants because they were surprised to see such a lush fertile valley after plodding through miles of dry arid desert.[6]

They passed Warm Springs, known today as Leonard Hot Springs.[7] Pringle camped at Warm Springs on the night of September 18. He woke the next morning to find one of his oxen shot with an arrow. Two cows in the company were also shot.[8] One was driven off the trail and the other soon died.[9]

They passed another hot springs while traveling toward Middle and Upper (Alkali) Lake.[10] They traveled across the south side of Upper (Alkali) Lake.[11] The scenery was changing even more. They were starting to see more trees.[12]

While Pringle was camping at Warm Springs, Scott was probably camped at a stream on the east side of Upper (Alkali) Lake. Upper Lake was also known to some emigrants as Plum Lake.[13] Scott called the stream Trout Creek.[14] He also said it was near a thick growth of plums. Later diaries refer to a Plum Creek that flowed into the east side of Upper (Alkali) Lake.[15]

Benjamin F. Burch, William G. Parker and Charles Putnam from the Applegate road party were waiting here for the first wagons.[16] Burch had taken ill and the other two men stayed behind with him. Two of the men were former exploring party members. They must have been glad to see their old friend Levi Scott again.

Saturday, September 19 Pringle traveled across the south side of Upper (Alkali) Lake.[17] After eight miles of this saline plain and dry alkaline waste, they found themselves on the side of a wooded mountain, covered with magnificent lofty pines.[18] They made their camp two miles further along on the east side of Upper Lake by a clear, clean, mountain stream flowing down the side of the Warner Mountains.[19]

Days later Thornton reached the alkali lakes:

> We passed over the dry bed of former lakes, which are probably covered with water during the season at which the snows melt. We crossed one that was about ten miles wide, having upon its western side a cool stream of water of great beauty, and ran down the side of a wooded mountain, and spread itself out in the grassy plane below. Here we saw some pine trees of a large size. They were the first we had seen, in many a weary league....[20] (Thornton, 1848)

From this point on Thornton wrote from memory. He said he had his third volume of notes taken by an Indian.[21] I'm not sure what an Indian would have wanted with Thornton's journal.

Next the emigrants had to climb Fandango Pass.[22] Fandango Pass was probably one of the steepest uphill grades the emigrants had encountered. It was known by some at the time as Goose Mountain Pass.[23] It was also known later as Lassen Pass,[24] named after Peter Lassen who found another route to California in 1848 using part of the Applegate Trail as his road.[25] The ascent of Fandango Pass was about two miles long.[26]

Pringle arrived on September 20. He considered this pass to be "quite steep."[27] Depending on the weight of the wagon and how much it was carrying, the emigrants might have shared their teams. By putting their teams together with their neighbor, they could help each other to get up the hill. This was called double teaming.[28] They would have also moved along behind the wagon with wheels stops to give the oxen a chance to rest climbing the hill.[29] This was known as "chocking the wheels." The descent down Fandango Pass was steep, but not as steep as Fly Canyon had been.[30] Fandango Pass probably got its name because the emigrants, thinking they had just crossed the Sierra Nevada Mountains, would hold a celebration which they called a fandango. Some later wagon trains would have a dance around the camp fire after reaching this point.[31]

After reaching the summit they traveled down Fandango Valley along Willow Creek to reach Goose Lake. They traveled on the lake bed of Goose Lake as they headed south around this very shallow lake. They had to keep the wagons near the shore of the lake because the exposed bed of the lake was too cracked and dried up.[32] The 1926 photograph taken by the Getty Studio of Lakeview, Oregon shows the original trail across Goose Lake toward present day McGinty Point.[33] This is now covered with about three or four feet of water across Goose Lake.[34]

When the foremost party reached Goose Lake they camped for the night. Scott said the water level was so low that some of the men waded out for as much as half a mile to do some duck hunting.[35]

Rev. Garrison recalled that while at Goose Lake they lost several head of cattle: "we soon found ourselves at Goose Lake, here the Indians made a break on us, killing several head of our cattle and driving off quite a number, leaving many wagons without a team, here my old friend Mr. Lancefield lost several of his oxen but supplied the place with cows...."[36] This incident was not mentioned by any other diarists. It also sounds a lot like a situation that happened a little further on the trail at Lost River, which we will get to soon. The Piute Indians occupied everything east of Fandango Pass as far as Humboldt River, while the Pitt River Indians occupied everything west of Fandango Pass as far as the Goose Lake Valley.[37]

Pringle traveled about fourteen miles around the south side of Goose Lake and along the beach of the lake Tuesday, September 22. He considered it a good road.[38] He camped that night near present day McGinty Reservoir.[39]

When Scott and the lead wagons left Goose Lake they headed west across a heavily timbered high plain.[40] They probably camped somewhere along "Canion Creek."[41] This today is called Fletcher Creek.[42] When they arrived, they found a man named Sevy. He was another member of the Applegate road party. He had fallen behind and had lost the trail. After finding a ravine to hide in, he decided to play it safe and wait until the first wagons came.[43] He had only a few provisions and was afraid Indians might find him if he tried to hunt, so he was not only glad to see the wagons, but equally as glad when he was offered some cooked venison.[44]

After camping on the west side of Goose Lake, Virgil Pringle traveled east about twelve miles to camp at Pool

Figure 1 Photograph of wagon ruts crossing the south end of Goose Lake during the drought of 1926 courtesy of George Burrell, professional land surveyor.

Levi Scott camped at Goff's Spring.[50] It is also known as Pot Hole Springs.[51] Here he found a note left by Jesse Applegate.[52] It was at the bottom of a large pine tree. Scott said this note on the trail was "at a very difficult place we reached."[53] It may have contained directions for locating the trail. This note was the last Scott heard from Captain Applegate until reaching the end of the Applegate Trail.[54] They stayed at Goff's Spring two days.[55]

After camping on Pool Creek or Canion Creek, Pringle traveled fourteen miles further and camped at a good spring.[56] This could have been Goff's Spring or it may have been the spring at Steel Swamp.[57]

Creek, which was also the same as present day Fletcher Creek.[45] This is the same creek Jesse Applegate called "Canion Creek."[46] They resumed their journey the next day along Pool Creek for about eight miles. The Geography was a "high plane and very stony and well timbered with pine and cedar."[47] (Virgil Pringle, 1846) This area was known years later as "the Devil's Garden."[48] It is within what is known today as Modoc National Forest.[49] (U.S.G.S. Maps)

Levi Scott and the company he was leading traveled from Goff's Springs to the Clear Lake Valley and camped on a spring near Clear River Marsh,[58] known today as Clear Lake.[59] Clear Lake was also known as Lost Lake or Modoc Lake.[60] They had crossed Boles Creek and traveled through a stretch of country covered with hundreds of acres of apaws, a main source of food for the Modoc Indians.[61] Now they

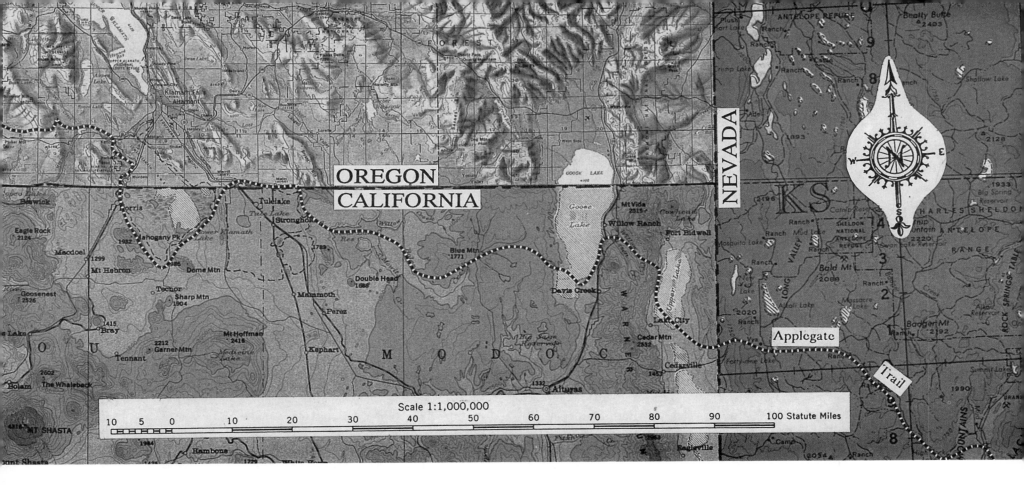

were beginning to see less timber.[62] In 1846 Clear Lake was a marsh land except later in the year.[63] Because the emigrants were traveling this stretch of the trail in late September, they considered this a good road.[64] Today Clear Lake is a reservoir[65] (U.S.G.S.Maps) so the water was lower in 1846 than it is today. The U.S.G.S. 15 minute series (topographic) map of Clear Lake Reservoir Quadrangle shows the location of the trail crossing the lake at the north shore.

The next day Scott and his group continued traveling from Clear Lake to the Tule Lake region, a distance of approximately twelve miles.[66] Pringle traveled eight miles through a generally level grade with only a few trees.[67] He probably made it to Clear Lake and camped at Mammoth Springs.[68]

On the following day Scott and the foremost company traveled to Lost River and camped a few miles before the Stone Bridge crossing. They made about twenty miles that day.[69] They had just crossed the 42nd parallel and entered Oregon Territory.[70] With today's state boundary lines they had entered the state of Oregon.[71]

- 53 -

That same day Pringle traveled across Clear Lake along the lake shore. He made about nine miles and camped beside the lake.[72] "We are now in the range of country of lakes of which the Klamath Lake is the largest known. Make nine miles and camp by a pretty lake. Road good and level. Weather fine."Ibid. (Virgil Pringle, September 27, 1846)

They were reaching the end of the tree lined countryside. From Clear Lake they resumed their journey east on the north side of Horse Mountain.[73] They traveled over a "Rocky Ridge"[74] called Modoc Mountains and along the eastern shore of Tule Lake.[75] Here they could see for miles. They could even see Mount Shasta. Thornton mentions seeing a mountain: "Around were many promontories and summits, of singular and varied forms, standing up against the horizon...."[76]

Monday evening, September 28, after traveling twenty-two miles from Clear Lake to Lost River[77] Pringle camped with the foremost company near present day Malin, Oregon.[78] This made a larger company of about fifty wagons strong.[79] Since Pringle mentioned having twenty-nine wagons ahead of him, this would mean that his company consisted of twenty-one wagons.[80] Tolbert Carter says that there were fifty-two wagons.[81] Young Henry Garrison said, "we were ninety wagons strong."[82]

A. E. Garrison's teamster, named David Tanner, had "pleurisy"[83] in his side and had a hard time walking. He was mainly taking care of the cattle that were being herded behind the wagons. Garrison had tried to get him to ride in the wagon, but he said he could not ride because the jolting of the wagon hurt his side. One evening he had fallen behind the train. This worried Garrison terribly so he scolded him and told him of the danger of falling behind.[84]

Tolbert Carter was another emigrant traveling with the forty-six wagon train. He was the teamster for a widow and her two small children.[85] Carter says that before now they had been traveling through a country of "a harmless, inoffensive tribe called Digger Indians...."[86] Because of this, the men let down their guard of the cattle and of camp.[87] This was actually Modoc Country.[88] That morning they found ten oxen missing. Four of them belonged to Washington Crowley.[89] Tolbert Carter also found that he was missing one of the steers he was in charge of. The steer belonged to the widow lady. Ten armed men mounted up and rode off to search for the culprits.[90]

While the men were off trying to recover the cattle, Young Henry Garrison went fishing with one of two brothers in the company. They went about a mile east of camp along Lost River. They sat on the bank of Lost River in the shade under a willow tree. The man whispered to Henry that he would kill an Indian.[91] By the time there was a fish biting on Henry's line, he looked up and noticed an Indian had just appeared across the river bank. The Indian did not see the two young men. He laid down by the river to get a drink of water. The young man Henry was with raised his rifle and shot the Indian for no reason. "The Indian made one dive, and when he came up, his body shot half his length out of the water, then sank and raised to sight no more...."[92]

The man that shot the Indian was a young single man. He could not realize the danger he was placing everyone in by his careless action.[93]

After the men in search of the lost cattle crossed Stone Bridge, they picked up the trail of five pairs of moccasins along the Lower Klamath Lake. There were tules that grew along the shore. This is where the Modoc Indians lived.[94] They also inhabited "both sides of Lost River below the Stone Bridge from a quarter of a mile on the right bank, to half a mile or more on the left bank."[95]

After following this trail of moccasins about fifteen miles, they found the place where the oxen had been slaughtered. It had been done crudely, possibly with arrowheads that they broke in the process. They found enough remains to conclude that these were seven of the ten oxen that were missing.[96]

The men proceeded further to find out what happened to the other three. They found a path leading into the tules.[97] The tules were at least ten feet high, so although there were not any trees or hills in the area this still created a significant visual barrier to see over.[98]

Fearing the worst, they decided to play it safe and split up.[99] Five men stood guard and held the horses while the other five followed the path into the tules. Carter was one of the five to enter this path, "on this foolhardy and hazardous trip."[100] In about a half mile the path led them to a large section of tules with a clearing that had five Indian dwellings. This was a village complete with pots, baskets, mats, and other belongings.[101] Assuming this village to be solely the habitation of the same people that had stolen and slaughtered the oxen, they went on to destroy everything in

Figure 2 Lower Klamath Lake

sight. "There was no signs of anything pertaining to the lost oxen in the lodges destroyed."[102]

After they had taken their frustrations out on this small village, they rejoined their comrades. When they came out of the tules, twenty or thirty Indians from the direction of the village ran to the lake shore out of shooting range and turned around in anger and started shouting at the men. The men started toward the Indians and they ran.[103]

The men moved on without finding the other three cattle. They split up into two groups again and went in two different directions to circle the lake. Carter went to the left with four others and the other five went to the right.[104]

Moments later Carter and the men he was with were called back to find that the other men had an Indian surrounded, lying face down in the sage brush. They decided to get the prisoner to his feet and take him back to camp and let everyone decide his fate. One man got off his horse with gun in hand and started to raise their captive. "A pitiful moan proceeded from the prisoner."[105] Once they could see the face of this prisoner, they realized they had captured an elderly Indian woman. Shame came over the men as they sat mounted on their horses. They all put their guns back in their holsters. It was obvious to them she not only had nothing to do with the theft of the cattle, but was not the recipient of any of the beef.[106]

In sign language she told them that she saw five Indians steal the ten head of cattle. They killed seven and packed the meat on the other three cattle, concealing them somewhere in the tule swamp. Carter also said, "lastly, she showed us by signs that could not be disputed, that she had not eaten of the meat."[107] "She expected nothing but death would atone for the manner in which we had been treated by the tribe, and perhaps some of her sons were engaged in the theft."[108] They left the old woman behind in the desert and rode quietly back to camp.

They got back about ten o'clock that night. By that time everyone had feared the worst. They were greatly relieved to see that all the men were back unharmed.[109]

After Levi Scott had led the emigrants this far and dealt with all of the encounters with the Indians, the emigrants insisted that he become their captain.[110] He did not want any part of it unless he could get all of them to agree to follow every order that he gave. They "pledged me that all of my orders should be strictly obeyed."[111] This made Levi Scott the captain of all the trains including both main companies that had just joined.[112] Up to now there had been more than one captain because there was more than one wagon company traveling separately. These captains probably became sub-captains.[113]

Because Thornton was missing his journal and writing from memory, it is hard to tell where he was and when he was at Lost River. He mentions losing a wagon. "We traveled over a country that was generally very barren, until we arrived at the Sacramento Valley, where my wagon was dashed in pieces upon an exceeding rough and dangerous road. Here I cast

aside some of my property.[114] He had probably arrived at Lost River, which is called Sacramento River in Jesse Applegate's 1848 Way Bill.[115] He also mentions that this happened before reaching, "dry beds of former lakes...."[116]

The foremost wagons got an early start the next morning and crossed Stone Bridge, "...we crossed the river on a ledge of rock that ran clear across the stream. It was called Stone Bridge."[117] (Lucy Ann Henderson Deady, 1923) There appeared to be one giant stone, a natural bridge that crossed the river which seemed to have water flowing under it and over it. The water was up to the hubs of the wagons.[118] It was the best way to be able to cross the river.[119] It was known by different names to different people. Scott called Stone Bridge "the Rock Bridge."[120] He called Lost River "Flat River," "Lost River" and "Rock Bridge River."[121] Pringle called it "a singular rock which made a shallow ford."[122] Young Henry Garrison referred to it as a "natural bridge."[123]

They got an early start the next morning and reached Klamath Lake.[124] Everyone had crossed Stone Bridge before noon.[125] Just one mile south of Stone Bridge they entered California once again. (U.S.G.S. maps)

They traveled through sage brush covered terrain to Klamath Lake and along the lake shore for the rest of the day.[126] Just before dark they came to a place where a steep grade projected out to the lake.[127] Scott went ahead to see which direction to take. He found it was not possible to pass around next to the lake. It was better to turn to the left and go a little out of the way into the hills to avoid such a steep grade.

Figure 3 Crossing Stone Bridge

When he returned, he found they had already taken their wagons past the point they would need to turn left to avoid the grade. The men felt they could take the grade and cross the ridge in less time than it would take to go back and around it. They hitched several teams together to one of the lighter wagons and made the grade.[128]

It was not long before the hillside was covered with wagons doing the same. No one wanted to retrace their steps. As they were all working their way up the hill, the king bolt snapped on Isaac Lebo's large, blue Conestoga style wagon. The wagon bed and hind wheels started rolling back down the hill that was by this time covered with wagons, oxen, men, women, and children.[129] There was a child inside the wagon that was moving back down the hill. Everyone was stunned. They could not move. In an instant Mrs. Lebo, the mother of the child, grabbed a large stone, ran behind the moving massive wagon, and stuck the stone under one of the wheels causing the wagon to whirl around and stop. She swept her baby into her arms and sank to the ground in relief. She had not only saved her child but many others below. It happened so fast that only a few were even aware of the event. They all finished ascending the hill and were all encamped by a little after dark. That evening as the campfires burned, things were once again back to normal.[130]

Days later when Thornton traveled around Lower Klamath Lake he had to climb the same steep grade. "Messrs. Baker, Butterfield, Putnam, and myself united our teams, and although we put from eighteen to twenty-three yoke of oxen to each wagon, it was with the utmost difficulty that we were able to take them up at all."[131] (Thornton, 1848)

Back at the foremost company camp, Rev. Garrison noticed that David Tanner had again fallen behind the train and not made it into camp. After a while he assumed that he had slept somewhere else in camp. He decided not to worry about him until morning.[132]

The next morning, Thursday, October 1, two men named Kelly and Hudson came into camp on foot. They had been with a wagon train that was further behind. About a week before they tried to catch up with the next group of wagons. When they were on Lost River, they shot a sage hen and about a dozen armed Indians appeared out of nowhere on the opposite shore. They made their getaway and had traveled all night without stopping to camp. Tired and hungry, they were given breakfast and were allowed to join the wagon train.[133]

That same morning it was discovered that David Tanner was still missing.[134] Henry Garrison said that he was last seen by several people on the side of the river.[135] When Tanner had not shown up for breakfast, Garrison started getting worried. The last place anyone had seen Tanner was after crossing Stone Bridge before noon. Scott sent the wagon train forward around lower Klamath Lake while he and some men went back to look for Tanner. The men who rode back with Scott were Charles B. Graves, David M. Guthrie, Chat Helms and Jesse Boone.[136]

They went back on the trail to just before Lost River and found his tracks. They recognized the tracks because he was missing a heel tap on one of his boots. After following the tracks they noticed he had started running. Then they noticed two Indian tracks, one on each side of him. The Indian tracks had closed in on Tanner's tracks.[137] Fifty to a hundred yards away, they found his body in a patch of sage brush.[138] He had been shot with nine arrows from two directions and stripped of all his belongings, including his clothes.[139] They buried him at that site.[140] The only tools they had to dig a grave were a butcher knife and their hands. They scraped out a hole about three feet deep in the sandy soil and buried David Tanner in the best blanket they had.[141]

Scott and the men caught up with the wagon company later that evening at the next camp and told them the grim news of Mr. Tanner.[142] They had made about twelve miles and were camping by a small stream on the south side of Klamath Lake.[143] Henry Garrison said, "Mr. Tanner was subject to fits, and we suppose that he having one, was the cause of his falling behind."[144]

The next morning while James Robinson was standing guard he shot at an Indian near the cattle. Robertson said the Indian was trying to drive off some of the cattle. They all thought he escaped without injury. The foremost party all resumed their journey and continued traveling around lower Klamath Lake. They camped near Klamath River.[145]

NOTES   Chapter 5

1. Helfrich, *Trails West*, p. 47.

2. Morgan, *Overland in 1846*, Vol. 1, pp. vi, vii.

3. Lavender, *Great West*, p. .

4. Ghent, *Road*, p. 86.

5. Morgan, *Overland in 1846*, Vol. 1, p. 393.

6. Brown, *Bloody Ground*, p. 11.

7.a) Applegate, *Way Bill*, p. 3.
b) Applegate, "Applegate Trail," p. 22.
c) Helfrich, "Applegate Trail," (1971), Vol. 9, p. 58.

8. Morgan, *Overland in 1846*, Vol. 1, p. 182.

9.a) Helfrich, "Applegate Trail," (1971), Vol. 9, p. 58.

10. Helfrich, "Applegate Trail," (1971), Vol. 9, p. 56.

11.a) Helfrich, "Applegate Trail," (1971), Vol. 9, pp. 58, 62.
b) Morgan, *Overland in 1846*, Vol. 1, p. 182.

12. Morgan, *Overland in 1846*, Vol. 1, p. 182.

13. Helfrich, "Applegate Trail," (1971), Vol. 9, p. 62.

14. Scott, *Independence*, p. 143.

15. Helfrich, "Applegate Trail," (1971), Vol. 9, p. 58.

16. Scott, *Independence*, p. 143.

17. a) Helfrich, "Applegate Trail," (1971), Vol. 9, pp. 58, 62.
b) Morgan, *Overland in 1846*, Vol. 1, p. 182.

18. Morgan, *Overland in 1846*, Vol. 1, p. 182.

19. Helfrich, *Trails West*, p. 48.

20. Thornton, *Or. and Ca. in 1848*, Vol. 1, p. 192.

21. Ibid., p.190.

22. Helfrich, *Trails West*, p. 48.

23. Garrison, "Reminiscences," p. 31.

24. Morgan, *Overland in 1846*, Vol. 1, p. 394.

25. Thomas H. Hunt, *Ghost Trails to California* (American West Publishing Company, 1974), p. 119.

26. a) Helfrich, "Applegate Trail," (1971), Vol. 9, p. 65.
b) Morgan, *Overland in 1846*, Vol. 1, p. 182.

27. Morgan, *Overland in 1846*, Vol. 1, p. 182.

28. McGlashan, *Donner Party*, p. 44.

29. Helfrich, "Applegate Trail," (1971), Vol. 9, p. 67.

30. Helfrich, *Trails West*, p. 140.

31. Helfrich, "Applegate Trail," (1971), Vol. 9, p. 65. [A fandango is a sort of celebration.]

32. Scott, *Independence*, p. 144.

33. Helfrich, "Applegate Trail," (1971), Vol. 9, pp. 71, 64.

34. Ibid., p. 71.

35. Scott, *Independence*, p. 144.

36. Garrison, *Life and Labours*, OHS Mss #1009, p. 32.

37. Helfrich, "Applegate Trail," (1971), Vol. 9, p. 65.

38. Morgan, *Overland in 1846*, Vol. 1, p. 183.

39. Helfrich, "Applegate Trail," (1971), Vol. 9, p. 73.

40. Morgan, *Overland in 1846*, Vol. 1, p. 183.

41. Applegate, *Way Bill*, p. 3.

42. Helfrich, "Applegate Trail," (1971), Vol. 9, p. 80.

43. Scott, *Independence*, p. 144.

44. Ibid., p. 145.

45. a) Morgan, *Overland in 1846*, Vol. 1, pp. 73, 183.
b) Helfrich, "Applegate Trail," (1971), Vol. 9, p. 394.

46. a) Applegate, *Way Bill*, p. 3.
b) Helfrich, "Applegate Trail," (1971), Vol. 9, p. 80.

47. Morgan, *Overland in 1846*, Vol. 1, p. 183.

48. Helfrich, "Applegate Trail," (1971), Vol. 9, p. 78.

49.a) Stone, "Southern Route," p. 141.
b) Helfrich, "Applegate Trail," (1971), Vol. 9, p. 78.

50. Scott, *Independence*, p. 145.

51. Helfrich, "Applegate Trail," (1971), Vol. 9, pp. 75, 80.

52. Scott, *Independence*, p. 135.

53. Ibid.

54. Ibid.

55. Ibid., p. 145.

56. Morgan, *Overland in 1846*, Vol. 1, p. 183.

57. Helfrich, "Applegate Trail," (1971), Vol. 9, pp. 72, 73.

58. Applegate, "Old Emigrant Road," p. 25.

59. Scott, *Independence*, p. 145.

60. Stone, "Southern Route," p. 141.

61. Helfrich, "Applegate Trail," (1971), Vol. 9, p. 79.

62. Morgan, *Overland in 1846*, Vol. 1, p. 183.

63. Helfrich, "Applegate Trail," (1971), Vol. 9, p. 79.

64. Morgan, *Overland in 1846*, Vol. 1, p. 183.

65. Helfrich, "Applegate Trail," (1971), Vol. 9, pp. 72, 79.

66. Scott, *Independence*, p. 146.

67. Morgan, *Overland in 1846*, Vol. 1, p. 183.

68.a) Helfrich, "Applegate Trail," (1971), Vol. 9, p. 75.
b) Morgan, *Overland in 1846*, Vol. 1, p. 394.

69. Scott, *Independence*, p. 146.

70. Morgan, *Overland in 1846*, Vol. 1, pp. vi, vii.

71. Helfrich, *Trails West*, p. 56.

72. Morgan, *Overland in 1846*, Vol. 1, p. 183.

73. Helfrich, "Applegate Trail," (1971), Vol. 9, pp. 82, 84.

74. Morgan, *Overland in 1846*, Vol. 1, p. 183.

75. Morgan, *Overland in 1846*, Vol. 1, p. 394.

76. Thornton, *Or. and Ca. in 1848*, p. 191.

77. Morgan, *Overland in 1846*, Vol. 1, p. 183.

78. Ibid., p. 394.

79. Ibid., p. 183.

80. Ibid., p. 182, 183.

81. Carter, *Pioneer Days*, p. 67.

82. Garrison, "Reminiscences," p. 24.

83. Garrison, *Life and Labours*, OHS Mss #1009, p. 32.

84. Ibid.

85. Carter, *Pioneer Days*, p. 78. [According to W. A. Moxley's Southern Route To Oregon," Tolbert Carter was a relative of Mr. Burns who died on the desert, and the widow was Mrs. Burns. (Moxley, OHS Mss #855, p. 32.)]

86. Ibid., p. 67.

87. Ibid.

88. Helfrich, "Applegate Trail," (1971), Vol. 9, p. 86.

89. Scott, *Independence*, p. 146.

90. Carter, *Pioneer Days*, p. 67.

91. Garrison, "Reminiscences," p. 25.

92. Ibid. [There was no reason for him to have shot this Indian. He could not blame any of the cattle that were missing on this Indian. They could not have blamed any other shootings on him. He was simply getting some water out of the river.]

93. Ibid.

94. Helfrich, "Applegate Trail," (1971), Vol. 9, p. 86.

95. Ibid.

96. Carter, *Pioneer Days*, p. 67.

97. Ibid., p. 68.

98. Harold William Rickett, *Wild Flowers of the United States* (New York, NY: McGraw-Hill Book Company, 1971), Vol. 5, p. 82.

99. Carter, *Pioneer Days*, p. 68.

100. Ibid.

101. Ibid.

102. Ibid., p. 69.

103. Ibid.

104. Ibid., p. 70.

105. Ibid.

106. Ibid., p. 71.

107. Ibid.

108. Ibid., p. 72.

109. Ibid.

110. Scott, *Independence*, p. 146.

111. Ibid.

112. Ibid.

113. Harry E. Chrisman, *The 1001 Most-Asked Questions About the American West* (Chicago, IL: Shallow Press, 1982), p. 316.

114. Thornton, *Or. and Ca. in 1848*, Vol. 1, p. 189.

115. a) Applegate, *Way Bill*, p. 3.
b) Helfrich, "Applegate Trail," (1971), Vol. 9, p. 85.

116. Thornton, *Or. and Ca. in 1848*, Vol. 1, p. 190. [This means he might have lost his wagon before the alkali lakes or Clear Lake.]

117. Lockley, *Pioneer Women*, p. 87.

118. Garrison, "Reminiscences," p. 25.

119. Applegate, "Applegate Trail," p. 9.

120. Scott, *Independence*, p. 146.

121. Ibid.

122. Morgan, *Overland in 1846*, Vol. 1, p. 183.

123. Garrison, "Reminiscences," p. 25.

124. Carter, *Pioneer Days*, p. 72.

125.a) Garrison, "Reminiscences," p. 25.
b) Scott, *Independence*, p. 146.

126. Scott, *Independence*, p. 146.

127. Garrison, "Reminiscences," p. 25.

128. Scott, *Independence*, p. 147.

129. Ibid., p. 148.

130. Ibid.

131. Thornton, *Or. and Ca. in 1848*, Vol. 1, p. 190.

132. Garrison, *Life and Labours*, OHS Mss #1009, p. 132.

133. Scott, *Independence*, p. 149.

134. Ibid.

135. Garrison, "Reminiscences," p. 25.   [Lost River]

136. Scott, *Independence*, p. 150.

137. Ibid., p. 151.
b) Garrison, "Reminiscences," p. 26.

138. Scott, *Independence*, p. 151.

139. Garrison, "Reminiscences," p. 26.

140. Ibid., pp. 25, 26.

141. Scott, *Independence*, p. 151.

142. Ibid., p. 152.

143. Morgan, *Overland in 1846*, Vol. 1, p. 183.

144. Garrison, "Reminiscences," p. 26.

145. Scott, *Independence*, p. 152.

Ch. 6 OVER the CASCADES

From the Klamath River to the Rogue Valley: Oregon

About five miles before leaving Lower Klamath Lake the foremost company once again journeyed into the Oregon Territory. This time they were here to stay. This was about ten miles south of the Klamath River. (U.S.G.S. maps)

The next day Scott and the foremost company crossed the Klamath River and traveled about eight miles.[1] Pringle and the company he was with made their last drive on the lake.[2] They made about twelve miles of good road that day and camped near Klamath River, "at a fine bold spring but not cold."[3] This was just south of present day Keno.[4]

We will now go forward to the road working party. Jesse Applegate and others in the road party decided he should go ahead to the settlements in the Willamette Valley to get help with provisions and more manpower to aid in opening the road before the winter rains.[5]

Before he left for the settlements, Jesse Applegate put a man in charge of the road party. This man was to make sure that the rest of the road party did everything necessary to make a passable trail before the wagons arrived.[6] The road party consisted of most of the original exploring party and the older sons of the pioneers who were traveling on this new trail. Jesse Applegate arrived back in the Willamette Valley on October 3rd. Shortly afterward, he sent out a party with oxen and horses to meet the emigrants and help them in reaching the Willamette Valley.[7]

The foremost wagon train journeyed through a crudely blazed trail in a thick growth of trees as they made their way

Figure 1 Klamath River crossing

up the wooded mountains between Buck and Hayden Mountain.[8] They were in the Cascade Mountains, known to some in the party as the Siskiyou Mountains[9] or, as some called them, "the Sis-que Mountains"[10] or "Siskia Mountains."[11] According to Bancroft, there was a fire somewhere in the Cascades.[12] These pioneers had to remove trees that had fallen from the fire into the path they were going.[13] It must have been rough for the first party, which was opening the road. The mountains were heavily

Figure 2 Along Beaver Creek

timbered[14] and steep.[15] The road party had blazed a rough trail but work still had to be done to get the wagons through.[16] The foremost company had to camp without water or grass the first night in the Cascade Mountains.[17]

The following day, Sunday, October 4, Pringle and the company he was with traveled another four miles and crossed Klamath River.[18] He said it was a "very rocky ford."[19] They made about eight miles and camped that night on the river.[20]

When Carter crossed the Klamath River he said it was "one of the worst crossings that wagons ever made -boulders from a foot through to the size of flour barrels- *[sic]* but no accidents occurred."[21]

Days later Thornton came as far as Klamath River before having any trouble with Indians.[22] Along the Klamath River they saw some Indians. "Indians appeared in considerable number among the trees, upon the opposite side.

They were fired upon and fled without receiving any harm."[23] These emigrants must have been firing on the Indians out of fear. The Indians all ran off.[24]

Going back to the foremost wagons, Levi Scott and the foremost company continued for the second day to cut their way through the dense wooded forest of Buck Mountain[25] (U.S.G.S. maps). They started at day break and worked until they reached Beaver Creek.[26] The foremost company traveled through Grouse Butte and along Beaver Creek, known today as Sheepy Creek.[27]

After two days traveling through the rugged mountains without any water, the emigrants in the foremost wagon company had grown irritable. That evening Levi Scott gave strict orders to have the livestock guarded at all times. Everyone felt this was unnecessary, and a guard was not posted. As a result the next morning a horse was missing.[28] Scott reminded them that he had agreed to be their captain only if they agreed to follow all of his orders. He therefore

- 64 -

resigned his post as captain. He did continue to guide them on the new trail as he had promised.[29]

Even after cutting through the trees, Pringle felt the road was "bad and rough."[30] The wagons he was with made ten miles that day and camped without water or grass.[31]

Carter wrote, "We then had the Siskiyou Mountains to cross; but fortunately we found plenty of timber, water and grass for the stock."[32]

Rev. A. E. Garrison wrote, "...a great job it was to cut a road across, but we had a long way back provisioned [sic] and sent young men ahead to open the road, so we got over the mountain quite well."[33]

The trail Levi Scott, Virgil Pringle and others helped cut went straight up a grade between Hayden Mountain and Buck Mountain.[34] The wagons wheels were tall to clear obtacles in their path. This higher center of gravity made them top heavy. They could not go on the side of a mountain because the wagons had to keep as level as possible. They went straight up and down the grades. Roads were later cut into the side of the mountains. The Cascade Mountains had a later route, the Southern Oregon Wagon Road, which was approximately the same as the present SS Fire Road for the last part of Hayden Mountain. The original wagon road went straight up at this location.[35]

Pringle started his second day through the Siskiyou Mountains Tuesday, October 6.[36] They made six miles that day. He considered the road to be fair.[37] He probably camped at the foot of Buck Mountain on Beaver Creek (Sheepy Creek).[38] (U.S.G.S. maps) There is no mention of water or grass at this camp.[39]

Rev. Garrison had a cow missing while camped at the dry camp. He and his friend, Mr. Lancefield, decided to go back to their last camp to see if they could catch the "Indians" with the cow. What they did find were a lot of Indian tracks. They hid out of sight and waited, but there was no sign of the cow or the "Indians." They returned to their new camp empty-handed. The next morning as they were preparing to leave, they noticed that the missing cow had been there all the time.[40]

The next major obstacle the foremost wagon company had to face was Jenny Creek.[41] It was known later as Jenny Creek Wagon Slide. Jenny Creek Slide had about a 45-degree angle, much like Fly Canyon in Nevada.[42] To go down the grade they would unhitch all their teams except one pair of their main working oxen. These were used to steer and hold the wagon back.[43] They would block the wheels to keep the wagon from rolling forward too fast. They would also tie the rear of the wagon to large trees by wrapping a rope around them and holding the other end. This helped to control the speed at which the wagon descended the slide. "And down they went!"[44] (Devere Helfrich, 1971)

Pringle arrived at Jenny Creek on October 7.[45] He said Jenny Creek Wagon Slide was, "...a steep hill to go down."[46] It took a lot of team effort to get each wagon down. After one wagon had made it down the slide, they would start the process all over again until all the wagons had gone down the slide, and crossed the creek.

By the end of the day all the teams were very weak. They pulled into camp at Round Prairie and rested their teams.[47] After Jenny Creek Slide there were Keene Creek Slide, Greensprings Summit, and Strychnine Hill just below Tyler Creek.[48]

The wagons were still spread out across the route. The first party of wagons was about three weeks ahead of the last.[49] Thornton was of course among the members of the last party. In later years he claimed, "...teams had to be

Figure 3 North of Tub Springs

doubled until eighteen to twenty yokes were put to a wagon to drag it up...." (Bancroft, 1886)[50] Thornton mentioneed how very steep the mountain was with its thick growth of trees. "...toiling up the steep and difficult ascent of the mountain....[51] We had entered the dense forest of fir-trees and pines, which covered the mountains with their thick and dark green foliage...."[52]

Although Thornton was with the last company to go on the Applegate Trail, his was not the last wagon. He paused at the top of the summit to view where he had been and where he was going.

> ...I stood and looked over the valley from which we ascended, yet below the covering of the dense and closely interwoven pine tops that grew upon the side of the mountain, all seemed to be dark; and all was silent, except the loud cry of drivers cheering the overwrought oxen to their toil.[53]

He waited some time for wagons belonging to Baker, Butterfield, Putnam, and Crump. Thornton was in the path of the only way through. Mr. Newton came up with his wagon and insisted that he move to allow the other wagons to keep moving.[54]

Lucy Ann Henderson later recalls,

> "Mr. Thornton was a lawyer, a sort of dreamer, not very well, very irritable and peevish. I lived with them later, when I was going to school at Oregon City, so I learned what a peculiar man he was. He was the type of man that always blamed someone else for misfortunes he himself had caused."[55]

Thornton later seemed to be wanting to turn people against "Captain Applegate"[56] for Thornton, himself, having

Figure 4 Following along Tyler Creek they eventually came to Emigrant Creek.

Figure 5 Just southeast of present day Emigrant Lake, along Emigrant Creek....

chosen[57] to go on "the Applegate cut-off."[58]   "We only knew that many fierce savages prowled among its rugged recesses, and we only wished that they had prevented Applegate from passing through it."[59] (Thornton 1898)

Along with Thornton some of the last party of wagons traveling through the Cascades were Butterfield,[60] Baker, Putnam, Crump,[61] Newton and Townsend.[62]

That night as Thornton camped, three of his cattle appeared to be very weak and in danger of dying.[63]   He chained them to the wheels of the wagon to prevent them from eating laurel "or being killed by Indians."[64]

When they continued their journey the next morning at about eleven o'clock, one of Thornton's oxen, Tom, sank down upon the road. He could not travel anymore. He was without water and too hungry to go any further.[65] Thornton left him in the wilderness to die, "I turned away to hurry forward, in order, if possible, to save the lives of the remainder of the cattle. I left him in the wilderness to famish and die...."[66] He continued to hurry forward over the rough mountain ridge and early that same afternoon he lost another ox, although he does not seem to have a name for this ox.[67]

We will now continue the journey with the foremost company. From the present town of Lincoln to Tub Springs, the Applegate Trail followed the same path as the existing Greensprings Highway does today.[68] It then went along the north side of the Cascade Mountains and descended down a steep grade to cross Keene Creek Wagon Slide.

According to Devere Helfrich of the Klamath Echoes, 1971, "At Tub Spring the trail led northwesterly up the swale back of the spring, to again join the highway at the point where the concrete covered canal leading to the Keene Creek Diversion Dam now crosses."[69] This means the trail crossed Keene Creek next to the location the dam is today. Scott mentions camping at a spring on the northwest side of the summit.[70]

On October 10, Virgil Pringle was working his way down the Greensprings Summit. He mentions that it took "...all day in making three miles, the Branch so near impassable. Found a tolerable route at last."[71] He was probably following the creek bed of Tyler Creek.[72] (U.S.G.S.)

Following along Tyler Creek they eventually came to Emigrant Creek.[73] (U.S.G.S. maps) Just southeast of present day Emigrant Lake, along Emigrant Creek, through present day Songer Gap, they joined the existing California Pack Trail.[74]

Carter was glad to see an existing trail. "We then struck the trail leading from Oregon to California, and it was a comfort to know that civilized men had traveled this road before...."[75]

The Applegate exploring party had used this former Indian trail as a route along with other Indian trails and pack trails to form this southern route to Oregon up to the point of turning left and going east across the Greensprings.[76] This turning point was later known as Klamath Junction. Today this intersection is under the waters of Emigrant Lake.[77] From here the valley opened and they could see what is today the present site of Ashland.

Now we will return to Thornton and the other wagons in the rear. It was about three o'clock on their second day through the Cascade Mountains. Thornton decided he could no longer take his wagon forward with what was left of his team. "Mr. David Butterfield took my blankets, bison robes, rifle, shot-pouch and a little food into his wagon, upon the condition that I would unite the remainder of my team with his, until we should arrive at water and grass."[78] He left his wagon with its contents in the mountains "with a great probability of its being robbed and burnt by the savages before morning."[79]

Duke was another ox of Thornton's. He only had one horn and was in the habit of letting people know of his

presence with it. Consequently, Thornton used to chastise him for it. About a half mile further "...Duke sank down upon the road...."[80] Thornton was feeling a little melancholy about how he had treated him in the past, as he left him to die on the side of the road.[81]

Figure 6 Today this intersection is under the waters of Emigrant Lake.

NOTES   Chapter 6

1. Scott, *Independence*, p. 152.

2. Morgan, *Overland in 1846*, Vol. 1, p. 184.

3. Ibid.

4. Morgan, *Overland in 1846*, Vol. 1, p. 394.

5. Scott, *Independence*, pp. 134, 135.

6. Ibid., p. 135, 153.

7.a) Applegate, "Old Emigrant Road," p. 41.
b) Helfrich, "Applegate Trail," (1971), Vol. 9, p. 21.
[According to Joseph Burk, a British botanist who was traveling with Jesse Applegate, they reached the Applegate farm on September 26th. (Morgan, *Overland in 1846*, Vol. 2, p. 767.)]

8.a) Morgan, *Overland in 1846*, Vol. 1, p. 394.
b) Helfrich, "Applegate Trail," (1971), Vol. 9, p. 93.
c) Stone, "Southern Route," p. 143.

9.a) Helfrich, "Applegate Trail," (1971), Vol. 9, p. 92.
b) Applegate, "Applegate Trail," p. 7.
c) Garrison, "Reminiscences," p. 26.

10. Morgan, *Overland in 1846*, Vol. 1, p. 184.

11. Thornton, *Or. and Ca. in 1848*, Vol. 1, p. 197.

12. Bancoft, Works, Vol. XXIX, p. 559.

13.a) Ibid.
b) Moxley, OHS Mss #855, p. 40.

14. Helfrich, "Applegate Trail," (1971), Vol. 9, p. 93.

15. Meacham, *Applegate Trail*, p. 13.

16. Scott, *Independence*, p. 152.

17. Ibid., p. 153.

18. Morgan, *Overland in 1846*, Vol. 1, p. 184.

19. Ibid.

20. Ibid.

21. Carter, *Pioneer Days*, p. 73.

22. Thornton, *Or. and Ca. in 1848*, Vol. 1, p. 196.

23. Ibid.

24. Ibid. [This certainly helped increase the animosity that the Indians must have started having toward the white man as he was invading their area and their land.]

25. Scott, *Independence*, p. 153.

26. Ibid.

27.a) Helfrich, "Applegate Trail," (1971), Vol. 9, p. 93.
b) Scott, *Independence*, p. 153.
[Jesse Applegate considered Beaver Creek to be the first camp and the first water after leaving Klamath River. (a) Helfrich, "Applegate Trail," (1971), Vol. 9, p. 93; b) Applegate, *Way Bill*, p. 3.)]

28. Scott, *Independence*, p. 153.

29. Ibid., p. 154.

30. Morgan, *Overland in 1846*, Vol. 1, pp. 184, 395.

31. a) Ibid., p. 184.
b) Helfrich, "Applegate Trail," (1971), Vol. 9, p. 93.

32. Carter, *Pioneer Days*, p. 73.

33.a) Garrison, *Life and Labours*, OHS Mss #1009, p. 33.
b) Helfrich, "Applegate Trail," (1971), Vol. 9, p. 92.

[Scott, Pringle and others did an enormous amount of work to open the road. Garrison and Carter sound as if they were on a different trail entirely. They must have been far back on the trail. They both thought this was all work of the road party.]

34. Helfrich, "Applegate Trail," (1971), Vol. 9, p. 97.

35. Ibid.

36. Morgan, *Overland in 1846*, Vol. 1, p. 184.

37.a) Ibid.
b) Helfrich, "Applegate Trail," (1971), Vol. 9, p. 93.

38. Helfrich, "Applegate Trail," (1971), Vol. 9, p. 93.

39. Morgan, *Overland in 1846*, Vol. 1, p. 184.

40. Garrison, *Life and Labours*, OHS Mss #1009, p. 33.

41. Morgan, *Overland in 1846*, Vol. 1, p. 395.

42. Helfrich, "Applegate Trail," (1971), Vol. 9, p. 98.

43. Ibid., p. 99.

44. Helfrich, "Applegate Trail," (1971), Vol. 9, p. 99.

45. Morgan, *Overland in 1846*, Vol. 1, pp. 184, 395.

46.a) Helfrich, "Applegate Trail," (1971), Vol. 9, pp. 93.
b) Morgan, Overland in 1846, Vol. 1, p. 184.

47.a) Ibid.
b) Mark Lawrence, *Applegate Trail Markers*, (Lawrence, 1979), p. 2. (Location not listed)
c) Morgan, *Overland in 1846*, Vol. 1, p. 395.

48.a) Helfrich, "Applegate Trail," (1971), Vol. 9, p. 99.
b) Lawrence, *Applegate Trail Markers*, p. 3.

49. Meacham, *Applegate Trail*, p. 13.

50.a) Bancroft, *Works*, Vol. XXIX, p. 562.
b) Meacham, *Applegate Trail*, p. 13.
c) Nichols, *South Road*, p. 92.
[I found no mention of this in his book, "Oregon and California in 1848."]

51. Thornton, *Or. and Ca. in 1848*, Vol. 1, p. 200.

52. Ibid.

53. Ibid., pp. 197, 198.

54. Ibid., p. 198.

55. Lockley, *Pioneer Women*, p. 88.

56. Thornton, *Or. and Ca. in 1848*, p. 165.

57. Ibid., p. 198.

58. Ibid., p. 170.

59. Ibid., p. 198.

60. Ibid., p. 190.

61. Ibid., p. 197.

62. Ibid., p. 198.

63. Ibid., p. 200.

64. Ibid., p. 198.

65. Ibid., p. 200.

66. Ibid. [I am sure that hurrying his animals in their condition did not help matters at all.]

67. Ibid., p. 200, 201.

68.a) Stone, "Southern Route," p. 143.

48.a) Helfrich, "Applegate Trail," (1971), Vol. 9, pp. 90, 103.

69. Helfrich, "Applegate Trail," (1971), Vol. 9, p. 103.

70. Scott, *Independence*, p. 154.

71. Morgan, *Overland in 1846*, Vol. 1, p. 184.

72. Helfrich, "Applegate Trail," (1971), Vol. 9, p. 99.

73.a) Helfrich, "Applegate Trail," (1971), Vol. 9, pp. 3, 4, 99, 102, 90, 103.
b) Morgan, *Overland in 1846*, Vol. 1, p. 395.
c) Lawrence, *Applegate Trail Markers*, p. 3, 4.

74. Helfrich, "Applegate Trail," (1971), Vol. 9, p. 105. [The pack trail they joined was not only a former Indian trail, but was also the Hudson's Bay Company's pack trail.]

75. Carter, *Pioneer Days*, p. 73.

76.a) Bancroft, *Works*, Vol. XXIX, p. 545.
b) Helfrich, "Applegate Trail," (1971), Vol. 9, p. 105.
c) Lawrence, *Applegate Trail Markers*, p. 4.
d) Applegate, "Applegate Trail," pp. 7, 21.

77. Helfrich, "Applegate Trail," (1971), Vol. 9, p. 105.

78. Thornton, *Or. and Ca. in 1848*, Vol. 1, p. 201.

79. Ibid., p. 202.

80. Ibid.

81. Ibid.

Ch. 7 The ROGUE its VALLEY and BEYOND

From Klamath Junction to Cow Creek: Oregon

The foremost company pushed on following the South Fork, today called Bear Creek.[1] They crossed Ashland Creek at about the location of the railroad tracks. "...below the railroad bridge, where the '46 wagon road had left its mark on the bank." (Jesse Applegate, Sunday, May 4, 1884)[2] After cutting down trees to make a road and traveling through intolerable terrain of mountains and wagon slides they had reached the Rogue Valley at the present site of Ashland.

> Some weeks later we camped in the rain on the present site of Ashland. I shall never forget this place. The wood was wet and I stood around shivering while father was trying to make a fire with flint and steel. Many years later, after I had married Judge Deady, Jesse Applegate showed me a big tree in Ashland and said, 'That is the tree you camped under in the Fall of 1846 on your way to the Willamette Valley.'[3] (Lucy Ann Henderson, 1922)

Pringle traveled down the South Fork (Bear Creek)[4] and probably camped where it intersects with Ashland Creek.[5] "...camp at a considerable sized creek, the best camp we have had for several. Road very good. High mountains around."[6] (Virgil Pringle, October 11, 1846)

Once they reached the Ashland area the road ahead looked clear. The South Fork was later called Stewart Creek.[7] The emigrants must have felt a sense of tranquility at the sight of such easy terrain ahead. "We decided to stop awhile in the Rogue Valley and let the cattle pick up and as a result of this delay we were caught in the Fall rains." (Grants Pass Daily Courier, Jan. 23, 1934. A. J. Richardson, narrative)[8] To make camp in the rain some emigrants fastened a canvas tarpaulin over the bows at the rear of their wagon. Tent poles held the opposite ends.[9]

The foremost company journeyed along present day Bear Creek through country that today makes up the present sites of downtown Talent, Phoenix, and Medford. Through Talent the Trail approximated Talent Avenue. Through Phoenix the trail was about the same as Old Highway 99. The trail through Medford followed the same route as present day Riverside Avenue.[10]

The company the Thorntons were with arrived on "the western side of the Siskia [sic] Mountains ..."[11] at about ten o'clock at night. This was days after the rest of the wagons had past. They had been without water for over two days. "...we arrived at a fine stream of beautiful clear water...."[12] Feeling quite content, Thornton decided to go back and get his wagon from the Greensprings. The company Thornton was with agreed to remain in camp another day for him to return. Mr. Hall agreed to carry his possessions and foodstuff in trade for two-fifths of his breadstuff. Josiah Morin agreed to carry the remainder of his clothing in trade for using John and Nig, Thornton's other two oxen. He gave Mr. Goff his "...medicine-chest, a set of cut-glass bottles filled with medicine for the journey, a cast-steel spade which I had carried up to this time, for the purpose of working the road where necessary, and a number of other articles, as a compensation for returning with me to the place where I had left the wagon."[13] (Thornton, 1848) He also wanted Mr. Morin to help clear the road where necessary to get his wagon off the

Figure 1 Once they reached the Ashland area the road ahead looked clear.

Greensprings. Thornton borrowed his own two oxen back from Josiah Morin and some of Morin's oxen to aid in getting his wagon.[14]

It was a sunny day coming down the hill after getting the wagon. From the hill Thornton and Morin could see the emigrant wagon camp below. Many people were going through their wagons sorting out what to leave behind to lighten their load.[15] While the first wagons were in the valley, it had rained.[16] Evidently it had cleared up when these emigrants got there.[17]

Thornton arrived back down in camp later that afternoon. He and Mrs. Thornton were up late that night going through the wagon deciding what articles they no longer needed. He worked until two o'clock in the morning deciding what to leave. Eventually they slept.[18]

The next morning when they prepared to leave, they left their wagon. They could not concede to abandoning everything at once. But eventually, by the time they left, they had abandoned most everything.[19] He felt somewhat relieved he would not have to deal with his team anymore. Instead he could leisurely walk along with the rest of the company, and only deal with getting himself, his wife, and their greyhound,[20] Darco, to the end of the trail.[21]

As the foremost party moved west across the valley, to their right in the distance they could see Upper Table Rock and Lower Table Rock. These locations have always been known in the valley as sacred places for the Indians.[22]

The company Virgil Pringle was with spent the day of October 13 camped[23] at Willow Springs just past present day Central Point. They could have seen the two Table Rocks from their camp. Pringle and the others spent the day exploring the region to decide the route of the trail. Present day Bear Creek flowed into the Rogue River just southwest of Lower Table Rock.[24] (U.S.G.S. maps) The Smith's were the only emigrants of 1846 that mention the Table Rocks.[25] They had followed Bear Creek and would now start following the Rogue River.[26] They were entering the territory of "the Rogue river Indians." (120-372)

The next day the foremost company moved west by northwest along the south side of the Rogue River. They stopped near Foots Creek Canyon just west to the present site of Gold Hill. The wagon company just behind them stopped at Rock Point just past the present site of Gold Hill.[27] The next morning as they were leaving camp an Indian ran up and shot one cow full of arrows and ran away.[28]

The lead wagons were camped near Foots Creek just west of Gold Hill. Mr. Vanderpool was known as a mountaineer. He had driven a herd of sheep across the plains and traveled all this way with them.[29] Some said there were twenty-five sheep[30] and some said there were fifty.[31]

The sheep disappeared while he was eating.[32] It was claimed that the Indians ran them off, although no one saw any Indians.[33] Carter did say there were moccasin tracks following the sheep.[34] They might have wandered off into Foots Creek Canyon.[35] Vanderpool had let the sheep out for grazing while he ate.[36] Tolbert Carter and others offered to go after them but Vanderpool thought it was too risky.[37]

They left the sheep, not knowing if they had been driven off by the Indians or just wandered off by themselves.[38] There were plenty of areas out of sight where the sheep could have wandered. Carter felt Vanderpool was more of a man of experience and sense than himself for not allowing the men to enter Foots Creek Canyon on "any such foolhardy expedition."[39]

Figure 2 ...to their right in the distance they could see Upper Table Rock and Lower Table Rock.

Figure 3 Some said there were twenty-five sheep and some said there were fifty. Some said he was having breakfast. Others said he was having dinner. Some said he had sons caring for the sheep. Some did not say.

They broke camp and traveled about a mile when it was reported a cow was missing in the company. Several men, including Levi Scott, went back to search for the cow.[40] When they were close to the last camp, they found Indians butchering her, and so the men returned to the train empty handed.[41]

Another camp was made somewhere near present day Grants Pass.[42] There were Indians all around but they stayed their distance. Pringle does mention losing some cattle to the Indians at this point on the trail.[43]

By now the two main forward wagon companies were probably all traveling together. The next day the lead wagons traveled about four miles down the Rogue River to Vannoy Creek.[44] They decided this was where they would cross the river. There were not many good places to cross. Even in early autumn there was a swift and rapid current.[45]

The emigrants were stepping up their guard. Captain Vanderpool went ahead with fifty men to scout out the crossing. He sent half across the river and the other half stayed on the south side. They stood guard on both sides of the river until all the emigrants had crossed.[46] The women and children rode across in the wagons holding some possessions to protect them from the water leaking in. Most emigrants had sealed their wagons before crossing the rivers of the Oregon Trail to help make them watertight.[47] The men waded across or rode their horses to drive their oxen across.[48] The oxen kept their heads down to pull the wagon. They had to turn their head sideways to get a breath of air.[49]

Water poured into the beds of some of the wagons as they crossed,[50] those in the wagons stuffed rags in the cracks of their wagons to keep water from leaking in.[51] The ford was "deep and rough,"[52] but all got over safely.[53] Pringle said it was a good ford.[54] They saw the Indians hiding, but none of them approached. After crossing they made camp on the other side.[55]

While they were camped, they heard a shot and someone yelled. They ran to find out what had happened. Mr. Poole was sitting on a log and noticed that there was an Indian close by.[56] Out of fear, he shot at the Indian without thinking. After shooting the Indian he realized there were many Indians around him. He immediately jumped inside the hollow log he had been sitting on and called for help. When the men ran down to see what was going on, the Indians ran off. They checked the area and found blood on the ground.[57] By this time everyone in camp was terrified. The Indians had done nothing. They were probably curious. This was their area. The location the emigrants crossed and camped was the best place to cross and was used by Indians to cross as well.[58] The Indians did shoot arrows at him after he had shot at them.[59]

There was another yell. John D. Wood came running back from the river bank. He had gone to get a pail of water and had some arrows zip by his head.[60] Rev. Garrison and others fired off their rifles. This ended the excitement for the night.

Figure 4 Rogue River

About the time they reached the Rogue River, Margaret Garrison. Rev. Garrison's wife, was feeling better. She had taken sick back on the desert. When they reached the Rogue River, she was getting up and around.[61]

The wagon company traveled north about eight miles and crossed Jump Off Joe Creek. They traveled along the creek on approximately the same route as present day Russell Road north of Merlin and camped in Pleasant Valley.[62] Pringle mentions that it was a good camp.[63]

From here the emigrants had to cross Sexton Mountain. The road builders traveling before them had done little to cut a road for the wagons. The wagons could not go any further without doing more to provide a road. Virgil Pringle, Levi Scott and others had to take their axes and cut through the undergrowth to clear a way for the wagons to cross.[64] In some places, the emigrants had to take down the wagon bows to get through.[65] They edged their way along in single file as Levi Scott and others cleared a path for the wagons to follow. They worked through the day and into the night. Sometime after dark they stopped having managed to make a total of about six miles through Sexton Mountain and beyond.[66] They chained their oxen to trees to camp for the rest of the night.[67]

While those ahead had stopped, the last wagons crept along in a single file through the new road that was cut. One wagon came to a halt while the others ahead kept moving. This caused all of the wagons behind to stop.[68] It took some time for everyone to find out what had happened. Mrs. Crowley's daughter, Martha Leland Crowley, had just past away.[69] Tolbert Carter said she died of typhoid fever.[70]

While the wagons were apart, the Indians took advantage of the situation and shot arrows at the wagon train. They hit Virgil Pringle's ox from the right while the animal was hitched to the team.[71] Three dogs chased after an Indian in the bushes on the left side of the train. There was a struggle and one dog was severely injured but not fatally. After the skirmish they moved the wagons forward to join forces.[72] Most did not get much sleep that night.[73] Pringle's ox later died as a result of the wound.[74]

Martha Leland Crowley was survived by her parents, Mr. and Mrs. Thomas Crowley.[75] The wagon behind her belonged to Mrs. Tabitha Brown. Mrs. Brown's brother-in-law, Captain John Brown, was traveling with her. Tabitha Brown was a widow. She was over sixty years of age and crippled. She was also the mother of Mrs. Virgil K. Pringle.[76]

The next morning all the wagons in the forward companies moved north about a mile to Grave Creek.[77] Mrs. Brown ordered the upper boards of her wagon to be removed and used for a casket for Miss Crowley to be buried in.[78] Theodore Parter, Mrs. Rachel Challinor and others assisted in giving her a proper burial.[79] The day was spent mourning and burying the young lady who was only fourteen years old.[80] Both wagon companies in the lead stopped to attend the funeral.[81] The creek they were on is still known as Grave Creek.[82] This was also later the location of a covered bridge that still stands today. This area is known today as Sunny Valley.[83]

The next day the foremost party worked through the thick timber, building a road from Grave Creek to Cow Creek. That evening, two men who were late getting into camp had arrows shot all around them. The arrows were shot close by them and stuck in the ground. After this, Levi Scott did not need to be called Captain. The emigrants listened to his every

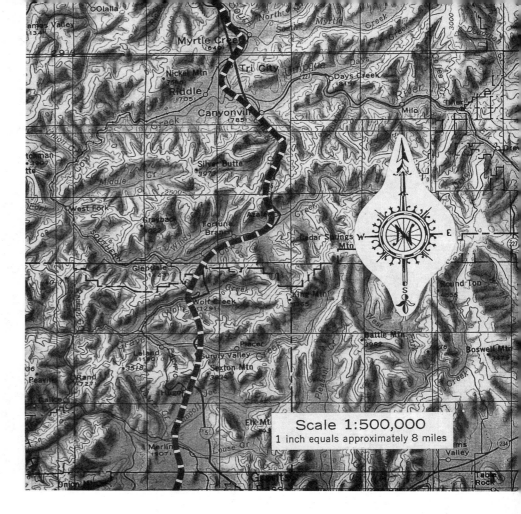

order and started standing guard every night.[84]

It took them three days to reach Cow Creek. They started just north of Wolf Creek. They traveled through thick timber and underbrush while moving slowly up the creek.[85] They camped for the night near Cow Creek.[86]

That morning as they were preparing to move on, they were visited by the first relief party, consisting of Jack Jones,

Figure 5 Both wagon companies in the lead stopped to attend the funeral. The creek they were on is still known as Grave Creek.

Tom Smith, Mr. Brown, Mr. Allen, John Jones and one or two others not mentioned.[87] These men had come with some fat cows. They had brought enough to sell to this camp and still had some to take to the emigrants coming up from further down the trail. These men were only selling enough for each person to have rations.[88] Their main purpose was to provide food to all those in need.[89] The people were fortunate to get this relief of food because they were starting to run out.

John Jones had been part of the Applegate road party. He had made it through and was coming back down with help.[90] Tom Smith had interests at Oregon City. He was genuinely concerned that the trail would be damaging to property values.[91] Believing this, he was trying to discourage the emigrants from using the new trail from southern Oregon.

Everyone stopped preparing to leave. They all started pursuing the men of the relief party with questions about the road ahead.[92] Tom Smith told the group that it was impossible for them to go more than another six miles. This caused the people of the train to have a feeling of hopelessness and despair. Levi Scott was the only one left who felt the urgency to keep moving forward. He was afraid the winter rains would soon start and the rivers would be too high to cross. He could only persuade them to go another two miles that day.[93]

The next day the Jones and Smith relief party left the foremost party and continued to travel south to supply food for more emigrants coming up the trail.[94] The foremost company only made another three miles that day along Cow Creek. They probably camped around Azalea.[95] Everyone seemed to be depressed about the stories the men had brought of the bad terrain ahead. This discouraged them so much they did not know what to do. Some did not want to go any further. Scott wanted to go ahead by foot and see what the road was like and how possible it would be for wagons to get through. No one else wanted to go.[96]

That next morning, as they left Cow Creek, young Garrison recalled that the widow Beaucham was riding behind him and a Mr. Andrew Davidson cut in front of the Ashley Beaucham wagon. Ashley Beaucham was the widow's only son. J. D. Wood, a 55-year-old pioneer jumped in to turn Davidson's team out of the way. This caused a fight between J. D. Wood and Andrew Davidson. Wood won the fight and Ashley Beaucham was able to continue following Garrison's wagon.[97] J. D. Wood had a son in his wagon who was sick and dying.[98]

They had gone another three miles. They were now at the entrance of the Umpqua Canyon. At this point, they did not want to go any further. Levi Scott called a meeting to order. He told them he was going in on foot the next morning. He was asking others to go with him. If no one wanted to go, he was just going on home. Otherwise, some men could follow him into the canyon to find out what it would take to get the wagons through.[99] This was around the 24th of October.

About this time the party of Jack Jones and Tom Smith had continued further south and probably made it to the Rogue River. They arrived at a camp Thornton was part of. "We met Messrs. Brown, Allen, and Jones, and some two or three other persons."[100] After leaving food for emigrants ahead, they still had two cows for this group.[101] Thornton said Brown and Allen were sons of the pioneer families of the Brown and Allen's whom he later found had continued on to

California. There was also possibly the son of Goff and Labin Morin in this party.[102]

The next day Brown, Allen, and Company persuaded some emigrants to go further south down the trail to find the families of Brown and Allen and some of their friends. Thornton and the others in this wagon train crossed the Rogue River at Vannoy Creek that day around noon. The two cows they obtained from Brown and Allen were butchered, dressed, cooked and consumed in camp that evening.[103] They were somewhere just north of Merlin. They moved camp the next day only a couple hundred yards

"...for the purpose of convenience."[104] This new location was probably Pleasant Valley, where most of the pioneers camped.

That afternoon Thornton spotted "a body of Indians" moving through the bushes. Suspecting they were trying to rustle some of their cattle he and others armed themselves and went after them.[105] Thornton was ready with gun in hand. They slowly approached by hiding in the bushes. When they got close enough, they jumped out at them. They found the Indians were some "squaws" returning from digging camas roots.[106]

NOTES   Chapter 7

1. Helfrich, "Applegate Trail II," (1976), Vol. 14, p. 22.

2. "The First Passenger Train." *Ashland (Oregon) Daily Tidings*, May 9, 1884, p. 3.

3. Lockley, *Pioneer Women*, pp. 86, 87.

4. Applegate, *Way Bill*, p. 3.

5.a) Morgan, *Overland in 1846*, Vol. 1, p. 395.
b) Helfrich, "Applegate Trail," (1971), Vol. 9, p. 99.

6.a) Morgan, *Overland in 1846*, Vol. 1, pp. 184, 395.
b) Helfrich, "Applegate Trail," (1971), Vol. 9, p. 99.

7. Helfrich, "Applegate Trail II," (1976), Vol. 14, p. 22.

8.a) Nichols, *South Road*, p. 93.
b) Leland, "Pioneer Days." p. 1.

9. Glen Rounds, *The Prairie Schooners* (New York, NY: Holiday House, Inc., 1968), p. 87.

10. Helfrich, "Applegate Trail II," (1976), Vol. 14, p. 22.

11. Thornton, *Or. and Ca. in 1848*, Vol. 1, p. 202.

12. Ibid.

13. Ibid., p. 204.

14. Ibid., p. 205.

15. Ibid.

16.a) Lockley, *Pioneer Women*, p. 86.
b) Nichols, *South Road*, p. 93.

17.a) Thornton, *Or. and Ca. in 1848*, Vol. 1, p. 205.
b) Lockley, *Pioneer Women*, p. 86.

18. Thornton, *Or. and Ca. in 1848*, Vol. 1, p. 206.

19. Ibid.

20. Malcolm Clark, *Eden Seekers: the Settlement of Oregon, 1818-1862* (Boston, MA: Houghton Miffin Company, 1981), p. 193.

21. Thornton, *Or. and Ca. in 1848*, Vol. 1, pp. 206, 207. [I never found a name for Mrs. Thornton in Thornton's writings. Thornton always called her Mrs. Thornton. Her name was Nancy. (Clark, *Eden Seekers*, p.193.) He did give the name of their dog. It was called Prince Darco. (Thornton, *Or. and Ca. in 1848*, Vol. 1, p. 218.)]

22. Atwood, "Takelma," Vol. 95, No.4, p. 519. [They probably kept a distance to avoid contact with the Indians. According to W. A. Moxley's "Southern Route To Oregon," the company camped that night at the later day "old" Jackson County Fair Grounds. (Moxley, OHS Mss #855, p. 43.)]

23.a) Morgan, *Overland in 1846*, Vol. 1, p. 184.
b) Helfrich, "Applegate Trail II," (1976), Vol. 14, p. 20.

24.a) Angeline (Smith) Crews, *Smith (William) Family, Recollections of Angeline Smith Crews* (Portland, OR: Oregon Historic Society Mss #1188, 1886), p. 10.
b) Atwood, "Takelma," Vol. 95, No.4, p. 522.

25. Crews, *Smith Family*, OHS Mss #1188, p. 10.

26. Morgan, *Overland in 1846*, Vol. 1, p. 185.

27. Helfrich, "Applegate Trail II," (1976), Vol. 14, p. 20. [They were still on the south side of the Rogue River. According to Young Henry Garrison, that evening at Rock Point, an Indian shot Miss Leland Crowley with a poisoned arrow as she was sitting by the fire baking bread. "The arrow was extracted, but no precautions were taken in regard to poison *[sic]* as we did not know at the time, that poisoned arrows *[sic]* was used." (Garrison, "Reminiscences," p. 26.)]

28. Garrison, "Reminiscences," p. 26.

29. Carter, *Pioneer Days*, p. 73.

30. Ibid.

31. Scott, *Independence*, p. 155.

32.a) Carter, *Pioneer Days*, p. 73.
b) Scott, *Independence*, p. 155.
c) Helfrich, "Applegate Trail II," (1976), Vol. 14, pp. 25, 28.
[Some said he was having breakfast. (a) Carter, *Pioneer Days*, p. 73; b) Scott, *Independence*, p. 155.) Others said he was having dinner. (Helfrich, "Applegate Trail II," (1976), Vol. 14, p. 28.) Some said he had his sons caring for the sheep. (a) Carter, *Pioneer Days*, p. 73; b) Helfrich, "Applegate Trail II," (1976), Vol. 14, p. 28.) Some did not say. (a) Scott, *Independence*, p. 155; b) Helfrich, "Applegate Trail II," (1976), Vol. 14, p. 22.) All agreed that while he was eating, the sheep disappeared.]

33.a) Helfrich, "Applegate Trail II," (1976), Vol. 14, p. 28.
b) Scott, *Independence*, p. 155.

34. Carter, *Pioneer Days*, p. 73.

35. Helfrich, "Applegate Trail II," (1976), Vol. 14, p. 25.

36. Ibid., p. 28.

37. Carter, *Pioneer Days*, p. 74.

38. Helfrich, "Applegate Trail II," (1976), Vol. 14, p. 25.

39. Carter, *Pioneer Days*, p. 74.

40. Scott, *Independence*, p. 155.

41. Helfrich, "Applegate Trail II," (1976), Vol. 14, p. 25.

42. Morgan, *Overland in 1846*, Vol. 1, p. 185.

43. Ibid.

44.a) Ibid.
b) Helfrich, "Applegate Trail II," (1976), Vol. 14, p. 23.

45. Scott, *Independence*, p. 155.

46.a) Garrison, *Life and Labours*, OHS Mss #1009, p. 34.
b) Garrison, "Reminiscences," p. 26.

47. Rounds, *Prairie Schooners*, p. 61.

48. Ibid., p. 62.

49. Chrisman, *1001 Questions*, p. 316.

50. Carter, *Pioneer Days*, p. 74.

51. Rounds, *Prairie Schooners*, p. 61.

52. Scott, *Independence*, p. 155.

53. Carter, *Pioneer Days*, p. 74.

54. Morgan, *Overland in 1846*, Vol. 1, p. 185.

55.a) Ibid.
b) Helfrich, "Applegate Trail II," (1976), Vol. 14, p. 23.

56. Garrison, "Reminiscences," p. 26.

57. Ibid.

58.a) Applegate, "Old Emigrant Road," p. 18.
b) Scott, *Independence*, p. 108.

59. Garrison, "Reminiscences," p. 26.

60. Garrison, *Life and Labours*, OHS Mss #1009, p. 34.

61. Garrison, "Reminiscences," p. 24.

62. Helfrich, "Applegate Trail II," (1976), Vol. 14, p. 23.

63. Morgan, *Overland in 1846*, Vol. 1, p. 185.

64. Scott, *Independence*, p. 155.

65. Cornwall, *Capt. Dunbar's Co. 1846*, OHS Mss #1509, p. 35.

Figure 6 Wolf Creek

66.a) Morgan, *Overland in 1846*, Vol. 1, p. 185.
b) Carter, *Pioneer Days*, p. 74.

67. Carter, *Pioneer Days*, p. 74.

68. Scott, *Independence*, p. 155.

69.a) Morgan, *Overland in 1846*, Vol. 1, p. 185.
b) Carter, *Pioneer Days*, p. 74.

70. Carter, *Pioneer Days*, p. 74. [Young A. H. Garrison later said the wound that she had received at Rocky Point was fatal. (Garrison, "Reminiscences," p. 26.) She was also said to have died of tuberculosis. (Meacham, *Applegate Trail*, p. 15.)]

71. Scott, *Independence*, p. 156. [This might have been the same Indians from the Rogue River retaliating for the Indian that was shot.]

72. Ibid.

73. Morgan, *Overland in 1846*, Vol. 1, p. 185.

74. Scott, *Independence*, p. 156.

75. Garrison, *Life and Labours*, OHS Mss #1009, p. 31.

76. Meacham, *Applegate Trail*, p. 17.

77. Morgan, *Overland in 1846*, Vol. 1, p. 185.

78.a) Helfrich, "Applegate Trail II," (1976), Vol. 14, p. 29.
b) Scott, *Independence*, p. 157.

79. Lockley, *Pioneer Women*, p. 87.

80. Morgan, *Overland in 1846*, Vol. 1, p. 185.

81.a) Carter, *Pioneer Days*, p. 74.
b) Garrison, "Reminiscences," p. 26.
c) Morgan, *Overland in 1846*, Vol. 1, p. 185.
d) Scott, *Independence*, p. 156.

82.a) Lockley, *Pioneer Women*, p. 87.

b) Helfrich, "Applegate Trail II," (1976), Vol. 14, p. 32.
c) Meacham, *Applegate Trail*, p. 15.
d) Francis Haines, *The Applegate Trail: Southern Emigrant Route* (Ashland, OR: The American Revolution Bicentennial Commission of Oregon, 1976), p.16.

83. Helfrich, "Applegate Trail II," (1976), Vol. 14, pp. 30, 31.

84. Scott, *Independence*, p. 157.

85.a) Scott, *Independence*, p. 158.
b) Morgan, *Overland in 1846*, Vol. 1, p. 185.
c) Helfrich, "Applegate Trail II," (1976), Vol. 14, p. 28.

86. Scott, *Independence*, p. 158.

87.a) Helfrich, "Applegate Trail II," (1976), Vol. 14, p. 28.
b) Scott, *Independence*, p. 158.
c) Thornton, *Or. and Ca. in 1848*, Vol. 1, p. 209.

88. Thornton, *Or. and Ca. in 1848*, Vol. 1, p. 210.

89. Helfrich, "Applegate Trail II," (1976), Vol. 14, p. 28.

90.a) Ibid.
b) Applegate, "Applegate Trail," p. 5.
c) Applegate, "Old Emigrant Road," p. 43.

91. Scott, *Independence*, p. 158.

92. Ibid.

93. Ibid., p. 159.

94. Helfrich, "Applegate Trail II," (1976), Vol. 14, p. 28.

95. Ibid.

96. Scott, *Independence*, p. 159.

97. Garrison, "Reminiscences," p. 26.

98. Scott, *Independence*, p. 161.

99. Ibid., p. 159.

100. Thornton, *Or. and Ca. in 1848*, Vol. 1, p. 208. [Thornton said he met with Brown, Allen and Jones on October 18th. Because Brown, Jones, and Allen's rescue party met with the foremost company on about the 22nd or 23rd, it was not possible for them to have met with Thornton on the 18th. (a) Thornton, *Or. and Ca. in 1848*, Vol. 1, p. 208.; b) Helfrich, "Applegate Trail II," (1976), Vol. 14, p. 28.) This is another reasons for determining that Thornton was probably wrong on his dates. (a) Thornton, *Or. and Ca. in 1848*, Vol. 1, pp. 210, 213.; b) Helfrich, "Applegate Trail II," (1976), Vol. 14, p. 28.)]

101. Ibid., p. 210, 211.

102. Ibid., p. 211.

103. Ibid.

104. Ibid.

105. Ibid. Ibid., p. 212.

Ch. 8 The UMPQUA CANYON

From Cow Creek to the South Umpqua River: Oregon

We return now to the foremost party. Levi Scott was ready very early the next day to go on foot to search out the canyon. Four men came forward to go with him. The men hiked down into the dreaded canyon and found it was as bad as Tom Smith had described. Scott considered this the worst ten miles he had ever seen to build a road, but it could be done. After inspecting this creek bed, the men decided they would build a road. When these men made their minds up to do something, they did it.[1]

Carter said that they laid over a day to give their "lean, jaded oxen a rest."[2] The night before entering the canyon, the oxen were corralled without feed.[3]

The next day everyone's thoughts were on getting through the dreadful canyon. With pioneer spirit, every man who was able and could be spared, went to work building a road.[4] Pringle referred to it as "working the road through the pass, which is nearly impassable."[5]

The evening before the wagons entered the great canyon, Rev. Garrison's brother, Joseph, brought a yoke of fresh oxen and some pack horses.[6] He also brought them food. They only had about ten pounds of flour left.[7]

The following day, October 27th, the rainy season commenced. It rained a little at first, then increased and rained steadily all week.[8]

They sent the cattle through the canyon, ahead of the wagons. Young Garrison was a part of that group.[9] Sixty-eight years later, Mrs. E. B. Foster recalled that she and her sister, Mrs. Humphrey also helped drive the cattle through ahead of the wagons.[10] They were the first women on this first wagon train through "Cow Creek Canyon."[11] She also said Mrs. Humphrey's brother, Hanley Currier, drove the first wagon through. It poured down rain that night.[12]

Rev. Garrison started early and entered the great canyon. He put two yoke of weak oxen with one existing yoke to an empty wagon. He put his brother's fresh oxen on a packed wagon together with the two yoke of weak oxen from the empty wagon.[13] It was a rugged descent into the rock and tree filled creek bed. Only one wagon went down at a time.[14] Men held on ropes fastened to the rear of the wagon as each wagon took the grade.[15] They camped that evening with oxen chained to trees.[16]

The rains also began where Thornton was traveling. It rained hard as they worked their way through the woods of Sexton Mountain.[17] The Brown, Allen and Jones rescue party returned to Thornton's camp on their way back to the Willamette Valley. They had gone as far as the Siskiyou Mountains without finding their relatives and friends. While they camped, Thornton hired Allen to carry a bag of clothes to the settlements.[18]

The rain drove the Thorntons out of their beds that night. The Thorntons were drenched; they did not have a tent.[19] They left early the next morning, "...through a dense forest of pine and firs, and down a hillside, [sic] where we picked up several arrows that were shot at us by ambushed savages."[20] "...all day through rain and mud, and over a broken country, of alternate prairie and timber lands, encamped near the foot of the Umpqua Mountains."[21] The

Umpqua Mountain they were about to ascend is known today as Sexton Mountain.

While Thornton was near the Umpqua Mountains, the foremost company was in the Umpqua Canyon. It is known today as Canyon Creek. Levi Scott was on his third day of road building and assisting wagons through. He had also repaired the road in places after he and the others had blazed it through.[22] The road was not much of a trail. With boulders from a foot to five feet wide, they turned a creek bed into a path. The pioneers moved boulders as much as they could to level out the bottom. They cut brush and logs to fill the gaps between the boulders. They made it passable, which was all they could do with what they had. Scott wished he had some dynamite.[23] Pringle referred to "a series of hardships, breakdowns and being constantly wet, and laboring hard."[24] They were also about out of food in the whole company.[25]

Virgil Pringle mentions leaving one wagon in his party.[26] This belonged to Mrs. Pherne Pringle's mother, Tabitha Brown.[27] The Pringles insisted on her going ahead. They divided the last of their food. Her portion was three slices of bacon and a cup of tea, but there was no bread.[28] After losing her wagon the day before, she started through on horseback with her brother-in-law, John Brown.[29] "Captain John Brown," as he was known, was seventy-eight years old.[30] "Captain Brown was too old and feeble to render any assistance to me."[31] (Tabitha Brown, 1854)

Tolbert Carter was in the middle of the wagons journeying toward the canyon entrance. They traveled in single file edging slowly along. When a wagon in front stopped, all the wagons behind had to stop. He and the widow woman he was with, did not know what caused the delay.[32] After some time, they finally reached the canyon entrance.

The entrance was a very steep grade. At the bottom of the grade was a large boulder protruding from the ground. As the day went on, the boulder kept getting more exposed. By the time Carter arrived it was protruding from the dirt about two feet. There was a man in front of Carter that had been with typhoid fever for twenty days. They "rough locked"[33] the wagon wheels with a man on each side of the hind wheels, and proceeded down the steep grade. When the wagon hit the rock, it broke loose and crashed down the bank; it landed upside down and broke the wagon bows.[34]

They ran down as fast as they could to find what they believed would be a dead man but found that he had lived through it all. They righted the wagon, bedded him in the back and moved it out of the way.[35]

A large ox came down the canyon packed with blankets and hit the same rock. The ox rolled over into the creek below. The men had to help the animal up.[36] Now Carter knew what caused such a delay, and it was finally his turn to take the grade- "...down the steepest hill, or rather bank, that wagons were ever known to pass."[37]

They continued to camp with their oxen chained to trees. It rained hard that night, causing the creek to rise. Mrs. Calvin Crowley gave birth that night in the rain.[38] The conditions in the canyon were unbearable. The child died in a few hours, and the mother soon followed.[39]

Lucy Ann Henderson, who was later known as Mrs. Mathew P. Deady, recalled, "The cattle could hardly keep their feet, on account of the smooth water-worn boulders in the bed of the stream, and the wagons would occasionally tip over."[40] There was a meeting of the men. They decided to discard any unnecessary items to reduce the surplus weight. They would make better time and the wagons behind would not be held back by "one over laden wagon."[41]

Figure 1 After some time, they finally reached the canyon entrance.

Rev. Garrison's son was with a man named Albright, who was hired by Garrison's brother Joseph. They were both camped at the end of the canyon looking after the cattle. That night young Garrison was concerned about their bread being stolen. Albright said that he would keep it under his sleeping bag and no one would ever get it there. The next morning it was gone. Garrison milked one of the cows for a cup of milk and that was his breakfast.

Albright went fishing and Garrison went hunting. Garrison shot a deer on the crest of the canyon. According to Garrison, the deer ran down the canyon into camp and fell dead.[42]

While J. D. Wood was traveling in the canyon his son, Alonzo, died in the wagon. Shortly after he died, the wagon turned over with his corpse in it, along with bee hives that Wood had brought all the way across the trail.[43] The bees drowned in the creek.[44]

Also about this time, someone set fire to a dead fir tree and the cinders came down all around. Some landed on Isaac Zumwalt, a four or five-year-old boy.[45] His mother was away from the wagon at that moment, so she was not able to help him get the cinders off in time. He was severely burned and scarred for life.[46]

Further back on the trail the Smith Company had made it through Cow Creek.[47] This was originally part of the Dunbar Company.[48] They arrived at a place where the canyon narrowed. The only way through was down a grade and into the creek bed. They had reached the canyon entrance.[49]

It had been raining for two days. The fallen trees in the Creek looked like impossible obstacles to them.[50] The rains had washed through the creek bed. There had also been many wagons through the creek bed, shifting logs and tramping the brush and debris as they went. They made camp and there they stayed.[51]

There were many sick people in the Smith camp. They needed the wagons to carry the sick. After looking at the creek, they did not think the wagons would make it through. They set up camp and stayed for several days.[52]

The company Thornton was with traveled all day through the rain and mud over broken country. That night they camped on Cow Creek, approximately where Woodford Creek Rest Area is today. "Mr. Hall did not get his team into camp until after dark."[53] This was about October 29. According to Thornton they remained in this camp for several days.[54] He was there at least two days.

Meanwhile, Scott left the canyon with about ten wagons.[55] Scott and his small company probably only crossed the South Umpqua River once. After crossing a ridge, they camped along the Umpqua River next to where Cow Creek comes in from the west.[56] Mrs. E. D. Foster recalled that in the Umpqua Valley, Mr. Stewart's daughter died, and they cut down and split saplings for a coffin[57]

Pringle probably got through the canyon around October 29th or 30th. There was "great loss of property and suffering...."[58] Mrs. Pringle carried her most cherished possessions over her head when she waded through the canyon creek.[59] They had nothing to eat except beef.[60]

Young Garrison said he was in camp five days before the wagons came through.[61] Hungry children constantly searching for berries,[62] were crying for food and his mother would give them bread, which was all she had.[63] Other people kept sharing their food. Some of these people were "Mr. Poole, Doctor Wood, Doctor Davis, Rev. Mr. Cornwall, Captain Vanderpool, the Pringles and others."[64]

Scale 1:500,000
1 inch equals approximately 8 miles

Rev. Garrison got through the canyon with two wagons. According to his son, Garrison was the fifth person out.[65] The Garrisons remained in camp to let the oxen rest and regain their strength. This was right outside the Canyon at the present site of Canyonville.[66]

Carter made it out of the canyon at about 3 o'clock in the afternoon. He saw extra wagons, tools and farm instruments lying along the road.[67] "The rain had ceased falling and the sun gave additional enchantment to the scene, and there was plenty of grass for the almost famished stock."[68] He made camp with other fellow emigrants who were exhausted after the ordeal of the canyon. This was the same main encampment outside the canyon.[69] Carter stayed in camp for two or three days.[70]

Tabitha Brown took three days to get through the canyon. All she had was the horse she was riding.[71] That night she caught up with families who had left the encampment that morning and camped in an oak grove,[72] probably on the Umpqua.

The Smiths were still at the entrance of the canyon. Discussion had begun about leaving their wagons. William Smith, their captain, would have nothing to do with abandoning the wagons. He pushed some logs together to build a large fire and gathered everyone around.[73] He simply did not want to abandon the wagons. While he was deliberating, he sank to his knees in the middle of the road and called out, "Lord, have murcy [sic] upon me."[74] At that moment, on that very spot, in the middle of the road, he dropped dead.[75]

William Smith was survived by his wife, Ellen, and nine children. Rufus, His oldest son, was 15. His father owned a little spring wagon he had wanted to carry his children in to go through the canyon. Rufus went to work building a coffin box for his dad using the little wagon. They buried him beside the creek close to where he had died,[76] and built a crude picket fence around his grave.[77]

The Thorntons were camped on Cow Creek. The next day Josiah Morin left all of his wagons except one, in camp. He decided to take his small, two-horse wagon. Morin had been carrying some of Thornton's belongings. He had to leave all of Thornton's and some of his own to care for his family. Thornton's reaction to this was, "I had, indeed, paid Mr. Morin for conveying my clothing as I have already stated; but he seemed to feel that his first duties were, nevertheless, due to his own family, and the preservation of his own property."[78]

Meanwhile, in the canyon the Cornwalls were plodding through the creek bed. They traveled along until about the middle of the afternoon through a "drenching rain."[79] They were fairly chilled. When they came to a more open area, they built a large fire and decided to camp overnight.[80]

The next morning they found several of their oxen had died during the night, so they remained at this camp. Two wagons traveling with them journeyed forward. The Cornwalls kept a large fire in the open area and made a large encampment there.[81]

Sunday, November 1, was a partly fair day. The Pringles traveled three miles that day. Their oxen were "very stiff and sore from scrambling over" wet rocks.[82]

Rev. Garrison sent his wife Margaret and four children forward to the settlements. They left on horseback with his brother Joseph.[83] His two older sons, David and A. H. Garrison stayed with their father to help him with the wagons. They remained in camp for a few days.[84]

Further forward, Tabitha Brown was trying to overtake three wagons ahead. Captain Brown felt sick that afternoon as they traveled along at as fast a pace as she could get him to move.[85]

Brown fell off his horse. He tried but could not remount. She was afraid to dismount her horse because it had not been ridden by a woman before. He held on to his horse's mane, and she led his horse by the bridle. They made it another few miles to the foot of a mountain.[86]

After resting a little, Tabitha and Captain John eventually made it over the mountain and into a large valley. "The sun was now setting, the wind was blowing, and the rain was drifting upon the sides of the distant mountain."[87]

The sun set and the starlight was covered by dark, overhead clouds. Captain Brown was sick and "bewildered."[88] Tabitha Brown no longer saw the wagon tracks. She decided to camp for the night. After unsaddling both their horses, she fashioned a tent by using the canvas she had saved from her wagon. Tabitha "flung it over" the branch of a large tree and covered the "Captain" with blankets. She had him sit on the bare ground, and then she crouched on her feet against the tree with his back against her. They sat through the cold wet night without a fire. She thought he would probably die by morning.[89]

Meanwhile, when Thornton made it to the entrance of the canyon, he came upon the company of Smiths still encamped there. "Upon approaching near the entrance of the close Canyon, we came to where many most miserable, forlorn, haggard, and destitute-looking emigrants were encamped."[90]

Thornton decided he and his wife were going to go through the canyon that day. While he was at the Smith encampment, for some reason he especially noticed a young couple with a child. Their names were Mr. and Mrs. Smith.

...a Mr. Smith, had lost every thing, and he appeared to be overwhelmed. His wife had on a coarse and tattered calico-dress. She was thinly clad, and the covering for her head was an old sun-bonnet. Her child was not in a better condition, while that of her husband was, perhaps, even more pitiful. They had not a cent of money; though had it been otherwise, it would not have purchased food, for there was none to be sold.[91]

Mr. and Mrs. Smith had lost their captain. They were probably related to William Smith. Thornton consoled them and told them it would not help to stay. Eventually he persuaded them to move on and continue their journey down into the canyon:[92]

He seemed to see at once the folly of remaining there.... He immediately took up his child, and about a pound of food, and desired his afflicted and almost helpless companion to follow him.[93]

By looking around it appeared to Thornton that most of the wagon companies had abandoned their wagons and moved on. Josiah Morin's wagon was among the wagons he saw.[94] Mrs. Burns eldest daughter, Lettie,[95] had died here, also a Mr. Brisbane.[96] Thornton decided it was time to move on. "Reluctantly leaving our unhappy fellow-travelers, we proceeded on until we came near the entrance of the canon [sic]."[97] After descending the steep grade, they took refuge under a large fir tree near the creek bed and shared their few morsels of food.[98]

In his writings Thornton twice mentions their possessions before entering the canyon.[99] "I had little remaining, save our buffalo robes, blankets, arms, ammunition, watch, and the most valuable part of our wardrobe...."[100] Thornton had paid another man to carry two bags of clothes

---

Figure 2 Canyon Creek

on his horse.[101] He does not mention it at the time, but they had hidden more food in these two bags.[102]

Meanwhile, deep in the heart of the canyon were the Cornwalls. Narcissa Cornwall said, "Our camp made a nice stopping place for the tired and hungry immigrants."[103] (Narcissa Cornwall, 1926) They had made a roaring fire and kept it going day and night. Many emigrants making it through stopped by and most stayed overnight. The Cornwalls continued to provide others what little they had to eat.[104]

After resting under the fir tree close to the entrance of the canyon, the Thorntons with their dog Prince Darco, decided to continue, so they finally had to enter the Canyon Creek stream. They walked through the stream, each with a staff to steady them. Darco swam some of the way, resting on large boulders. According to Thornton they crossed the creek forty-eight times, wading in water from eighteen inches to waist deep.[105] Mrs. Thornton lost her sense of feeling on one side and then became temporarily blind. The water was very cold. They felt chilled to the bones. Many cattle were dead all around.[106]

They came out of the "narrow gorge" and into the open area of the canyon, where Rev. Cornwall was encamped. The Cornwall tent was filled with other emigrant refugees from the canyon trail. They stood warming themselves by his fire.[107]

Thornton found the Smith family, whom he had persuaded to continue. It had stopped raining so they could dry out next to the fire in the open air.[108]

NOTES   Chapter 8

1. Scott, *Independence*, p. 159. [I believe the days they delayed in not wanting to go any further were some days that Pringle referred to in his diary as getting, "to the foot of the Umpqua Mountain...." (Morgan, *Overland in 1846*, Vol. 1, p. 184.) Part of the time was in not wanting to go any further and they spent one day exploring the canyon. (a) Ibid.; b) Scott, *Independence*, p. 160.)]

2. Carter, *Pioneer Days*, p. 75. [This is probably the day they explored the canyon.]

3. Carter, *Pioneer Days*, p. 76.

4. Scott, *Independence*, p. 160.

5. Morgan, *Overland in 1846*, Vol. 1, p. 185.

6. Garrison, *Life and Labours*, OHS Mss #1009, p. 44.

7. Garrison, "Reminiscences," p. 26.

8.a) Scott, *Independence*, p. 160.
b) Morgan, *Overland in 1846*, Vol. 1, p. 185.
c) Helfrich, "Applegate Trail II," (1976), Vol. 14, p. 45.

9. Garrison, "Reminiscences," p. 27.

10. Helfrich, "Applegate Trail II," (1976), Vol. 14, p. 45.

11. Ibid.

12. Ibid.

13. Garrison, *Life and Labours*, OHS Mss #1009, p. 38.

14. Carter, *Pioneer Days*, p. 76.

15. Garrison, *Life and Labours*, OHS Mss #1009, p. 38.

16. Carter, *Pioneer Days*, p. 75. [After the rains had started in the Umpqua Canyon around October 27th, they also started at Sutter's Fort in Sacramento on October 28 according to Edwin Bryant, a 1846 California emigrant. (Helfrich, "Applegate Trail II," (1976), Vol. 14, p. 29.) While on the new Applegate Trail, the pioneers of 1846 could not have known how severe the weather would be across the entire west coast. This was the same storm that trapped the Donner party in the Sierra Nevada Mountains. The Donners were snowed in by October 28. (a) McGlashan, *Donner Party*, p. 56.; b) Helfrich, "Applegate Trail II," (1976), Vol. 14, p. 28.) The rains also started in Oregon City on October 28th, according to George Gary of Oregon City. (Helfrich, "Applegate Trail II," (1976), Vol. 14, p. 29.)]

17. Thornton, *Or. and Ca. in 1848*, Vol. 1, p. 212. [The fact that Thornton refers to the rains beginning somewhere between the 21st and 26th is another reason that Thornton is probably wrong on his dates. (a) Thornton, *Or. and Ca. in 1848*, Vol. 1, pp. 210-213.; b) Helfrich, "Applegate Trail II," (1976), Vol. 14, p. 28.)]

18. Thornton, *Or. and Ca. in 1848*, Vol. 1, p. 212.

19. Ibid., p. 213.

20. Thornton, *Or. and Ca. in 1848*, Vol. 1, pp. 212, 213. [I believe these arrows were the ones shot at the men in the foremost company when they were near Wolf Creek. That was about where Thornton was when he found the arrows.]

21. Ibid., p. 214.

22. Scott, *Independence*, p. 161.

23. Ibid., p. 160.

24. Morgan, *Overland in 1846*, Vol. 1, p. 185.

25. Ibid. [I find no mention of the foremost party seeing Jones, Smith or Allen on their way back through to the settlements. They might have traveled over the "high, wooded ridges" of the Umpqua Mountains avoiding the Canyon Creek. (Bancroft, *Works*, Vol. XXIX, p. 545.)]

26. Morgan, *Overland in 1846*, Vol. 1, p. 185.

27. Meacham, *Applegate Trail*, p. 17.

28. Brown, "Brimfield Heroine," p. 201.

29.a) Helfrich, "Applegate Trail II," (1976), Vol. 14, p. 47.
b) Brown, "Brimfield Heroine," p. 201.

30.a) Meacham, *Applegate Trail*, p. 17.
b) Brown, ed., *Man*, p. 101.

31. Brown, "Brimfield Heroine," p. 201.

32. Carter, *Pioneer Days*, p. 77.

33. Ibid. [chocked]

34. Ibid.

35. Ibid. [According to W. A. Moxley's "Southern Route To Oregon," this man's name was James Kirkendall. (Moxley, OHS Mss #855, p. 55.)]

36. Ibid.

37. Ibid., p. 76.

38.a) Moxley, OHS Mss #855, p. 56.
b) Carter, *Pioneer Days*, p. 80.

39.a) Carter, *Pioneer Days*, p. 80.
b) Helfrich, "Applegate Trail II," (1976), Vol. 14, p. 44.

40. Lockley, *Pioneer Women*, p. 87.

41.a) Ibid., p. 88.
b) Helfrich, "Applegate Trail II," (1976), Vol. 14, p. 45.

42. Garrison, "Reminiscences," p. 27.

43.a) Lockley, *Pioneer Women*, p. 88.
b) Scott, *Independence*, p. 161.

44.a) Scott, *Independence*, p. 161.
b) Carter, *Pioneer Days*, p. 79.
[Rev. Garrison refers to him as Woods. (Garrison, *Life and Labours*, OHS Mss #1009, p. 34.)]

45. Scott, *Independence*, p. 161.

46. Ibid.

47. Crews, *Smith Family*, OHS Mss #1188, p. 14.

48. Ibid., p. 35.

49. Ibid., p. 14.

50.a) Crews, *Smith Family*, OHS Mss #1188, p. 16.
b) Scott, *Independence*, p. 160.
c) Morgan, *Overland in 1846*, Vol. 1, p. 185.

51. Crews, *Smith Family*, OHS Mss #1188, p. 14.

52. Ibid.

53. Thornton, *Or. and Ca. in 1848*, Vol. 1, p. 216.

54. Ibid.

55. Scott, *Independence*, p. 162. [From what I can tell, Pringle was not with them.]

56. Ibid.

57. Helfrich, "Applegate Trail II," (1976), Vol. 14, p. 45.

58. Morgan, *Overland in 1846*, Vol. 1, p. 185.

59. Sarah Hunt Steves, *Book of Remembrance of Marion County, Oregon, Pioneers 1840-1860* (Portland, OR: The Berncliff Press, 1927), p. 78.

60. Morgan, *Overland in 1846*, Vol. 1, p. 185.

61. Garrison, "Reminiscences," p. 27.

62. Moxley, OHS Mss #855, p. 53.

63. Garrison, "Reminiscences," p. 30.

64. Ibid.

65. a) Helfrich, "Applegate Trail II," (1976), Vol. 14, p. 45.
b) Garrison, "Reminiscences," p. 27.

66. Helfrich, "Applegate Trail II," (1976), Vol. 14, p. 45.

67. Carter, *Pioneer Days*, pp. 77, 79.

68. Ibid., pp. 77, 78.

69. Ibid., pp. 75, 78.

70. Ibid., p. 80.

71. Brown, "Brimfield Heroine," p. 201.

72. Ibid., pp. 201, 199.

73.a) Crews, *Smith Family*, OHS Mss #1188, p. 17.
b) Thornton, *Or. and Ca. in 1848*, Vol. 1, p. 219.

74. Ibid., p. 18.

75.a) Ibid.
b) Brown, ed., *Man*, p. 104.
b) Meacham, *Applegate Trail*, p. 19.
[James Smith, who was the brother of Henry Smith, had mentioned moments before to William, "Boy, you better take a look at the sun; maybe it will be the last time you see it...." There had not been much sun that day either. (Steves, *Book of Remembrance*, p. 88.)]

76. Crews, *Smith Family*, OHS Mss #1188, p. 18.

77. Steves, *Book of Remembrance*, p. 89.

78. Thornton, *Or. and Ca. in 1848*, Vol. 1, p. 216.

79. Cornwall, *Capt. Dunbar's Co. 1846*, OHS Mss #1509, p. 36.

80. Ibid.

81. Ibid.

82. Morgan, *Overland in 1846*, Vol. 1, p. 185.

83. Garrison, "Reminiscences," p. 27.

84.a) Ibid.
b) Garrison, *Life and Labours*, OHS Mss #1009, p. 40.

85. Brown, "Brimfield Heroine," p. 210.

86. Ibid., p. 212.

87. Ibid.

88. Ibid.

89. Ibid.

90. Thornton, *Or. and Ca. in 1848*, Vol. 1, p. 218. [Not to mention what he and his wife must have looked like by then.]

91. Ibid., p. 219.

92. Ibid., p. 220.

93. Ibid., p. 219.

94. Ibid., p. 220.

95. Moxley, OHS Mss #855, p. 53.

96. Thornton, *Or. and Ca. in 1848*, Vol. 1, p. 220.

97. Ibid.

98. Ibid., p. 221.

99. Ibid., pp. 217, 218.

100. Ibid., p. 217.

101. Ibid.

102. Ibid., p. 227.

103. Cornwall, *Capt. Dunbar's Co. 1846*, OHS Mss #1509, p. 36.

104. Ibid.

105. Thornton, *Or. and Ca. in 1848*, Vol. 1, p. 223.

106. Ibid., p. 224.

107. Thornton, *Or. and Ca. in 1848*, Vol. 1, p. 225.

108. Ibid.

From the South Umpqua River to the Willamette Valley: Oregon

Monday, November 2nd, Pringle was probably camped about two miles south of Myrtle Creek. He had made five miles that day. There was no rain, but it was partly cloudy.[1]

Somewhere near Myrtle Creek or Round Prairie, Tabitha Brown was up at the crack of dawn. Captain Brown had lived through the night. She packed her tent, saddled their horses and was able to get "Captain" on his feet.[2] Then, a man showed up from the same wagon train she had tried to overtake. He was out hunting for venison. They were camped about half a mile away. They noticed fresh tracks of Indians within eight feet of where she and Captain Brown had slept. The Indians had come that close without disturbing them. Tabitha Brown and Captain Brown joined this group of pioneers for a few days.[3]

The emigrant pioneers had already been through the worst.[4] After leaving the canyon they no longer felt threatened by the Indians. The emigrants were traveling in smaller numbers.[5] They were beginning to communicate with the Indians and they found them "friendly."[6] They were also in smaller groups because they wanted to travel at their own pace.[7] They were not as united as they had been.[8] This caused some to be ahead and some to be further behind.[9] Some had also joined different groups of wagons than they had started with.[10]

Rev. Garrison and his sons were still in the encampment outside the canyon and about ready to leave. They had seven yokes of oxen.[11] He and his friend Mr. Lancefield had gathered up most of their things in preparation to leave. At that moment, Garrison was told there had been a committee formed. They had decided they must have the fat oxen Garrison's brother had left for him to eat. Garrison wanted to use these oxen to drive his wagons so he begged them to accept a couple of heifers; they did so gladly. People were out of food and getting hungry. He felt fortunate that he could talk them out of taking his oxen.[12]

By the time the food supply issue was resolved, another large group of emigrants had come through the canyon and had made a large encampment. Rev. Garrison heard he had a nephew in camp. He had been traveling on the same wagon train all this time.[13] They had a good talk, and Garrison stayed over another day. One heifer the emigrants in the encampment had slaughtered belonged to Rev. Garrison's son, A. H. Garrison. "After the killing of my cow, we left then."[14]

On Tuesday, November 3rd,[15] Pringle sent his fourteen-year-old son,[16] Octavius, ahead for provisions. They were virtually out of food.[17] The deer in the valley were mainly does and fawns.[18]

The Pringles were camped around Round Prairie, south of present day Roseburg. There were eight wagons in their small company.[19] They made seven miles that day.[20] It rained most of the day.[21]

Octavius rode the only horse left in the company. He was escorted by two young men who needed to go to the other side of the Calapooya Mountains,[22] a distance of about forty miles.[23]

Tolbert Carter was traveling with the Pringles. He loaned his overcoat to Octavius. Octavius agreed to let Carter have a share of the provisions, "...poor venison boiled or roasted without seasoning, not even salt, is about as poor a repast as I ever undertook to satisfy the cravings of a hungry stomach...."[24]   Carter agreed to pay Octavius for the food after crossing the mountains.[25]

Young A. H. Garrison: "In about six or eight miles we came to the South Umpqua and forded, it was a rough crossing on account of boulders...."[26]   One of Rev. Garrison's oxen died during the day while traveling. That evening he sent his son back to save the hide for making ropes to help in crossing the rivers.   When his son found the ox, some emigrants had already taken some of the best parts of the meat off to cook and eat.[27]

Figure 1 Old road coming from Canyon Creek.

Back in the canyon, the Thorntons had left the Cornwalls' camp and continued forward. He said they waded another thirty-nine times across the creek bed. They came to a pack trail that led up the side of the canyon wall, "...clamoring along the side of the mountain."[28]

They came out to the encampment outside the canyon about noon. The Thorntons journeyed along the left bank of the Umpqua River. There were more abandoned wagons and dead oxen all around. "Mr. Humphrey was the only man who, so far as I have since been able to learn, got to this point with a whole wagon and a complete team."[29] He said Mr. Hall left two wagons, Mr. Lovelin left one, Mr. Boone one or two.[30]   Thornton did not know that others had made it through the canyon with their wagon and part of their team. Other belongings left behind were: beds and bedding,[31] carpets, books, household and kitchen furniture, cooking utensils,[32] tools, farm implements[33] clothing[34] and a rolling pin.[35]

Thornton retrieved the two packs of clothes, along with the provisions they had hidden in the packs.[36]   The Thorntons figured they would both have three meals a day for ten days if they conserved what they ate.

> We had two pounds of good tea, as many of loaf sugar, one pint of rice, one pint of beans, about half a pint of dried peaches, sixty table-spoonfuls of the dust or flour of crackers, about one pint of flour, and a half a pound of dried beef.[37]

According to Thornton, the emigrants in camp had started eating the dead cattle in the canyon, "But single men, who knew of the condition of the companies, had gone forward on mules, and we hope[d] *[sic]* these would in some way be instrumental in sending to us the necessary supplies."[38]

Further back in the depths of the canyon were the Cornwalls. Narcissa Cornwall recalled, "We remained in this camp several weeks."[39] Rev. Cornwall took several loads of their books and belongings further through the canyon. Mr. Culver, their hired hand, helped move the belongings.[40]

One day Rev. Cornwall, Isreal Stoley, Richard Chrisman[41] and Daniel Culver were moving some of their belongings, and a mule kicked Rev. Cornwall. Three of his ribs were broken.[42] This slowed things down considerably.

The Smith Company, still at the entrance of the canyon, decided to send two young men to the settlements. They were not to stop for anything. If they came to a stream, they should swim it or build a raft. They each took a hatchet, knife, and a sack of dried beef and began their journey.[43]

The forward body of emigrants proceeded along the south bank of the South Umpqua River. They forded the river three times within one mile to avoid steep hills on both sides.[44] Pringle was probably crossing the three fords of the Umpqua about the same time Scott was heading toward Deer Creek at present day Roseburg.[45] Pringle camped near present day Myrtle Creek. Some emigrants probably camped at Round Prairie south of Roseburg.

Rev. Garrison helped Mr. Lancefield cross the hills north of Myrtle Creek. Lancefield's team was very weak, and Garrison was helping by lending some of his team after he had crossed a major hill.[46]

Scott was leading the remainder of the foremost company. He had ten wagons with him ahead of all others.[47] Some of them were probably Bounds, Linville and Crowley.[48] They reached the North Umpqua about where he had crossed with the exploring party at the beginning of the year.[49] This was about where Fisher Road is today.[50] They found the river was too rough to cross,[51] so they went back along the river about five miles, near the present location of Brown's Bridge,[52] and camped for the night.[53]

Figure 2 Three fords of the South Umqua River.

The Pringles came to the present day Fisher Road location at the North Umpqua River. They made six miles that day. They also found they could not cross, and camped for the night.[54]

The next day Scott hired canoes from the Indians and managed to get the women, children and belongings over. Next they drove the empty wagons over with the teams.[55]

About this time the Garrisons were probably reaching the top of Roberts Mountain. After reaching the top,

Figure 3 Trail north of Myrtle Creek.

that day. He had nothing to eat. "Mr. Pringle tried to shoot a wolf, but he was too weak and trembling to hold the rifle steady."[58] (Tabitha Brown, 1846)

They brought the wagons over the next day. They went one mile and camped.[59] Carter also mentions crossing the North Umpqua with canoes furnished by the Indians. "This was severe on the poor oxen, the water being very cold."[60]

Not long after Lancefield abandoned his wagon, Garrison had to abandon one of his. They traveled along until reaching the North Umpqua River that evening.[61] They noticed that there were people camped across the river. "There was [sic] a few wagons ahead of us and the Indians had assisted them in crossing...."[62]

The next morning there were no Indians about to help them cross. There was an emigrant camped on the other side of the river. There was also a canoe on that side of the river. He called to the man for help with the canoe. The man told him he had no food and had not eaten breakfast. Garrison replied, "Bring it over and I will give you your breakfast." The

Garrison's son took three yokes back down to help Mr. Lancefield bring his wagon up the hill. Garrison had been helping him for two or three weeks. Mr. Lancefield told young Garrison to tell his father it was too hard on his oxen to keep helping him. He was leaving his wagon and packing everything on his team.[56] Young Garrison said, "...that night we camped where Roseburg now stands."[57]

Pringle got to the lower ford of the North Umpqua River and crossed in the canoes. He made about five miles man brought the canoe over, and soon after a number of Indians showed up to helped ferry his wagon over.[63]

After crossing the North Umpqua River, Garrison climbed a steep hill by placing his oxen at the top and pulling the wagon up with several long log chains.[64]

Pringle ate the last of his tripe. He met some Indians and got six venison hams. Octavius returned with half a bushel of peas and forty pounds of flour.[65] This was probably on Sutherlin Creek[66] near Deady[67] or Wilbur. Tabitha Brown met with the Pringle family on the same day Octavius came back.[68] This was quite a reunion for all of them.

Carter got his share of provisions from Octavius. "Our share consisted of a small portion of flour, not exceeding 20 pounds, and about half that amount of peas."[69] Carter could hardly wait as he watched Mrs. Pringle take the flour, knead it into dough, and place the dough into the frying pan to cook. He did not realize the wheat tramped by oxen to thrash it had also gotten mixed with wild weeds called anise. The bread also had some dirt in it. He did not enjoy the bread any more than the unseasoned meat.[70]

Octavius told his family of his adventures. It had taken three days for Octavius and the two men to reach a warehouse of stored food. There was no one he could return with, so he braved it himself. He followed the pack trail south and for a distance a "very large bear track came into the trail...."[71] After camping he woke about midnight to the sounds of branches breaking. He spent the rest of the night above his camp on a high limb of a large fir tree.[72] After hearing the animal roam his camp all night, that morning he found it "was an old, emaciated immigrant cow, left, because she could go no further...."[73] The next night was spent with Indian people who were camped by the pack trail. They took him in and fed him venison. He left with a carcass of a deer

Scale 1:500,000
1 inch equals approximately 8 miles

which he was to pay for with "powder, lead and caps."[74] Hearing about all of Octavius' risky adventures, Mrs. Pringle decided she would never let "one of her children go alone into such a wilderness...."[75]

They were traveling toward the Calapooya Mountains. Scott felt that it was a reasonably good road in open country. The teams were so jaded that it took longer than he expected.[76] Pringle found good feed for the cattle around Elk Creek, now known as Calapooya Creek. It was rainy and cold. He had gone five miles that day.[77]

Figure 4 Looking north toward Elk Creek.

They stayed on Elk Creek about three days[78] with the same Indian families that Octavius had stayed three nights before on his wilderness adventure.[79] This was just south of present day Oakland.[80] Their teams were able to graze and build up their strength. There was another death in the train, an eighteen-year-old girl. She was buried nearby.[81]

The Cornwalls were still in the canyon after several weeks.[82] By now the original road out was not even passable on foot. The stream had swollen so much they felt they might not escape. They crossed the stream several times. Rev. Cornwall was carrying books on his back and still managing to help the children when the stream was so deep their feet no longer touched the ground. They eventually found the pack trail up alongside the Canyon and made their way to the top of the ridge after dark.[83]

The Thorntons were traveling along the Umpqua Valley. Early one morning Mr. Kirquendall, Asa Williams and others arrived. They were a relief party sent out by Jesse Applegate. They brought some fat cows and flour to aid the emigrants still on the trail.[84] They were all extremely glad to get these provisions. Kirquendall made sure everyone got a share.[85]

The Kirquendall, Williams relief party decided to help the Thorntons into the settlements. Thornton hired a horse from Mr. Kirquendall. He and his wife used this horse to take turns riding into the Willamette Valley. Thornton traded one of his very fine suits of clothes to Asa Williams for another horse. He used this horse to carry the two packages of his finest clothing he had managed to get this far.[86]

The Thorntons packed their things and began to journey toward the settlements with the Kirquendall relief party. After traveling for a while, they reached the top of a mountain, probably Roberts Mountain. Thornton turned and saw some people behind him at a distance. He asked Mr. Kirquendall who these people were. Kirquendall said they were Mr. and Mrs. Newton and Sutton Burns. They were probably trying to catch up with him.[87] The Newtons traveled until after dark, unable to catch up with the Kirquendall relief party.[88] Thornton said, "We resumed our journey the following morning; and Mr. Newton resumed his."[89]

Mr. Newton had lost his wagon. His wife rode on the only mare they had. His brother Thomas was with him and also Sutton Burns, an orphan boy. They packed their tent and what provisions they had on their only ox.[90]

The following evening the Newtons camped by a creek in what is now part of Roseburg. They were completely out of food, and Mr. Newton was sick. Thomas went back to the wagons south of their camp to ask for medicine and food.[91]

That evening just before sunset three Indians came up to their camp.[92] These Indians were renegades, not part of any tribe.[93] One of them spoke English. He offered to hunt down a deer if Mr. Newton would lend him his rifle. This seemed reasonable to Mr. Newton who was too sick to hunt for himself. The Indians were also out of food. Mr. Newton had already shared what little food he had in camp with the three Indians. Imagining fresh venison on an open fire, he agreed to lend them his rifle.[94]

They only pretended to go hunting. Instead, they came back to John Newton's camp and shot him. Newton sprang up and tried to go into his tent for another gun. One Indian grabbed an axe and hit Newton in the leg, drawing blood.[95] The Indians took Newton's mare and his gun. They fled, leaving his wife unharmed.[96]

Mrs. Newton and Sutton Burns spent the night nursing Mr. Newton. He died early the next morning with his wife at his side. The boy ran five or six miles to the next camp for help.[97] The creek they were camped on is known today as Newton Creek.[98]

After Pringle and the others rested their livestock for three days, their teams were more able to pull the wagons, "...our teams much improved and ourselves rested. Pringle received a Salmon from the Indians at this camp.[99] He and his son Octavius were shoemakers and had cobbler tools and leather in their wagon. They made a pair of shoes for an Indian in trade for three large deer carcasses.[100]

Pringle was by now a part of Scott's foremost party. Friday, November 13th, Mrs. Elizabeth Lovelady Bounds died.[101] They traveled about a mile to the north side of Calapooya Creek and buried her in a beautiful little spot near the present town of Oakland.[102]

The next day they were crossing a little creek, possibly today Cowan Creek or Wilson Creek.[103] It was rainy and the crossing was deep. They had to cut the bank to form a ramp for the wagons.[104] The wagons were usually held back on each side with a rope. If there was not an even amount of tension on both sides of the wagon while crossing, it could upset.[105]

Richard Linville's wagon was the first to try the crossing.[106] The wagon turned over with his wife Mary inside. Unfortunately, she drowned before she could be helped. She was an elderly woman and could not easily help herself.[107]

Carter recalled, "...laid over one day to recruit our exhausted team before surmounting this dreaded mountain, the summit of which was covered with snow."[108] They probably stayed about where Scotts Valley is today.[109]

Lucy Ann Henderson's uncle, Mr. Holman, came to the rescue of her family. He came with food and horses to help them into the settlements. Her mother rode to the settlements on one horse with her six week old baby in her lap and one of her daughters riding behind. Lucy rode with Mr. Holman, and her sisters rode with the other men.[110]

It had been a few weeks since the Smith Company had sent the two boys toward the settlements for help. More of the sick in the company had died. They decided to try going forward on foot. Henry Smith was chosen to be their captain. His first order was to abandon their wagons.[111]

Along with the Smiths, there were many others still with the Cornwalls. Some had abandoned their wagons after losing their teams. Some still had their teams after losing their wagons.[112] One of the men who still had a team offered Rev. Cornwall three oxen in trade for one of Cornwall's wagons. He gladly accepted the offer. This allowed the Cornwalls to bring both their wagons out of the canyon. The wagons still contained most of his precious book collection.[113] Trading a wagon also limited his possibility of moving his books any further toward the settlements.

Mrs. Cornwall had caught typhoid fever helping others. Some later died of the "mountain fever." She did not feel well enough to travel further. Almost every day, those who regained their strength started toward the settlements a few at a time.[114] This enabled the Cornwalls to move a little further north.

The Smiths were among those starting toward the settlements. Ellen Smith had her three children put on the back of their family ox, Darby. There was one-year-old Marion, three-year-old Thaddeus, and Louisa Smith. Louisa had been ill and getting sicker every day.[115]

There was an elderly man in the Smith Company named James Curtendall who was too sick to travel. He asked to be left behind. His only request was a glass of water. He had a son in his twenties and a teen-aged daughter. They protested but eventually agreed to let him remain.[116]

After getting through the canyon and stopping for the night, Curtendall's son and a friend ran back to see his father breathe his last breath. The two young men built a coffin box out of one of the wagon beds and sometime before midnight held a funeral service for their loved one.[117] Young Curtendall and his friend caught up with their company sometime the next day.[118]

We will now resume our journey with the foremost wagons. They had made it to the foot of the Calapooya

Figure 5 Almost every day, those who regained their strength started toward the settlements a few at a time.

Mountains.[119]   It was about the 17th of November.[120] They started cutting a trail up the mountain and through the woods. Carter mentions, "About this time three men left us all on foot, with blankets on their back, to press on to the settlement...."[121]   They traveled forward on the Indian trail through the Calapooya Mountains for relief and supplies.[122] These men did not have any provisions to take with them. They had a shotgun and thought they could hunt, but there was no game to be found.

On the third day after leaving, they met a man named Durbin who had some provisions on his pack horse. He pointed out some wild berries growing in abundance near where they stood. They had not tried these berries because they thought they were poisonous. Durbin told them the Indians ate them all the time. They called them "salad berries" while in season. The men gorged themselves. The man who ate the most was a portly young man named Dan Toole.[123]

The Calapooya Mountains were quite a task to undertake. Those emigrants still with wagons could not get through without first cutting a road.[124]   Rev. Garrison had also halted to help build a road: "...all hands went to work to cut the road across, our old friend Mr. Scott the pilot yet remaining and working like a good fellow...."[125]

Tabitha Brown grew weary of waiting and plodding through the mountains, "We were many days crossing the Calipose [sic] Mountain, able to go ahead only a mile or two each day. The road had to be cut open for us, and the mountain was covered with snow."[126]   There were also winter rains at the time.[127]   It took five days to make it through about sixteen miles.[128]

The Thorntons entered the Willamette Valley Wednesday, November 18.[129]   Mr. Thornton felt he had thrown a load of care and concern off his shoulder upon descending the Calapooya Mountains and entering the valley.[130]   They traveled the pack trail through the mountains.[131]   Other than the existing pack trail, there had not been any road cut for the emigrants since the entrance of the canyon.[132]

Rev. Garrison's brother Enoch arrived to help them with the road cutting into the settlements. Working next to Enoch, Garrison felt fatigued in comparison, "...it did appear to me he was able to do as much work as three of us....it was several days before we got to the summit...."[133]   With the help of Enoch, the pioneers made a trail.[134]

There were two main ridges to cross through the Calapooya Mountains. They made it over one and then worked their way up the other.[135]   Scott helped cut down trees with others while also stopping to scout the direction ahead to blaze more of the trail. Then he would return to continue helping cut trees and build more road.[136]   They finally managed to get to the top of the second ridge around November 19th.[137]   They double teamed their oxen at the steep grades on the last ridge.[138]   Carter was pleased to reach the top, "... we reached the summit and passed the belt of snow; then we camped and chained our oxen to trees...."[139]

When they finished cutting the road through the Calapooya Mountains they returned for their wagons and worked their way up and over the summit.[140]   They made four miles that day. It rained, and one steer died in camp.[141]

Carter was full of joy the morning they descended the mountain. "We were glad when day appeared and all hands prepared to make the downgrade."[142]   While descending the mountain, they passed a few Indians who were on their way south and traveling through the snow. "These aborigines were scantily dressed and barefooted, but appeared comfortable."[143] They all exchanged greetings and went on their way; "Heha-Hi-Um," which means "How do you do."[144]

Saturday, November 21st, most of the emigrants in the foremost company reached the foot of the Calapooya Mountains.[145] Scott probably pushed on to what is today the Cottage Grove area.[146] It took most of the day to reach the valley floor. It was all downhill, but the soft ground caused the wagon wheels to sink, which helped slow them down as they descended the mountain. This also made it easier for the teams.[147] They had at long last reached the border of the Willamette Valley.[148]

About this time the Smith Company was journeying through the Umpqua Valley. They were traveling by foot, packing their belongings and their sick, on oxen. Louisa knew she was dying. She told her mother to bury her six feet deep so the wolves would not get her. She had seen shallow graves while on the Oregon Trail. They had been dug up by wolves.[149]

Somewhere near present day Roseburg Louisa died. Her mother Ellen selected a spot for her burial.[150] They dug the grave down a few feet and said they would not dig any deeper. Full of anguish and love for her daughter, Ellen Smith dropped down in the burial pit and started digging herself.[151] She told the men she had promised her daughter, and she was going to dig until the grave was deep enough. Their new captain, Henry Smith, told her not to worry; he would see that the grave was dug as deep as she wanted. They dug the grave deeper until she was satisfied that it was deep enough. Three or four days were spent burying Louisa.[152]

Meanwhile, the foremost wagon train had managed to make it to the head of the Willamette Valley.[153] This is about where Cottage Grove is today.[154] "I had performed the duties I had assumed, and had led the immigration into the Great Valley at the head of the Willamette River...."[155] (Levi Scott, c.1886)[156]

Rev. Garrison helped finish the road through the mountains and all got their wagons down.[157] "...now for the first time I place my foot on soil for which I had been so long in traveling, that of the Willamette...."[158]

Albert L. Alderman was one of the single men on the first Applegate Trail wagon train. He recalled, "Coming in broken parties out of the Calapooia [sic] Mountains, they at length all got into the Willamette valley alive...."[159] After making it this far there was no sign of the settlements. Winter was upon them and they would need supplies to pull through.

Scott mentioned that a wagon with provisions came to greet them.[160] Rev. Garrison obtained some flour at a high price. His brother Enoch and his father Jeptha took his son David ahead to the settlements.[161] Garrison's son Henry stayed to help with the wagon.[162] They all rested for a few days while they fed their teams.[163]

Rev. Garrison heard that Mr. Lancefield was at the south end of the mountain. He was going to carry him some flour. The man selling provisions came by to deliver flour, and Mr. Lancefield bought the flour he needed. Mr. Lancefield was traveling with Mr. Isaac Lebo. He had his belongings in Mr. Lebo's wagon. He also had joined the rest of his oxen with Lebo's team. Garrison helped both of them to the top of the mountain.[164]

Mr. Lancefield, Mr. Lebo, and their families got to the Willamette River, dug out a large canoe[165] and headed down the river with their families. This was the last time Rev. Garrison saw them until he reached the settlements. Later that year, he saw them on a farm in the Willamette Valley.[166]

Wednesday, November 25th, the Thorntons arrived at the house of Mr. Lewis. They had a "renewed cause to be grateful."[167]

"The track made by the wagons that met us could be followed into the settlements by the immigrants...."[168] (Levi Scott, c.1886)[169]

Pringle had also helped build the new road. As he journeyed to the Willamette River, he observed, "All charmed with the prospects and think they will be paid for their sufferings."[170] The next day Pringle lost two steers to the cold, so he rested his team for a day.[171] He was probably northeast of Creswell on Hill Creek.[172]

Most emigrants had run short of supplies. Carter was traveling with seven or eight wagons, "...more complaining was heard for the want of tobacco than for the lack of provisions."[173] Carter said those who were good at hunting could add wild geese to their diet of venison and poor beef. Carter got some geese and a raccoon. His dog helped corner the raccoon in a hollowed out log.[174]

About four days from their mountain camp, Thomas Crowley died of typhoid fever.[175] He was the fourth of the Crowley family that had died in the train. He was buried without a coffin. "All turned sorrowfully from his grave."[176] (Tolbert Carter, c.1896)

NOTES   Chapter 9

1. Morgan, *Overland in 1846*, Vol. 1, p. 186.

2. Brown, "Brimfield Heroine," p. 202.

3. Ibid. [This was probably Levi Scott's group.]

4.a) Carter, *Pioneer Days*, p. 77.
b) Garrison, *Life and Labours*, OHS Mss #1009, p. 38.
c) Thornton, *Or. and Ca. in 1848*, Vol. 1, p. 220.

5.a) Scott, *Independence*, p. 162.
b) Carter, *Pioneer Days*, p. 80.

6.a) Garrison, *Life and Labours*, OHS Mss #1009, p. 39.
b) Carter, *Pioneer Days*, p. 84.

7.a) Garrison, *Life and Labours*, OHS Mss #1009, p. 39.
b) Carter, *Pioneer Days*, p. 79.
c) *Hist. of the Pac. N. W.*, Vol. II, p. 191.

8.a) *Hist. of the Pac. N. W.*, Vol. II, p. 191.
b) Garrison, "Reminiscences," p. 28.

c) Garrison, *Life and Labours*, OHS Mss #1009, p. 41.

9.a) Garrison, *Life and Labours*, OHS Mss #1009, p. 40.
b) Carter, *Pioneer Days*, pp. 77, 81.

10.a) Brown, "Brimfield Heroine," p. 201.
b) Garrison, "Reminiscences," p. 21.
c) Thornton, *Or. and Ca. in 1848*, Vol. 1, p. 238.
d) *Hist. of the Pac. N. W.*, Vol. II, p. 191.

11. Garrison, *Life and Labours*, OHS Mss #1009, p. 41.

12.a) Ibid., p. 40.
b) Garrison, "Reminiscences," p. 28.

13. Garrison, *Life and Labours*, OHS Mss #1009, p. 40.

14. Garrison, "Reminiscences," p. 28.

15. Morgan, *Overland in 1846*, Vol. 1, p. 186.

16. Steves, *Book of Remembrance*, p. 80.

17. Morgan, *Overland in 1846*, Vol. 1, p. 186.

18. Carter, *Pioneer Days*, p. 80.

19. Ibid.

20. Morgan, *Overland in 1846*, Vol. 1, p. 186.

21. Carter, *Pioneer Days*, p. 80.

22. Steves, *Book of Remembrance*, p. 81.

23. Morgan, *Overland in 1846*, Vol. 1, p. 186.

24. Carter, *Pioneer Days*, p. 81.

25. Ibid., p. 82.

26. Garrison, "Reminiscences," p. 28.

27. Garrison, *Life and Labours*, OHS Mss #1009, p. 40.

28. Thornton, *Or. and Ca. in 1848*, Vol. 1, p. 225, 226. [This was probably the same path the trail blazers had taken coming south to find the new route. (Applegate, "Old Emigrant Road," p. 16.)]

29. Thornton, *Or. and Ca. in 1848*, Vol. 1, p. 226. [This may have been true as far as having a complete team, but as we know he was not the only man to get through the canyon with a wagon and a team.]

30. Ibid., p. 227

31.a) Ibid., p. 218.
b) Brown, "Brimfield Heroine," p. 201.

32. Thornton, *Or. and Ca. in 1848*, Vol. 1, p. 218.

33. Carter, *Pioneer Days*, p. 79.

34. Brown, "Brimfield Heroine," p. 201. [Was some of the clothing more of the Thornton's ?]

35. Lockley, *Pioneer Women*, p. 88.

36. Thornton, *Or. and Ca. in 1848*, Vol. 1, p. 228.

37. Ibid.

38. Ibid., pp. 228, 227.

39. Cornwall, *Capt. Dunbar's Co. 1846*, OHS Mss #1509, p. 36.

40. Ibid.

41. Ibid., p. 35.

42. Ibid., p. 36. Crews, *Smith Family*, OHS Mss #1188, p. 20.

43. Crews, *Smith Family*, OHS Mss #1188, p. 20.

44. Helfrich, "Applegate Trail II," (1976), Vol. 14, p. 53.

45.a) Morgan, *Overland in 1846*, Vol. 1, p. 187.
b) Scott, *Independence*, p. 162.
c) Brown, "Brimfield Heroine," p. 200. [Tabitha Brown was possibly with this group of wagons.]

46. Garrison, *Life and Labours*, OHS Mss #1009, p. 41.

47. Scott, *Independence*, p. 163.

48. Kay Alsing, Conversations with author, Ashland, OR, 1995-1996.

49. Scott, *Independence*, p. 163.

50. Helfrich, "Applegate Trail II," (1976), Vol. 14, p. 59.

51.a) Scott, *Independence*, p. 163.
b) Morgan, *Overland in 1846*, Vol. 1, p. 186, 397.

52. Helfrich, "Applegate Trail II," (1976), Vol. 14, p. 59.

53. Scott, *Independence*, p. 163.

54. Morgan, *Overland in 1846*, Vol. 1, p. 186, 397.

Figure 6 North along the Willamette River in Cottage Grove

55. Scott, *Independence*, p. 164. [He was possibly just a few miles ahead of Pringle. This would explain Tabitha Brown's whereabouts.]

56.a) Garrison, "Reminiscences," p. 28.
b) Garrison, *Life and Labours*, OHS Mss #1009, p. 41.

57. Garrison, "Reminiscences," p. 28.

58. Brown, "Brimfield Heroine," p. 202.

59. Morgan, *Overland in 1846*, Vol. 1, p. 186.

60. Carter, *Pioneer Days*, p. 82.

61. Garrison, *Life and Labours*, OHS Mss #1009, p. 41.

62. Ibid.

63. Ibid.

64. Ibid.

65. Morgan, *Overland in 1846*, Vol. 1, p. 187.

66. Helfrich, "Applegate Trail II," (1976), Vol. 14, p. 59.

67. Morgan, *Overland in 1846*, Vol. 1, p. 396.

68. Brown, "Brimfield Heroine," p. 202.

69. Carter, *Pioneer Days*, p. 82.

70. Ibid. [Anise is a kind of licorice.]

71. Steves, *Book of Remembrance*, p. 82.

72. Ibid., p. 82, 83.

73. Ibid., p. 83.

74. Ibid.

75. Ibid., p. 84.

76. Scott, *Independence*, p. 154.

77. Morgan, *Overland in 1846*, Vol. 1, p. 186, 396.

78. Ibid.

79. Steves, *Book of Remembrance*, p. 78, 84.

80. Morgan, *Overland in 1846*, Vol. 1, p. 186, 396.

81. Steves, *Book of Remembrance*, p. 78, 84.

82. Cornwall, *Capt. Dunbar's Co. 1846*, OHS Mss #1509, p. 36.

83.a) Applegate, "Applegate Trail," p. 6.
b) Applegate, "Old Emigrant Road," p. 16.
c) Cornwall, *Capt. Dunbar's Co. 1846*, OHS Mss #1509, p. 37.
[This was the same original Hudson's Bay pack trail the Thorntons had taken out of the canyon. It was probably originally an Indian trail.]

84. Thornton, *Or. and Ca. in 1848*, Vol. 1, p. 234.

85.a) Meacham, *Applegate Trail*, p. 18.
b) Brown, ed., *Man*, p. 103.

86. Thornton, *Or. and Ca. in 1848*, Vol. 1, p. 235. [I guess we all have our priorities ?]

87. Ibid., p. 237.

88. Ibid.

89. Ibid., p. 238.

90. Scott, *Independence*, p. 162.

91. Ibid.

92.a) Ibid., p. 163.
b) Thornton, *Or. and Ca. in 1848*, Vol. 1, p. 238.
c) Meacham, *Applegate Trail*, p. 21.

93. Scott, *Independence*, p. 163.

94.a) Scott, *Independence*, p. 163.
b) Thornton, *Or. and Ca. in 1848*, Vol. 1, p. 238.
c) Meacham, *Applegate Trail*, p. 21.

95.a) Thornton, *Or. and Ca. in 1848*, Vol. 1, p. 238.
b) Scott, *Independence*, p. 163.
c) Meacham, *Applegate Trail*, p. 21.

96.a) Helfrich, "Applegate Trail II," (1976), Vol. 14, p. 41.
b) Scott, *Independence*, p. 163.

97. Thornton, *Or. and Ca. in 1848*, Vol. 1, p. 237.

98.a) Helfrich, "Applegate Trail II," (1976), Vol. 14, p. 41.
b) Scott, *Independence*, p. 163.

99. Morgan, *Overland in 1846*, Vol. 1, p. 186.

100. Steves, *Book of Remembrance*, p. 79, 84.

101.a) Morgan, *Overland in 1846*, Vol. 1, p. 187.
b) Scott, *Independence*, p. 164.

[She had been feeding her food to the children, and did not nourish herself. (Kay Alsing, Conversations with author, Ashland, OR, 1995-1996.)]

102.a) Morgan, *Overland in 1846*, Vol. 1, p. 187, 396.
b) Scott, *Independence*, p. 164.
[They must have thought much of her because not only did Levi Scott mention her, but Virgil Pringle also mentioned her in his diary. There are many people that died along the trail that Virgil Pringle did not mention.]

103. Scott, *Independence*, p. 164.

104. Carter, *Pioneer Days*, p. 85.

105. Rounds, *Prairie Schooners*, p. 58.

106. Carter, *Pioneer Days*, p. 85.

107.a) Scott, *Independence*, p. 164.
b) Carter, *Pioneer Days*, p. 85.

108. Ibid., p. 84.

109.a) Morgan, *Overland in 1846*, Vol. 1, p. 187.
b) Helfrich, "Applegate Trail II," (1976), Vol. 14, p. 59.

110. Lockley, *Pioneer Women*, p. 89. [This was probably between November 15th and 17th.]

111. Crews, *Smith Family*, OHS Mss #1188, p. 20. [Henry Smith was not related to their former deceased captain, William Smith.]

112. Thornton, *Or. and Ca. in 1848*, Vol. 1, p. 226.

113. Cornwall, *Capt. Dunbar's Co. 1846*, OHS Mss #1509, p. 37.

114. Ibid.

115.a) Crews, *Smith Family*, OHS Mss #1188, p. 21.
b) Meacham, *Applegate Trail*, p. 19.

116. Crews, *Smith Family*, OHS Mss #1188, p. 22.

117. Ibid., p. 23.

118. Ibid., p. 24.

119.a) Morgan, *Overland in 1846*, Vol. 1, p. 187.
b) Carter, *Pioneer Days*, p. 84.

120. Morgan, *Overland in 1846*, Vol. 1, p. 187, 396.

121. Carter, *Pioneer Days*, p. 83.

122. Scott, *Independence*, p. 164.

123. Carter, *Pioneer Days*, p. 83.

124. Garrison, "Reminiscences," p. 29.

125. Garrison, *Life and Labours*, OHS Mss #1009, p. 42.

126. Brown, "Brimfield Heroine," p. 203.

127. Scott, *Independence*, p. 164.

128. Morgan, *Overland in 1846*, Vol. 1, p. 187.

129. Thornton, *Or. and Ca. in 1848*, Vol. 1, p. 239.

130. Ibid. [They must have passed the other wagons which were all working their way through the Calapooya Mountains. He may have taken the pack trail to Fort Umpqua.]

131. Ibid., p. 239.

132. Scott, *Independence*, p. 165.

133. Garrison, *Life and Labours*, OHS Mss #1009, p. 42.

134. Scott, *Independence*, p. 165.

135.a) Morgan, *Overland in 1846*, Vol. 1, p. 396.

b) Helfrich, "Applegate Trail II," (1976), Vol. 14, p. 71.

136. Scott, *Independence*, p. 165.

137. Morgan, *Overland in 1846*, Vol. 1, p. 187.

138.a) Scott, *Independence*, p. 165.
b) Morgan, *Overland in 1846*, Vol. 1, p. 187.

139. Carter, *Pioneer Days*, p. 84.

140.a) Scott, *Independence*, p. 164.
b) Garrison, *Life and Labours*, OHS Mss #1009, p. 42.
c) Morgan, *Overland in 1846*, Vol. 1, p. 187.

141. Morgan, *Overland in 1846*, Vol. 1, p. 187.

142. Carter, *Pioneer Days*, p. 84.

143. Ibid.

144. Ibid.

145.a) Morgan, *Overland in 1846*, Vol. 1, p. 187, 396.
b) Garrison, *Life and Labours*, OHS Mss #1009, p. 42.
c) Carter, *Pioneer Days*, p. 84.
[This is probably present day Divide.]

146. Scott, *Independence*, p. 165.

147. Carter, *Pioneer Days*, p. 84.

148.a) Garrison, *Life and Labours*, OHS Mss #1009, p. 42.
b) Carter, *Pioneer Days*, p. 84.

149. Crews, *Smith Family*, OHS Mss #1188, p. 26.

150. Ibid.

151. Ibid., p. 27.

152. Ibid., p. 28.

153. Scott, *Independence*, p. 165.

154. Morgan, *Overland in 1846*, Vol. 1, p. 396.

155. Scott, *Independence*, p. 165.

156. Ibid., p. 133.

157.a) Garrison, *Life and Labours*, OHS Mss #1009, p. 42.
b) Morgan, *Overland in 1846*, Vol. 1, p. 396.
c) Carter, *Pioneer Days*, p. 84.

158. Garrison, *Life and Labours*, OHS Mss #1009, p. 42.

159. *Hist. of the Pac. N. W.*, Vol. II, p. 191.

160. Scott, *Independence*, p. 165.

161. Garrison, *Life and Labours*, OHS Mss #1009, p. 42.

162. Garrison, "Reminiscences," p. 29.

163.a) Morgan, *Overland in 1846*, Vol. 1, p. 187.
b) Carter, *Pioneer Days*, p. 84.

164. Garrison, *Life and Labours*, OHS Mss #1009, p. 43.

165.a) Morgan, *Overland in 1846*, Vol. 1, p. 188.
b) Garrison, *Life and Labours*, OHS Mss #1009, p. 43.

166. Garrison, *Life and Labours*, OHS Mss #1009, p. 43.

167. Thornton, *Or. and Ca. in 1848*, Vol. 1, p. 239.

168. Scott, *Independence*, p. 165.

169. Ibid., p. 133.

170. Morgan, *Overland in 1846*, Vol. 1, p. 187.

171. Ibid.

172. Helfrich, "Applegate Trail II," (1976), Vol. 14, p. 73.

173. Carter, *Pioneer Days*, p. 85. [This goes to show that in 1846 tobacco was as hard a habit to quit as it is today.]

174. Ibid.

175. Garrison, *Life and Labours*, OHS Mss #1009, p. 31. [According to W. A. Moxley's "Southern Route To Oregon," Thomas Crowley died from a high fever he caught after crossing a stream to retrieve two oxen and traveling all day in his wet clothes. (Moxley, OHS Mss #855, p. 62.)]

176. Carter, *Pioneer Days*, p. 86. [Mrs. Crowley later married Mr. Fulkerson of Polk County. (a) Lockley, *Pioneer Women*, p. 87.; b) Helfrich, "Applegate Trail II," (1976), Vol. 14, p. 32.)]

The Settlements in the Willamette Valley: Oregon

On Sunday, November 29th, the Thorntons arrived at Forest Grove. They were "cheerful and happy."[1] About this time the foremost party was somewhere around present day Eugene.[2] Pringle was somewhere west of present day Springfield in south Eugene.[3] Carter mentions that he came to Eugene Skinner's cabin. "A small pole cabin .... without door or window, looked homelike, in deed."[4]

Many families were abandoning their wagons and making canoes because the next major obstacle was the Long Tom River.[5] Pringle started building a raft with Mr. Lancefield and Isaac Lebo.[6]

Scott mentioned a Herman Buckingham had lost his team and had to abandon his wagon. He built a raft near Junction City on the Middle and Coast Forks of the Willamette. He and his family went about ten miles. The raft overturned and they lost everything, but they all survived.[7]

Carter was still caring for the widow and her two children. She was expecting a third child. This was the last trimester of her pregnancy. Carter needed the wagon to make things as comfortable as possible for her at the time.[8] "We went from this camp to what is now known as Long Tom River - a stream running crosswise of the valley, with much swampy land. It is now being in December...."[9]

Lucy Ann Henderson mentioned that another family crossing either the Long Tom River or Mary's River in Corvallis had a trunk with the last of all their possessions swept off a horse never to be seen again.[10]

It was the beginning of December. Rev. Garrison had traveled through the Willamette Valley with his wheels in the mud sometimes up to the hubs.[11] "The first sign of civil[iz]ation *[sic]* we saw was in Skinner Bute, *[sic]* [now Eugene City] Mr. Skinner had built a hewed log house but was not covered as yet. It was now raining nearly all the time...."[12]

Carter and his widow friend were in the vicinity of the Long Tom River. Their wagon was getting stuck in the mud as they traveled on.

We will now go back to the Smith Company. The Smiths were slowly plodding along somewhere in the Calapooya Mountains, probably on present day Pass Creek. They had packed their belongings on oxen and were traveling by foot. As they nooned, they discussed which cow they would slaughter to eat next.[13] Everyone in the company heard Henry Smith yelling. He was jumping up and down on a log and waving his hat in the air. Next they saw what he was yelling about. It was a relief party. The two young men the Smith Company had sent for relief earlier had reached the Willamette Valley and brought a rescue party back with them.[14] They had brought a pack train loaded with much needed provisions for the hungry emigrants. The supplies were first rationed out to be sure no one ate too much and made themselves sick; they had been a long time without much food.[15]

Figure 1 North of Eugene

Scale 1:500,000
1 inch equals approximately 8 miles

The Cornwalls had managed to get to the vicinity of present day Oakland. The man who had traded them three of his oxen for one of their wagons had helped them get there. Here Rev. Cornwall decided to stay for the winter,[16] rather than abandon his library which they had managed to transport this far. Rev. Cornwall's library was one of his most cherished possessions.[17] The spot he selected was a pleasant one with a stream, known today as Cabin Creek.[18]

We will now return to the Long Tom River. The Garrisons had arrived, and this was the first stream they had seen full bank to bank. They were traveling with three wagons in their company. Rev. Garrison saw a large tree and decided if he felled the tree, it might get all the way across. They could use it for a foot bridge. He started cutting down the tree while other emigrants traveling with him went to find trees to cut into canoes.[19]

He felled the tree and it crossed to the other side but broke before getting all the way. He got across to the other side and felled a couple of smaller trees. By joining them together he made a makeshift bridge. They dismantled the wagons and carried everything over this bridge, piece by piece one wheel at a time. Next, they swam their teams across. After getting everything over they reassembled the wagons.[20] The next day they finished setting up the wagons, replenished the contents and went on their way.[21]

Tolbert Carter and the pregnant mother with her two children were on their way to the Long Tom River with their wagon. The oxen got stuck in the muddy road and had to be pulled out. After the oxen were pulled out by force, some were not able to stand up. They had to be left behind. It took several days for Tolbert Carter to reach the Long Tom River crossing.[22]

Virgil Pringle and his family were still in the Eugene area. He spent three days working on a canoe. They had run out of provisions in their company. Pringle decided to go on horseback to the settlements for food.[23]

Thomas Holt had come to Oregon in 1844 and was living north of the Rickreall River.[24] He heard about the plight of the emigrants. His heart went out to them. He got some people together to form a rescue party. Thursday, December 3, Holt left, along with five French-Indians and one Frenchman. They took thirty-four horses packed with flour, bacon and salt pork. Some of the provissions were from Rev. J. B. Baldroach and some were donated by Holt.[25] Other donations came from relief centers in Salem, the French Prairie and a large portion from the Catholic Mission at Saint Paul.[26]

The next day Pringle arrived at the Long Tom "Bath" and started making another canoe.[27] Scott was also at the Long Tom about this time and started making a canoe.[28]

Back on Cabin Creek the Cornwalls started building a cabin. Isreal Stoley and Richard Chrisman[29] used cedar timber they cut nearby.[30] It was about the middle of winter. The tools they used were an axe, crosscut saw, and a froe.[31] In the 1800's this was all that was needed to get the job done.

Rev. Garrison and his son were crossing Mary's River by present day Corvallis. They found it overflowing. Again they took their wagons apart, and ferried them over using what Garrison called, "the smallest canoe I ever saw."[32] About this time Pringle was on his second day along the Long Tom "Bath" working on a canoe.[33] Scott may very well have been working on a canoe with Pringle.[34]

Thomas Holt crossed the north and south forks of the "Luckemute" *[sic]* River. He said it was "swimming and bad crossing." He made about ten miles that day and met Mr. Goff who was also bringing Mrs. Newton in.[35]

The Garrisons got about seven miles north of Mary's River and came to the McFuller's home. Mr. McFuller and his wife let them stay for the night. They ate at a real table and slept inside the McFuller's house, the first house young Garrison had slept in "since leaving old Missouri."[36]

Pringle was working as hard as he could to finish his canoe to get further north for provisions to bring back to his family. His family had run out of food. As a last resort, Mr. Pringle's eldest son Clark shot one of their best working oxen, dressed it and they had it for dinner that night.[37]

Three days after he arrived at the Long Tom, Pringle finished his canoe and crossed the Long Tom River that evening.[38] After crossing he met Orus Brown, Tabitha Brown's son. Brown was coming back with four pack horses and provisions for his family and others.[39] Pringle joined up with Orus Brown and crossed the Long Tom River again.[40]

Carter finally reached the Long Tom River. The stream was about fifty feet

Figure 2 Near the Long Tom River.

wide. There were rafts made for crossing the river. Carter got help from others at the river to join two rafts with a pine log to make a ferry much like the one they made on the North Umpqua River.[41]

It was about three o'clock in the afternoon and they were just about ready to start crossing. The women and children went first. At that moment, the woman that Carter had been traveling with went into labor. Carter was fortunate that he was traveling with others. Mrs. Crowley, Mrs. Linville and Mrs. Vanderpool[42] helped with the delivery and she gave birth that night to a little baby girl.[43]

The next day they got the women and children across. The contents of the wagons went next.[44] The livestock had to be swum over.[45] The wagons, one at a time, were wheeled down onto the ferry made from rafts.[46] There were ropes on both sides of the river that helped guide the wagons across.[47] If they needed to, they pulled a wagon out by attaching long chains to the teams on the other side.[48]

The people helped Carter, the woman and her children across the river. After making sure the woman and child were all right, these emigrants moved on. It snowed about four inches that night.[49]

Holt crossed Mary's River by present day Corvallis. He first sent the packs across, in probably the same small canoe the Garrisons mentioned. They camped on the south bank. They had gone five miles that day. He said they ran into five families with their wagons and one family carrying their belonging.[50] He probably ran into the Garrisons who had already crossed Mary's River and were somewhere north of where Corvallis is now located.[51]

The Garrisons reached the Luckiamute River and again had to take their wagons apart and ferry them across, probably using the same canoe that Holt had used.[52] Garrison's son mentions that their cook left them that day.[53]

Pringle was still heading back to his family with Orus Brown.[54]

Now the Garrisons were crossing the Rickreall River. They said their bedding was all but ruined because it rained nonstop.[55]

Virgil Pringle and Orus Brown arrived at the Pringle family camp. It was night and everyone had already retired, so they let out a "halloo."[56] Everyone immediately recognized their voices and sprang from their tents with joy to greet them.[57]

The last recollection that Lucy Ann Henderson Deady had of being on the trail was spending the night at A. C. Avery's place in present day Corvallis.[58] It was a log cabin, and they slept on the floor. What she remembered most were the sounds all that night of Indians nearby who were mourning for their loved one that had died. Lucy was eleven years old at the time.[59]

When Holt continued south and crossed the Long Tom River, he caught up with Captain Campbell, Mr. Goodman, Mr. Jenkins, and Mr. Harris.[60] They were on their way to the canyon with provisions to help others. They also had twenty-five horses with them. Traveling together, they all met three families packing their belongings and one family that still had a wagon. They had not eaten, and their children were crying for bread, so Holt gave them about fifty pounds of flour.[61]

The Pringles traveled about five miles and ran into some French-Indians with pack horses. Tabitha Brown said, "We hired six of them and pushed ahead."[62]

The Garrisons got to Salt Creek and slept in the house of James Riggs and family, who had come to the territory on the Oregon Trail in 1845.[63]

Carter journeyed to Mary's River. It had stopped snowing further north. He again ferried the river. This is possibly later the location of the old grist mill.[64] One ox got caught in the brush on the other side. Carter jumped into the cold river and tied a rope around the ox's horns. Some of the others helped pull it out.[65] Carter camped that night at the present site of Corvallis. They met A. C. Avery, who had the first dwelling in Corvallis. It was a "pole cabin."[66]

After leaving the Rickreall River, the Garrisons went to the Applegate farm and spent the night there.[67] Although the father, Rev. Garrison, mentioned Applegate; his son only mentioned staying at Salt Creek.[68]

Wednesday, December 9th, Thomas Holt met eight families with eight wagons along the Willamette River. He gave them ten pounds of flour and camped for the night.[69]

Carter left Mary's River and traveled with only one other wagon. This belonged to his thirty-five-year-old cousin. Carter's younger brother was driving the loose stock. They camped in the foothills near the cabin of H. C. Lewis.[70] The Garrisons spent the night with Solomon Eads.[71]

When Holt arrived on Goose Creek on December 10th, he found families camped there waiting for assistance. Their teams had given out. They still had their wagons. At this time more relief parties showed up coming from the settlements. Their names were Mr. Owens, Mr. Patton, Mr. Duskins, Mr. Hutchins, Mr. Howell, and a Mr. Burrows. These men also had twenty-four horses to help bring people in.[72]

The next day the Frenchmen and the three French-Indians, who were traveling with Holt, decided to turn back to the settlements. They were concerned about getting caught by winter storms in the mountains. Holt persuaded the

Figure 3 Luckiamute River

Frenchman, Jean Baptiste Gardepie and one French-Indian named Q. DeLore to stay.[73] He told them, when they returned they could try to raise money to help pay for their efforts.[74] Around noon that same day they found four or five more families around Creswell Butte. These people were unable to go further without assistance. Mr. Goodman, Mr. Hutchins and Mr. Howell stayed to help them.[75]

Meanwhile, Carter made camp near the residence of Thomas Reed. Mr. Reed visited them. When he found they were out of bread and flour, he returned to his cabin and brought some bread to share with them. Words cannot express how grateful they were for his generosity. Between the two wagons there were not only four people but also five children to feed.[76]

After talking a while, Mr. Reed told them of a cabin not far away that was unoccupied. He also gave them directions to the person in charge of the cabin.[77]

That next morning they left in the direction of the cabin and found it. Carter's cousin decided he would go talk to the person in charge, so he took off in the direction he thought they lived. He went about two miles and found the man in charge of the cabin.[78]

It was raining hard that day. Carter's hunger for shelter could not wait. He looked through the cracks in the walls and saw dry ground inside. Without thinking of the consequences he took his axe and cut open a door. Next he built a fire and improvised a bed. By using one corner of the room for two sides, he only needed one leg to support the bed from the floor. After helping the mother and the child to the bed, he turned the teams loose to graze on the lush green grass. All this was done before his cousin returned to tell him it was okay to occupy the cabin. Soon after, they all had permanent homes in the same vicinity.[79] After about a year the woman married a "well-to-do farmer" and later raised a large family.[80]

The Garrisons also reached the end of their trail. They arrived at Uncle Enoch Garrison's place near Salt Creek about a mile southeast of present day Amity.[81] This was the end of their long "heart-rending" journey.[82]

Rev. Garrison said,

The next day which was the 13th day of December 1846 the same day of the same month I was married, I stopped my wagon under a large fir tree, here I took a claim, *[sic]* it was a wilderness country only one family above me on the Yamhill River....[83]

A. H. Garrison, his son, said it was December 12.[84]

Holt was at the foot of the Calapooya Mountains. They saw carcasses of dead animals as they crossed the mountains. There was one family on top of the mountain

Figure 4 Rickreall River

packing without their wagon. Their teams had given out and they had no provisions.[85] The emigrants were walking in the heavy rains and most were not dressed for winter conditions. Their clothes were unavoidably drenched by the rains as they walked. It was hard to build a fire to dry out in the wet weather.[86]

There were two families on the south side of the mountain also without food. Mr. Campbell let them all have some flour. They camped on a small creek in the Umpqua Valley. They made about twelve miles that day.[87]

Monday, December 14th, Thomas Holt made it to the North Fork of Elk River, known today as Cabin Creek, and camped on the north side. He had made fifteen miles that day. Holt met five families who were all out of provisions.[88] He gave them fifty pounds of flour.[89]

The next day Holt crossed the north fork of Elk River. He traveled to the south fork of Elk Creek, now known as

Calapooya Creek.[90] Mr. Campbell met his family here. The Campbell family decided to leave nearly all of their possessions with the Cornwalls. The Campbells started back toward the settlements.[91]

Mr. Harris and Mr. Jenkins stopped here to help Mr. Cornwall and Mr. Dunbar. Mr. Campbell also helped move the Dunbar family but there were not enough horses to move the Cornwalls.[92]

Mr. Burrows packed Mr. Loveland's family in.[93] Q. Delore, the French-Indian traveling with Holt, killed a deer for the families to eat.[94]

Thursday, December 17th, Mrs. Henderson, her new baby girl and her children, arrived at Broadmead on horseback with her brother.[95] They were just in time to enjoy Christmas. They stayed with another relative who had come to Oregon the year before.[96]

Still traveling south, Thomas Holt met five more families of emigrants stranded on Roberts Creek west of the Umpqua Canyon. They were the James Townsend family, the John Baker family, the David Butterfield family with the widow Butterfield, and the Crump family.[97] These families had all traveled with the Thorntons earlier. They were probably all late getting through the canyon.[98]

Holt now felt that he had found everyone. It was December 18th. He put everyone to work making pack saddles so they could start heading north the next day.[99] Since there were other rescuers with him, he decided to divide them up with the emigrants. These families had been out of bread, their teams had given out, and they were planning to take their empty wagons as far as the Umpqua River.[100] They got as far as Rock Creek and camped. Rock Creek is probably known today as Parrott Creek south of Roseburg.[101] They made about nine miles that day.[102]

The next day they were missing three more horses and a mule belonging to Mr. Owens, Mr. Patton, and Mr. Duskins. They chased after them and managed to get the mule back from an Indian.[103] They camped on the Spring branch south of Winchester and made about six miles that day.[104]

Monday, December 21st, Holt and his party arrived at the North Umpqua River. They probably saw the same Indians here who helped the others cross the river. By now the Indians were just tired of helping, no matter what they paid them. They said the river could not be forded. After considerable negotiations, Mr. Q. Delore traded his rifle for the use of the canoes.[105] Holt and his party spent the day crossing the river, got about nine miles and camped on the north bank.[106]

Thursday, December 24th, Holt and his group journeyed to Calapooya Creek and spent all day crossing. They did not travel that day because it took so much time to cross with the wagons. Two oxen drowned in the process. They camped that night on the north bank of the Calapooya Creek.[107] It was Christmas Eve.

Mr. Henderson arrived at Broadmend with the wagons on December 25th, Christmas Day, to be rejoined with his family.[108]

Tabitha Brown recalled, "On Christmas Day, at 2 P. M. I entered the house of a Methodist minister, the first house I had set my feet in for nine months."[109]

Thomas Holt and the Baker family spent their Christmas just south of the Cornwall's encampment. It had snowed all night, and there was a foot of snow on the ground the next morning. They decided not to travel that day.[110]

Saturday, December 26, Holt and his group traveled one mile and arrived with the Bakers to make a second visit to the Cornwall encampment. This was on the north fork of Elk River, now known as Cabin Creek.[111]

Seeing their famished situation, Holt persuaded Mr. Baker to let Mr. Kennedy and Mr. Hall have three oxen he had been using to pull his wagon. Mr. Baker agreed, and Mr. Kennedy's family got one ox, Mr. Hall's family got one, and Mr. Croizen's family got one. There must have been four oxen because after dividing those three; the Cornwalls got three quarters of an ox. Holt traded fifty pounds of beef for an axe to two men encamped there, and gave the axe to Mr. Townsend. It was such cold weather, and he had no axe to cut firewood. Mr. Baker and Mr. Townsend both got eighty pounds of beef. Mr. Owens and Mr. Duskin went on ahead that day and the rest stayed.[112]

Sunday, December 27th, was the first clear day that month. Holt and others stayed at the Cornwalls.[113] They probably helped on the Cornwalls' cabin.

Monday, December 28, Holt and the others left the Cornwalls and traveled toward the settlements.[114] The Cornwalls had their cabin finished after Christmas. Narcissa Cornwall was ten years old at the time.

> Our cabin was finished after Christmas and we moved in. It was real warm and we found it quite a change from camping out in the rain and snow. There was a large fireplace and a place for our beds, made after the style of the camp meeting scaffold running all the way across the end of the cabin. Under this we stored our trunks and things left by the immigrants.[115]

This area where the Cornwalls were, was a common area for the various Indian tribes. The Calapooia[116] (or Calapuya)[117] Indians lived north of Cornwalls cabin,[118] and the Upper Umpqua tribes[119] lived south of their cabin.[120] The Calapooia Indians must have used this area for wintering,

although it was mainly the Umpqua Valley. "We learned the country where we were was called the Umpqua Valley, but there were about as many Calapooya Indians as there were Umpqua living there, but I suppose the country really belonged to the Umpqua Indians."[121] (Narcissa Cornwall, 1926)

Holt spent from December 29th to January 1st traveling ten miles to the Calapooya Mountains. They had been out of bread for some time. Holt had hidden some flour in the Calapooya Mountains on his way south. They finally reached the spot where he had stored it for safe keeping and found it still there. Their mouths watered at the thought of having some bread so they made it to the foot of the mountain where they made camp and had a feast.[122] This was about where Cottage Grove is today. They had gone about ten miles.[123] It was New Year's Day, January 1st, 1847.

Friday, January 8th, there was a freeze. This was hard on everyone still traveling. The wet clothes they were wearing froze as they walked. This caused more suffering and hardship to those emigrant still on foot.[124] Albert L. Alderman recalled the early winter month of 1847. "That winter the brother, M. R. Alderman, also met with a great misfortune,- having his feet so frozen while on an express tour for the Hudson's Bay Company as to necessitate the amputation of one of them."[125]

Thursday, January 21st, Holt arrived at home after fifty days on the road.[126] Thursday, March 18th, The Oregon Spectator printed a plea for people to help the relief parties:

> A subscription has been opened at this office for the relief of Thomas Holt and others, who went to the succor of the immigrants by the southern route, and thereby incurred indebtedness which they cannot sustain. Call and subscribe.[127] (*Oregon Spectator*, March 18, 1847)

The Cornwalls survived very well in their little cabin. Rev. Cornwall's ribs healed. Mrs. Cornwall eventually regained her strength from being sick. Narcissa and Joseph Cornwall's cousin Stoley constantly hunted for deer. He managed to get more than enough to keep them fed.[128]

By April the Cornwalls were getting anxious to leave. They started getting things together to go forward to the settlements. They decided to send Daniel Culver. The Cornwalls packed him some deer meat, and he started toward the settlements in the Willamette Valley to bring help to the Cornwalls.[129] He had not gone far when he ran into Joseph Hess, Clark Rogers and Joshua Nelson, who were coming to the rescue.[130]

Friday, April 9th, 1847, at 10 a.m. help arrived at the Cornwalls cabin. It was Mr. Culver with Hess, Rogers, and Nelson. They had brought two yokes of oxen,[131] flour,[132] sugar,[133] coffee, salt,[134] and bacon.[135] By noon, with the help of her daughters, Mrs. Cornwall had put an "old time dinner" on the table.[136]

The next morning they prepared to leave. The Indian Chief of the nearby Umpqua Tribe came to bid them farewell. The Chief was called "Captain" by the Indians. He came with his "subchief", who went by the name of "Joe."[137]

More of the emigrants who had left things with the Cornwalls also arrived.[138] Narcissa Cornwall, who was ten years old at the time, later recalled, "Our preparations for our journey were short, and we bade adieu to our neighbors, some of them looking sorrowful with tears in their eyes when they saw us drive away."[139] Their neighbors were the Indians.

Captain and Joe were among the Indians who stayed to see them leave. Joseph Cornwall, Jr., who was fourteen at the time, recalled, "Father gave his cabin to Capitan, [sic] and I always remember him as a noble Indian, a good friend, honest and reliable."[140]

THE END

1. Thornton, *Or. and Ca. in 1848*, Vol. 1, p. 239. [I'm not sure whether this is the Forest Grove of today or the Forest Grove he said he named and decided to live at or both.]

2.a) Morgan, *Overland in 1846*, Vol. 1, p. 188.
b) Carter, *Pioneer Days*, p. 86.

3. Morgan, *Overland in 1846*, Vol. 1, p. 187, 397.

4. Carter, *Pioneer Days*, p. 86.

5. Ibid.

6. Morgan, *Overland in 1846*, Vol. 1, p. 188.

7. Scott, *Independence*, p. 166.

8. Carter, *Pioneer Days*, p. 87.

9. Ibid., p. 86.

10. Lockley, *Pioneer Women*, p. 89. [The Long Tom River was a wider river to cross; Although, Mary's river could have risen higher by the time they arrived.]

11. Garrison, *Life and Labours*, OHS Mss #1009, p. 34.

12. Garrison, "Reminiscences," p. 29.

13. Crews, *Smith Family*, OHS Mss #1188, p. 30. ["Nooned" is an old expression for stopping for a rest around noon.]

14.a) Crews, *Smith Family*, OHS Mss #1188, p. 30.
b) Meacham, *Applegate Trail*, p. 21.

15.a) Crews, *Smith Family*, OHS Mss #1188, p. 30.
b) Meacham, *Applegate Trail*, p. 22.

16. Cornwall, *Capt. Dunbar's Co. 1846*, OHS Mss #1509, p. 37.

17. Ibid., p. 33.

18.a) Helfrich, "Applegate Trail II," (1976), Vol. 14, p. 64.
b) Morgan, *Overland in 1846*, Vol. 1, p. 398.

19.a) Garrison, *Life and Labours*, OHS Mss #1009, p. 44.
b) Garrison, "Reminiscences," p. 29.

20. Ibid.

21. Garrison, "Reminiscences," p. 30.

22. Carter, *Pioneer Days*, p. 87.

23.a) Morgan, *Overland in 1846*, Vol. 1, p. 188.
b) Brown, "Brimfield Heroine," p. 203.

24. Morgan, *Overland in 1846*, Vol. 1, pp. 190, 191.

25. Ibid., p. 191.

26. Moxley, OHS Mss #855, p. 69.

27. Morgan, *Overland in 1846*, Vol. 1, p. 188.

28. Scott, *Independence*, p. 166.

29.a) Scott, *Independence*, p. 35.
b) Moxley, OHS Mss #855, p. 75.

30. Cornwall, *Capt. Dunbar's Co. 1846*, OHS Mss #1509, p. 34.

31. Ibid.

32. Garrison, *Life and Labours*, OHS Mss #1009, p. 34.

33. Morgan, *Overland in 1846*, Vol. 1, p. 188.

34. Scott, *Independence*, p. 165.

35. Morgan, *Overland in 1846*, Vol. 1, p. 191.

36. Garrison, "Reminiscences," p. 30.

37. Brown, "Brimfield Heroine," p. 203.

38. Morgan, *Overland in 1846*, Vol. 1, p. 188.

39.a) Brown, "Brimfield Heroine," p. 203.
b) Morgan, *Overland in 1846*, Vol. 1, p. 188.

40. Helfrich, "Applegate Trail II," (1976), Vol. 14, p. 79.

41. Carter, *Pioneer Days*, p. 87.

42. Moxley, OHS Mss #855, p. 71.

43. Carter, *Pioneer Days*, p. 87. [According to W. A. Moxley's "Southern Route To Oregon," the baby girl was named Olivia. (Moxley, OHS Mss #855, p. 72.)]

44. Ibid.

45. Rounds, *Prairie Schooners*, p. 57.

46. Carter, *Pioneer Days*, p. 87.

47. Rounds, *Prairie Schooners*, p. 58.

48. Ibid., p. 59.

49. Carter, *Pioneer Days*, p. 87.

50. Morgan, *Overland in 1846*, Vol. 1, p. 192.

51. Garrison, "Reminiscences," p. 30.

52. Garrison, *Life and Labours*, OHS Mss #1009, p. 45.

53. Ibid., pp. 44, 45.

54. Morgan, *Overland in 1846*, Vol. 1, p. 188.

55. Garrison, *Life and Labours*, OHS Mss #1009, p. 45. [It was about December 8, 9th, or 10th.]

56. Brown, "Brimfield Heroine," p. 203.

57. Ibid.

58.a) Lockley, *Pioneer Women*, p. 89.
b) Carter, *Pioneer Days*, p. 89.

59. Lockley, *Pioneer Women*, p. 89.

60. Morgan, *Overland in 1846*, Vol. 1, pp. 192, 398. ["Mr. Harris" was probably Moses "Black" Harris.]

61. Ibid., p. 192.

62. Brown, "Brimfield Heroine," p. 203.

63. Garrison, "Reminiscences," p. 30.

64.a) Carter, *Pioneer Days*, p. 88.
b) Morgan, *Overland in 1846*, Vol. 1, p. 397.

65. Carter, *Pioneer Days*, p. 88.

66. Carter, *Pioneer Days*, p. 89. [Corvallis means "heart of the valley."]

67. Garrison, *Life and Labours*, OHS Mss #1009, p. 45.

68. Garrison, "Reminiscences," p. 30.

69.a) Morgan, *Overland in 1846*, Vol. 1, p. 192.
b) Meacham, *Applegate Trail*, p. 23.

70. Carter, *Pioneer Days*, p. 89.

71.a) Garrison, "Reminiscences," p. 30.
b) Garrison, *Life and Labours*, OHS Mss #1009, p. 45.

72. Morgan, *Overland in 1846*, Vol. 1, pp. 192, 193. [Goose Creek is in present day Eugene.]

73. Ibid., pp. 193, 398.

74. Ibid., p. 193.

75. Ibid., pp. 193, 398.

76. Carter, *Pioneer Days*, p. 89.

77. Ibid.

78. Ibid.

79. Ibid., p. 90.

80. Ibid., p. 88.

81. Garrison, "Reminiscences," p. 30, 31.

82. Garrison, *Life and Labours*, OHS Mss #1009, p. 37.

83. Ibid., p. 45.

84. Garrison, "Reminiscences," p. 37.

85. Morgan, *Overland in 1846*, Vol. 1, p. 193.

86. Moxley, OHS Mss #855, p. 77.

87. Morgan, *Overland in 1846*, Vol. 1, p. 193.

88. Morgan, *Overland in 1846*, Vol. 1, pp. 194, 398. [Mr. Ezekiel Kennedy, Mr. R. B. Hall, Mr. Henry Croizen (or Croysnt) (Ibid., p. 398.) and Mr. Lovlin (a) Ibid., p. 398.; b)Bancroft, *Works*, Vol. XXIX, p. 568.; c)Thornton, *Or. and Ca. in 1848*, Vol. 1, p. 188.) (or Lovelen) (Morgan, *Overland in 1846*, Vol. 1, p. 194.)]

89. Ibid., p. 195.

90. Ibid., pp. 194, 398.

91. Ibid., p. 194.

92. Ibid.

93. Ibid., p. 196.

94. Meacham, *Applegate Trail*, p. 23.

95. Lockley, *Pioneer Women*, p. 89.

96. Ibid., p. 89.

97. Morgan, *Overland in 1846*, Vol. 1, p. 398.

98. Thornton, *Or. and Ca. in 1848*, Vol. 1, pp. 197, 198.

99. Morgan, *Overland in 1846*, Vol. 1, p. 194.

100. Ibid., p. 195.

101. Ibid., p. 398.

102. Ibid., p. 195.

103. Ibid.

104. Ibid., p. 399.

105. Ibid., pp. 195, 399.

106. Ibid., p. 195. [It is sort of hard to believe, but according to Holt, they kept the wagons with them crossing the North Umpqua River. They did not leave the wagons until they reached Calapooya Creek. This creek took all day to cross.]

107. Ibid. [They must have felt their wagons would be safer being closer to the Cornwalls.]

108. Lockley, *Pioneer Women*, p. 89.

109. Brown, "Brimfield Heroine," p. 203.

110. Morgan, *Overland in 1846*, Vol. 1, p. 195.

111. Morgan, *Overland in 1846*, Vol. 1, p. 195. [Cabin Creek was later named after the Cornwall's cabin. (Helfrich, "Applegate Trail II," (1976), Vol. 14, p. 66.)]

112. Ibid., p. 196.

113. Ibid.

114. Ibid.

115. Cornwall, *Capt. Dunbar's Co. 1846*, OHS Mss #1509, p. 37.

116. *Indians of the Rogue Valley*, p. 7.

117. Dicken, *Making of Oregon*, p. 42.

118. Schlesser, *Fort Umpqua*, p. 9.

119.a) Zucker, *Oregon Indians*, p. 9.
b) *Indians of the Rogue Valley*, p. 4.
c) Dicken, *Making of Oregon*, p. 42.

120. Schlesser, *Fort Umpqua*, p. 8.

121. Cornwall, *Capt. Dunbar's Co. 1846*, OHS Mss #1509, p. 38.

122. Morgan, *Overland in 1846*, Vol. 1, p. 196.

123. Ibid., pp. 399, 196.

124. Moxley, OHS Mss #855, p. 77.

125. *Hist. of the Pac. N. W.*, Vol. II, p. 191. [Albert Alderman was an emigrant from the Applegate Trail of 1846. (*Hist. of the Pac. N. W.*, Vol. II, p. 191.)]

126. Morgan, *Overland in 1846*, Vol. 1, p. 197.

127. Ibid., p. 399.

128. Cornwall, *Capt. Dunbar's Co. 1846*, OHS Mss #1509, p. 33.

129. Ibid., p. 39.

130. Ibid., p. 34.

131. Cornwall, *Capt. Dunbar's Co. 1846*, OHS Mss #1509, p. 34.

132. Ibid., pp. 40, 34.

133. Ibid., p. 34.

134. Ibid., pp. 40, 34.

135. Ibid., p. 34.

136. Ibid.

137. Ibid.

138. Ibid., p. 40.

139. Ibid.

140. Ibid., p. 34.

APPENDIX OF NAMES

OTHER TRAIL NAMES
FOR THE ORIGINAL SOUTHERN EMIGRANT ROUTE TO OREGON

This is a list of additional names that have been given to the Applegate Trail through the years. This list includes names mentioned in this book as well as names found while doing the research for the book. There are at least as many historians and trail enthusiasts who would prefer the trail be called "the Southern Route" as there are those who started naming it "the Applegate Trail." The problem with this favored historic name is it only works if you are in Oregon. If you look at this name outside of Oregon, the name is too generic. A name I came up with that might make some people happy is "the Applegate Scott Trail."

"the Applegate Trail"[1]
"Southern Immigrant Road"[2]
"The 'Southern' Route"[3]
"Scott's and Applegate's Old South Road"[4]
"South Immigrant Road"[5]
"The Applegate Trail: 1846-1883 The Southern Route"[6]
"the Applegate Cut-off"[7]
"the Applegate route"[8]
"cut-off of Applegate's"[9]
"Applegate Road"[10]
"The Southern Rout to Oregon"[11]
"The Southern Rout from the United States to Oregon"[12]
"Applegate Trail"[13]

"Applegate Cut-off"[14]
"Applegate Route"[15]
"Applegate Road"[16]
"the southern route"[17]
"Scout-Applegate Trail"[18]
"California-Oregon Trail"[19]
"The old '46 wagon road"[20]
"Southern Pass"[21]
"The Southern Route Into Oregon"[22]
"The Applegate Route"[23]
"The new Southern Road"[24]
"the Applegate Trail, Cut-off, Route, Road"[25]
"a new route"[26]
"the southern route to Oregon"[27]

EXPLORING PARTY

This was second expedition to explore an alternate route to Oregon from the east. They were the first succesful exploring party to find a southern route from the Willamette Valley to Fort Hall. These men arrived in time to find emigrants who were willing to attempt this new proposed southern trail to Oregon.

Levi Scott
Jesse Applegate
Moses Harris
David Goff
Robert Smith
William Sportsman
William G. Parker
John M. Scott

Benjamin F. Burch[28]
John Owens[29]
Lindsay Applegate[30]
John Jones[31]
Samuel H. Goodhue[32]
Henry Bogus[33] (or Boygus)[34]
Bennett Osborne[35] (Osborn[36] or Osburn)[37]

THE VOLUNTEER ROAD PARTY

This is a list of those who went foreword for the purpose of blazing a trail ahead of the emigrants.[38] The road working party began with all but three of the original exploring party[39] as well as some older sons of the emigrants who were traveling on this first wagon train.[40]

Jesse Applegate
Moses Harris
Robert Smith
William Sportsman
William G. Parker
John M. Scott
Benjamin F. Burch[41]
John Owens[42]
Lindsay Applegate[43]
John Jones[44]
Samuel H. Goodhue[45]
Henry Bogus[46] (or Boygus)[47]
Bennett Osborne[48] (Osborn[49] or Osburn)[50]

William Scott[51]

Thomas Powers
Joseph Burke
Powell
Perrin
Alfred Stewart
Shaw
Carnahan[52]

Charles Putnam
William Kirquendall[53]

Bannock Indian[54]

Sevy[55]

LIST OF EMIGRANTS

This is a list of the emigrants who were on the first wagon train to take the original southern route to Oregon known later as the Applegate Trail. It includes Levi Scott and David Goff who stayed behind from the exploring party to help guide the emigrants. Those from the road working party who later fell back and joined the wagon train are also included. The list may not be complete and includes only those young people who were acting the role of an Adult. I did not have enough information to include most of the children, so I chose not to include the few I had.

Albright, Mr.[56]
Alderman, Albert L.[57]
Baker, Mr. and Mrs. John[58]
Barnard, Mr.[59]
Beaucham, Mrs.[60]
Beaucham, Ashley[61]
Boone, Alphonso[62]
Boone, Jesse[63]
Bosworth, J. H.[64]
Bounds, Mr. and Mrs.* John D.[65]
Bridges, Mr. and Mrs. J. H.*[66]
Brisbane, Mr.*[67]
Brown, Alvin C.[68]
Brown, Captain John[69]
Brown, Mrs. Tabitha[70]
Buchanan, John A.[71]
Buckingham, Herman[72]
Burns Senior, Mr.* and Mrs. Sutton[73]
Burns, Mr. and Mrs. William[74]
Butterfield, Mr. and Mrs. David[75]
Butterfield, Mrs., (widow)[76]
Byrd, Lorenzo[77]
Calahan, Mr.[78]

Caldwell, Richard S.[79]
Campbell, Mr. and Mrs.* James
    and Margaret[80]
Carter, Tolbert[81]
Challinor, Rachel[82]
Clarke[83]
Collins, Mr. and Mrs. Smith[84]
Colwell, Mrs., (widow)[85]
Cornwall, Rev. & Mrs. J. A.[86]
Chrisman, Richard[87]
Croizen, Mr. and Mrs. Henry[88]
    (Croysnt,[89] Croizers,[90]
    Croisan[91] or Croysant)[92]
Crowley, Mr.* and Mrs. Calvin[93]
Crowley, Martha Leland*[94]
Crowley, Mr.* and Mrs. Thomas[95]
Crump, Mr. and Mrs. James[96]
Curtendall, James[97]
Curtendall, Mr. (son)[98]
Culver, Daniel[99]
Davis, Dr. Samuel[100]
Davidson, Andrew[101]
Dodd[102]

Dunba, Judge O. R.[103]
Dunbar, Mr. and Mrs. Rice[104]
Dunlava, Mr. and Mrs.[105]
Duskin, Mr.[106]
Faulkner, Absalon[107]
Foster, Mrs. E. B.[108]
Garrison, Mr. and Mrs. Rev. Abraham
    Elison and Margaret[109]
Garrison, Abraham Henry[110]
Gates, Mr.[111]
Gilliam, Robert[112]
Goff, David[113]
Goode, Daniel[114]
Graves, Charles B.[115]
Guthrie, David[116]
Hall, John[117]
Hall, Mr. and Mrs. Reason B.[118]
Harley, Ira[119]
Helms, Chat[120]
Henderson, Lucy Ann[121]
Henderson, Mr. and Mrs. Robert
    and Ronda[122]
Hoover, Martin*[123]

Hudson, Mr.[124]
Humphrey, Mr.[125]
Jacobs, Mr.[126]
Jenkins, Mr.[127]
Kelly, Mr.[128]
Kennedy, Mr. and Mrs. Ezekiel[129]
Kiethly, William[130]
Kirquendall, William[131]
Lancefield, Robert A.[132]
Lebo, Mr. and Mrs. Isaac[133] (or
    Leabo)[134]
Lee, Mr. and Mrs. Wilson[135]
Linville, Mr. and Mrs. Harrison[136]
    (or Loveland)[137]
Lippincott, Mr.[138] (or Lippincot)[139]
Long, Mr. and Mrs. John[140]
Lovelady, Thomas J.[141]
Lovlin, Mr. and Mrs.[142] (Lovelady[143]
    or Lovelen)[144]
Miller, Richard[145]
Morin, Josiah[146]
Morin, Labin[147]
Newton, Mr.* and Mrs. John[148]
Newton, Thomas[149]
Nye, Mr.[150]
Owens, Mrs.[151]
Parker, W. G.[152]
Pratcer, Theodore[153]
Patton, Mr.[154]
Perkins, Mr. and Mrs.[155]
Poole[156] (or Pool)[157]
Powers, Thomas[158]
Pringle, Mr. and Mrs. Virgle K. and
Pherne[159]
Pringle, Octavius[160]
Pringle, William[161]
Putnam, Charles[162]

Robey, Rubert*[163]
Robinson, James[164]
Robinson, John[165]
Ruth, Samuel[166]
Sallee, Mr.[167]
Savage, Mr. and Mrs. Morgan[168]
Scales[169]
Scott, Levi[170]
Sevy, Mr.[171]
Shaw, Mr.[172]
Shelbysingee, Mr.[173] (or Shelby)[174]
Shelton, Mr.[175]
Smith, G. W.[176]
Smith, Mr. and Mrs. Henry, [177]
Smith, James S.[178]
Smith, William M.[179]
Social, Miss Adeline[180]
Stokes, William[181]
Stoley, Israil[182]
Tanner, David*[183]
Thornton, Mr. and Mrs. J. Quinn
    and Nancy[184]
Toole, Dan[185] (or Tool)[186]
Townsend, Mr. and Mrs. David[187]
Townsend, Mr. and Mrs. James[188]
Turnedge, Harrison[189] (or
Turnidge)[190]
Turnedge, Joseph[191] (or Turnidge)[192]
Underwood[193]
Van Bibber, Mr. and Mrs.[194]
    (or Van Biber)[195]
Vanderpool, Larkin[196]
Vanderpool, Mr. and Mrs. Medders
    and Margaret[197]
Vanderpool, Miles[198]
Ware, J. M.[199]
Whately, Mr.[200]

White, R.[201]
Wood, Dr.[202]
Wood, John D.[203] (or Woods)[204]
Zumwalt, Mrs.[205]

*Indicates those
who died on the trail.

RELIEF PARTIES

This is a list of the people who came with provisions, supplies fresh oxen and pack animals to rescue the emigrants from starvation and cold weather setting in. This includes those from the settlements, the road building party, and emigrants from the wagon train who went forward to the settlements and returned with relief.

Jack Jones[206]
Tom Smith[207]
Mr Brown
Mr. Allen
John Jones[208]

Joseph Garrison[209]

Octavius Pringle[210]
Virgil Pringle
Orus Brown and three other men
      (including Moses "Black" Harris)[211]
Mr. Kirquendall
Asa Williams[212]

Uncle of Lucy Ann Henderson
Mr. Holman[213]

Mr. Durbin[214]

Enoch Garrison[215]

Man in Calapooya Mountains with a wagon of
      provisions he was selling[216]

Two young men from the Smith company[217]
Thomas Holt[218]
Jean Baptiste Gardepie[219]
Q. Delore[220]
Two French Indians[221]

Captain Campbell
Mr. Goodman
Mr. Jenkins
Mr. Moses "Black" Harris[222]

Mr. Owens[223]
Mr. Patten[224]
Mr. Duskins[225]
Mr. Hutchins[226]
Mr. Howell[227]
Mr. Burrows[228]

Mr. Campbell[229]

Mr. Duskins[230]

Daniel Culver[231]
Joseph Hess
Clark Rogers
Joshua Nelson[232]

1.a) Brown, ed., *Man*, p. 10.
b) Frederica Coons, *The Trail to Oregon*, (Portland, OR: Binfords & Mort, 1954), p. 127.

2.a) Corning, *History*, p. 318.
b) Willis B. Merriam, "Notes on Historical Geography of Rogue River Valley," *Oregon Historical Quarterly*, Vol. 42, No. 4 (Portland, OR: Oregon Historical Society, December, 1941), p. 318.

3. Brown, "Brimfield Heroine," p. 336.

4. Burchard, "South Road," p. 4.

5. Merriam, "Rogue River Valley," p. 318.

6. *The Trail Marker*, Vol. 5, No. 1, p. 1.

7.a) Steves, *Book of Remembrance*, pp. 78, 88.
b) Thornton, *Or. and Ca. in 1848*, Vol. 1, pp. 170, 173.

8.a) Steves, *Book of Remembrance*, p. 88.
b) Eva Emery Dye, *The Soul of America: An Oregon Iliad* (New York, NY: The Press of the Pioneers, Inc., 1934), p. 162.

9. Thornton, *Or. and Ca. in 1848*, Vol. 1, p. 172.

10. Morgan, *Overland in 1846*, Vol. 1, p. 190.

11. Stone, "Southern Route," p. 148.

12. Ibid.

13. Meacham, *Applegate Trail*, p. 24.

14. Ibid.

15. Ibid.

16.a) Ibid.
b) Cornwall, *Capt. Dunbar's Co. 1846*, OHS Mss #1509, p. 30.

17. Stone, "Southern Route," p. 147.

18. Corning, *History*, p. 218.

19. Ibid., p. 40.

20. "Hon. Lindsay Applegate." *Ashland (Oregon) Daily Tidings*, December 12, 1892, p. 3.

21. Scott, *Independence*, p. 167.

22. Stone, "Southern Route," p. 1.

23. Cornwall, *Capt. Dunbar's Co. 1846*, OHS Mss #1509, p. 1.

24. Morgan, *Overland in 1846*, Vol. 1, p. 189.

25. Meacham, *Applegate Trail*, p. 24.

26. Ghent, *Road*, p. 86.

27. Stone, "Southern Route," p. 145.

28.a) Applegate, "Old Emigrant Road," pp. 14, 43.
b) Applegate, "Applegate Trail," pp. 5, 18.
c) Morgan, *Overland in 1846*, Vol. 1, p. 638.
d) Scott, *Independence*, p. 104.
e) *Hist. of the Pac. N. W.*, Vol. I, p. 371.
f) Bancroft, *Works*, Vol. XXIX, p. 544.
g) Sargent, "Sketch of the Rogue River Valley," p. 2.
h) Burchard, "South Road," p. 406.
i) Stone, "Southern Route," p. 138.

29.a) Applegate, "Old Emigrant Road," pp. 14, 43.
b) Applegate, "Applegate Trail," pp. 5, 18.
c) Scott, *Independence*, p. 104.
d) *Hist. of the Pac. N. W.*, Vol. I, p. 371.
e) Bancroft, *Works*, Vol. XXIX, p. 544.
f) Sargent, "Sketch of the Rogue River Valley," p. 2.
g) Burchard, "South Road," p. 406.
h) Stone, "Southern Route," p. 138.

30.a) Applegate, "Old Emigrant Road," pp. 14, 43.
b) Applegate, "Applegate Trail," pp. 5, 18.
c) Morgan, *Overland in 1846*, Vol. 1, p. 638.
d) Scott, *Independence*, p. 104.
e) *Hist. of the Pac. N. W.*, Vol. I, p. 371.
f) Bancroft, *Works*, Vol. XXIX, p. 544.
g) Burchard, "South Road," p. 406.
h) Stone, "Southern Route," p. 138.

31.a) Applegate, "Old Emigrant Road," pp. 14, 43.
b) Applegate, "Applegate Trail," pp. 5, 18.
c) Morgan, *Overland in 1846*, Vol. 1, p. 638.
d) *Hist. of the Pac. N. W.*, Vol. I, p. 371.
e) Bancroft, *Works*, Vol. XXIX, p. 544.
f) Sargent, "Sketch of the Rogue River Valley," p. 2.
g) Burchard, "South Road," p. 406.
h) Stone, "Southern Route," p. 138.

32.a) Applegate, "Old Emigrant Road," p. 14.
b) Applegate, "Applegate Trail," p. 5.
c) Morgan, *Overland in 1846*, Vol. 1, p. 638.
d) Scott, *Independence*, p. 104.
e) *Hist. of the Pac. N. W.*, Vol. I, p. 371.
f) Bancroft, *Works*, Vol. XXIX, p. 544.
g) Sargent, "Sketch of the Rogue River Valley," p. 2.
h) Burchard, "South Road," p. 406.
i) Stone, "Southern Route," p. 138.

33.a) Scott, *Independence*, p. 104.
b) *Hist. of the Pac. N. W.*, Vol. I, p. 371.
c) Bancroft, *Works*, Vol. XXIX, p. 544.
d) Moxley, OHS Mss #855, p. 1.

34.a) Sargent, "Sketch of the Rogue River Valley," p. 2.
b) Applegate, "Old Emigrant Road," p. 43.

35.a) Applegate, "Applegate Trail," p. 5.
b) Morgan, *Overland in 1846*, Vol. 1, p. 638.
c) *Hist. of the Pac. N. W.*, Vol. I, p. 371.
d) Bancroft, *Works*, Vol. XXIX, p. 544.
e) Moxley, OHS Mss #855, p. 1.

36. Stone, "Southern Route," p. 138.

37. Burchard, "South Road," p. 406.

38.a) Meacham, *Applegate Trail*, p. 10.
b) Bancroft, *Works*, Vol. XXIX, p. 558.

39. Meacham, *Applegate Trail*, p. 10.

40. Thornton, *Or. and Ca. in 1848*, Vol. 1, p. 165.

41.a) Applegate, "Old Emigrant Road," pp. 14, 43.
b) Applegate, "Applegate Trail," pp. 5, 18.
c) Morgan, *Overland in 1846*, Vol. 1, p. 638.
d) Scott, *Independence*, p. 104.
e) *Hist. of the Pac. N. W.*, Vol. I, p. 371.
f) Bancroft, *Works*, Vol. XXIX, p. 544.
g) Sargent, "Sketch of the Rogue River Valley," p. 2.
h) Burchard, "South Road," p. 406.
i) Stone, "Southern Route," p. 138.

42.a) Applegate, "Old Emigrant Road," pp. 14, 43.
b) Applegate, "Applegate Trail," pp. 5, 18.
c) Scott, *Independence*, p. 104.
d) *Hist. of the Pac. N. W.*, Vol. I, p. 371.
e) Bancroft, *Works*, Vol. XXIX, p. 544.
f) Sargent, "Sketch of the Rogue River Valley," p. 2.
g) Burchard, "South Road," p. 406.
h) Stone, "Southern Route," p. 138.

43.a) Applegate, "Old Emigrant Road," pp. 14, 43.
b) Applegate, "Applegate Trail," pp. 5, 18.
c) Morgan, *Overland in 1846*, Vol. 1, p. 638.
d) Scott, *Independence*, p. 104.
e) *Hist. of the Pac. N. W.*, Vol. I, p. 371.
f) Bancroft, *Works*, Vol. XXIX, p. 544.
g) Burchard, "South Road," p. 406.
h) Stone, "Southern Route," p. 138.

44.a) Applegate, "Old Emigrant Road," pp. 14, 43.
b) Applegate, "Applegate Trail," pp. 5, 18.
c) Morgan, *Overland in 1846*, Vol. 1, p. 638.
d) *Hist. of the Pac. N. W.*, Vol. I, p. 371.
e) Bancroft, *Works*, Vol. XXIX, p. 544.
f) Sargent, "Sketch of the Rogue River Valley," p. 2.
g) Burchard, "South Road," p. 406.
h) Stone, "Southern Route," p. 138.

45.a) Applegate, "Old Emigrant Road," p. 14.
b) Applegate, "Applegate Trail," p. 5.
c) Morgan, *Overland in 1846*, Vol. 1, p. 638.
d) Scott, *Independence*, p. 104.
e) *Hist. of the Pac. N. W.*, Vol. I, p. 371.
f) Bancroft, *Works*, Vol. XXIX, p. 544.
g) Sargent, "Sketch of the Rogue River Valley," p. 2.
h) Burchard, "South Road," p. 406.
i) Stone, "Southern Route," p. 138.

46.a) Scott, *Independence*, p. 104.
b) *Hist. of the Pac. N. W.*, Vol. I, p. 371.
c) Bancroft, *Works*, Vol. XXIX, p. 544.
d) Moxley, OHS Mss #855, p. 1.

47.a) Sargent, "Sketch of the Rogue River Valley," p. 2.
b) Applegate, "Old Emigrant Road," p. 43.

48.a) Applegate, "Applegate Trail," p. 5.
b) Morgan, *Overland in 1846*, Vol. 1, p. 638.
c) *Hist. of the Pac. N. W.*, Vol. I, p. 371.
d) Bancroft, *Works*, Vol. XXIX, p. 544.
e) Moxley, OHS Mss #855, p. 1.

49. Stone, "Southern Route," p. 138.

50. Burchard, "South Road," p. 406.

51. Scott, *Independence*, p. 131.

52.a) Applegate, "Old Emigrant Road," p. 39.
b) Helfrich, "Applegate Trail," (1971), Vol. 9, p. 7.

53. Thornton, *Or. and Ca. in 1848*, Vol. 1, p. 165.

54.a) Applegate, "Old Emigrant Road," p. 39.
b) Helfrich, "Applegate Trail," (1971), Vol. 9, p. 7.

55. Scott, *Independence*, p. 144.

56. Garrison, "Reminiscences," p. 26.

57.a) *Hist. of the Pac. N. W.*, Vol. 1, p. 26.
b) Cornwall, *Capt. Dunbar's Co. 1846*, OHS Mss #1509, p. 35.

58.a) Bancroft, *Works*, Vol. XXIX, p. 567.
b) Thornton, *Or. and Ca. in 1848*, Vol. 1, p. 197.
c) Morgan, *Overland in 1846*, Vol. 1, p. 194.
d) Moxley, *Southern Route*, p. 79.

59. Moxley, *Southern Route*, p. 79.

60. Garrison, "Reminiscences," p. 26.

61. Haines, *Applegate Trail*, p. 23.

62. Meacham, *Applegate Trail*, p. 10.

63.a) Bancroft, *Works*, Vol. XXIX, p. 567.
b) Thornton, *Or. and Ca. in 1848*, Vol. 1, p. 171.

64.a) Bancroft, *Works*, Vol. XXIX, p. 567.
b) Thornton, *Or. and Ca. in 1848*, Vol. 1, p. 188.

65.a) Scott, *Independence*, p. 164.
b) Moxley, *Southern Route*, p. 79.

66.a) Moxley, *Southern Route*, p. 79.
b) Steves, *Book of Remembrance*, p. 86.
c) Cornwall, *Capt. Dunbar's Co. 1846*, OHS Mss #1509, p. 30.

67.a) Thornton, *Or. and Ca. in 1848*, Vol. 1, p. 220.
b) Moxley, *Southern Route*, p. 79.
c) Cornwall, *Capt. Dunbar's Co. 1846*, OHS Mss #1509, pp. 30, 35.

68. Bancroft, *Works*, Vol. XXIX, p. 567.

69.a) Brown, "Brimfield Heroine," p. 199.
b) Meacham, *Applegate Trail*, p. 17.

c) Moxley, *Southern Route*, p. 79.

70. Ibid.

71. Corning, *History*, p. 37.

72. Scott, *Independence*, p. 166.

73.a) Meacham, *Applegate Trail*, p. 10.
b) Bancroft, *Works*, Vol. XXIX, p. 567.
c) Cornwall, *Capt. Dunbar's Co. 1846*, OHS Mss #1509, p. 35.

74. Moxley, *Southern Route*, p. 79.

75.a) Morgan, *Overland in 1846*, Vol. 1, p. 194.
b) Thornton, *Or. and Ca. in 1848*, Vol. 1, p. 188.
c) Moxley, *Southern Route*, p. 79.

76. Moxley, *Southern Route*, p. 79.

77.a) Steves, *Book of Remembrance*, p. 88.
b) Cornwall, *Capt. Dunbar's Co. 1846*, OHS Mss #1509, p. 35.

78. Moxley, *Southern Route*, p. 79.

79.a) Bancroft, *Works*, Vol. XXIX, p. 567.
b) Thornton, *Or. and Ca. in 1848*, Vol. 1, p. 188.

80.a) Morgan, *Overland in 1846*, Vol. 1, p. 194.
b) Bancroft, *Works*, Vol. XXIX, p. 567.
c) Moxley, *Southern Route*, p. 79.
d) Steves, *Book of Remembrance*, p. 86.
e) Cornwall, *Capt. Dunbar's Co. 1846*, OHS Mss #1509, pp. 30, 35.

81. Carter, *Pioneer Days*.

82. Lockley, *Pioneer Women*, p. 87.

83. Cornwall, *Capt. Dunbar's Co. 1846*, OHS Mss #1509, p. 30.

84.a) Arlie Holt, Conversation with author, 1995.
b) Bancroft, *Works*, Vol. XXIX, p. 567.
c) Helfrich, "Applegate Trail," (1971), Vol. 9, p. 27.

d) Morgan, *Overland in 1846*, Vol. 1, p. 181.
e) Steves, *Book of Remembrance*, p. 72.

85. Cornwall, *Capt. Dunbar's Co. 1846*, OHS Mss #1509, p. 35.

86.a) Bancroft, *Works*, Vol. XXIX, p. 567.
b) Moxley, *Southern Route*, p. 79.
c) Cornwall, *Capt. Dunbar's Co. 1846*, OHS Mss #1509, pp. 30, 34, 35.
d) Meacham, *Applegate Trail*, p. 22.
e) Morgan, *Overland in 1846*, Vol. 1, p. 194.
f) Steves, *Book of Remembrance*, p. 86.

87.a) Cornwall, *Capt. Dunbar's Co. 1846*, OHS Mss #1509, p. 35.
b) Moxley, *Southern Route*, p. 79.

88.a) Bancroft, *Works*, Vol. XXIX, p. 567.
b) Thornton, *Or. and Ca. in 1848*, Vol. 1, p. 188.
c) Morgan, *Overland in 1846*, Vol. 1, p. 194.

89. Morgan, *Overland in 1846*, Vol. 1, p. 398.

90. Moxley, *Southern Route*, p. 79.

91.a) Cornwall, *Capt. Dunbar's Co. 1846*, OHS Mss #1509, p. 35.
b) Dye, *Soul of America*, p. 164.

92. Jackson and Teeples, *Oregon Census Index*, p. 18.

93. Moxley, *Southern Route*, p. 79.

94.a) Lockley, *Pioneer Women*, p. 87.
b) Carter, *Pioneer Days*, p. 74.
c) Meacham, *Applegate Trail*, p. 15.
d) Moxley, *Southern Route*, p. 79.

95.a) Moxley, *Southern Route*, p. 79.
b) Garrison, *Life and Labours*, OHS Mss #1009, p. 31.

96.a) Bancroft, *Works*, Vol. XXIX, p. 567.
b) Thornton, *Or. and Ca. in 1848*, Vol. 1, p. 188.
c) Morgan, *Overland in 1846*, Vol. 1, p. 194.
d) Moxley, *Southern Route*, p. 79.

e) Cornwall, *Capt. Dunbar's Co. 1846*, OHS Mss #1509, pp. 30, 35.

97.a) Meacham, *Applegate Trail*, p. 20.
b) Helfrich, "Applegate Trail II," (1976), Vol. 14, p. 49.

98. Crews, *Smith Family*, OHS Mss #1188, p. 22.

99. Cornwall, *Capt. Dunbar's Co. 1846*, OHS Mss #1509, pp. 35, 40.
100. Garrison, "Reminiscences," p. 30.

101. Ibid., p. 26.

102.a) Bancroft, *Works*, Vol. XXIX, p. 567.
b) Thornton, *Or. and Ca. in 1848*, Vol. 1, p. 188.

103. Cornwall, *Capt. Dunbar's Co. 1846*, OHS Mss #1509, p. 35.

104.a) Morgan, *Overland in 1846*, Vol. 1, p. 194.
b) Cornwall, *Capt. Dunbar's Co. 1846*, OHS Mss #1509, pp. 30, 35.
c) Steves, *Book of Remembrance*, p. 86.

105. Steves, *Book of Remembrance*, p. 86.

106. Moxley, *Southern Route*, p. 79.

107. Ibid.

108.a) Helfrich, "Applegate Trail II," (1976), Vol. 14, p. 25.
b) Garrison, "Reminiscences," p. 10.

109. Garrison, *Life and Labours*, OHS Mss #1009, p. 10.

110. Garrison, "Reminiscences," p. 10.

111. Cornwall, *Capt. Dunbar's Co. 1846*, OHS Mss #1509, p. 35.

112. Scott, *Independence*, p. 145.

113. Helfrich, "Applegate Trail," (1971), Vol. 9, p. 7.

114. Cornwall, *Capt. Dunbar's Co. 1846*, OHS Mss #1509, p. 35.

115. Scott, *Independence*, p. 150.

116.a) Moxley, *Southern Route*, p. 79.
b) Scott, *Independence*, p. 150.

117. Moxley, *Southern Route*, p. 79.

118.a) Morgan, *Overland in 1846*, Vol. 1, pp. 195, 398.
b) Thornton, *Or. and Ca. in 1848*, Vol. 1, pp. 188, 216.
c) Moxley, *Southern Route*, p. 79.
d) Cornwall, *Capt. Dunbar's Co. 1846*, OHS Mss #1509, pp. 30, 35.

119. Cornwall, *Capt. Dunbar's Co. 1846*, OHS Mss #1509, p. 35.

120. Scott, *Independence*, p. 150.

121. Lockley, *Pioneer Women*.

122.a) Ibid., p. 81.
b) Moxley, *Southern Route*, p. 79.

123. Garrison, *Life and Labours*, OHS Mss #1009, p. 27.

124. Scott, *Independence*, p. 149.

125. Moxley, *Southern Route*, p. 79.

126. Ibid.

127. Ibid.

128. Scott, *Independence*, p. 149.

129.a) Morgan, *Overland in 1846*, Vol. 1, pp. 194, 195.
b) Bancroft, *Works*, Vol. XXIX, p. 567.
c) Meacham, *Applegate Trail*, p. 23.
d) Cornwall, *Capt. Dunbar's Co. 1846*, OHS Mss #1509, pp. 30, 35.

130. Moxley, *Southern Route*, p. 79.

131.a) Thornton, *Or. and Ca. in 1848*, Vol. 1, p. 165.
b) Moxley, *Southern Route*, p. 79.

132.a) Morgan, *Overland in 1846*, Vol. 1, p. 188.
b) Moxley, *Southern Route*, p. 79.

133.a) Scott, *Independence*, p. 148.
b) Steves, *Book of Remembrance*, p. 79.
c) Garrison, *Life and Labours*, OHS Mss #1009, p. 43.
d) Morgan, *Overland in 1846*, Vol. 1, p. 396.

134.a) Morgan, *Overland in 1846*, Vol. 1, p. 188.
b) Moxley, *Southern Route*, p. 79.

135. Moxley, *Southern Route*, p. 79.

136.a) Bancroft, *Works*, Vol. XXIX, p. 567.
b) Moxley, *Southern Route*, p. 79.

137. Cornwall, *Capt. Dunbar's Co. 1846*, OHS Mss #1509, p. 35.

138. Meacham, *Applegate Trail*, p. 11.

139. Moxley, *Southern Route*, p. 79.

140.a) Steves, *Book of Remembrance*, p. 88.
b) Cornwall, *Capt. Dunbar's Co. 1846*, OHS Mss #1509, p. 35.

141. Kay Alsing, Conversations with author, Ashland, OR, 1995-1996.

142.a) Morgan, *Overland in 1846*, Vol. 1, p. 194.
b) Bancroft, *Works*, Vol. XXIX, p. 567.
c) Thornton, *Or. and Ca. in 1848*, Vol. 1, p. 188.

143. Jackson and Teeples, *Oregon Census Index*, p. 45.

144. Morgan, *Overland in 1846*, Vol. 1, p. 194.

145.a) Bancroft, *Works*, Vol. XXIX, p. 567.
b) Helfrich, "Applegate Trail," (1971), Vol. 9, pp. 9, 22.

146.a) Bancroft, *Works*, Vol. XXIX, p. 567.

131.b) Thornton, *Or. and Ca. in 1848*, Vol. 1, p. 188.

147.a) Bancroft, *Works*, Vol. XXIX, p. 567.
b) Thornton, *Or. and Ca. in 1848*, Vol. 1, p. 211.

148.a) Bancroft, *Works*, Vol. XXIX, p. 567.
b) Thornton, *Or. and Ca. in 1848*, Vol. 1, pp. 188, 198.
c) Meacham, *Applegate Trail*, p. 21.
d) Moxley, *Southern Route*, p. 79.
e) Cornwall, *Capt. Dunbar's Co. 1846*, OHS Mss #1509, p. 35.

149. Scott, *Independence*, p. 162.

150. Cornwall, *Capt. Dunbar's Co. 1846*, OHS Mss #1509, p. 35.

151. Moxley, *Southern Route*, p. 79.

152. Scott, *Independence*, p. 143.

153. Lockley, *Pioneer Women*, p. 87.

154. Moxley, *Southern Route*, p. 79.

155. Cornwall, *Capt. Dunbar's Co. 1846*, OHS Mss #1509, p. 35.

156.a) Bancroft, *Works*, Vol. XXIX, p. 567.
b) Ronald Vern Jackson and Gary Ronald Teeples, *Oregon 1850 Territorial Census Index* (Bountiful, UT: Accelerated Indexing Systems, Inc., 1978), p. 58.

157. Garrison, "Reminiscences," pp. 26, 30.

158. Moxley, *Southern Route*, p. 79.

159.a) Bancroft, *Works*, Vol. XXIX, p. 567.
b) Morgan, *Overland in 1846*, Vol. 1, p. 181.
c) Moxley, *Southern Route*, p. 79.

160.a) Bancroft, *Works*, Vol. XXIX, p. 186.
b) Moxley, *Southern Route*, p. 79.

161. Bancroft, *Works*, Vol. XXIX, p. 567.

162.a) Ibid.

b) Thornton, *Or. and Ca. in 1848*, Vol. 1, p. 188.
c) Moxley, *Southern Route*, p. 79.
d) Cornwall, *Capt. Dunbar's Co. 1846*, OHS Mss #1509, p. 30.

163.a) Meacham, *Applegate Trail*, p. 10.
b) Brown, ed., *Man*, p. 96.
c) Moxley, *Southern Route*, p. 79.
d) Bancroft, *Works*, Vol. XXIX, p. 559.

164. Scott, *Independence*, p. 152.

165. Moxley, *Southern Route*, p. 79.

166. Steves, *Book of Remembrance*, p. 72.

167.a) Bancroft, *Works*, Vol. XXIX, p. 567.
b) Thornton, *Or. and Ca. in 1848*, Vol. 1, p. 171.
c) Meacham, *Applegate Trail*, p. 11.
d) Moxley, *Southern Route*, p. 79.

168.a) Moxley, *Southern Route*, p. 79.
b) Cornwall, *Capt. Dunbar's Co. 1846*, OHS Mss #1509, p. 35.

169. Cornwall, *Capt. Dunbar's Co. 1846*, OHS Mss #1509, p. 30.

170. Helfrich, "Applegate Trail," (1971), Vol. 9, p. 7.

171. Scott, *Independence*, p. 144.

172. Moxley, *Southern Route*, p. 79.

173. Cornwall, *Capt. Dunbar's Co. 1846*, OHS Mss #1509, p. 35.

174. Ibid., p. 30.

175. Moxley, *Southern Route*, p. 79.

176. Ibid.

177. Meacham, *Applegate Trail*, pp. 19, 21.

178.a) Moxley, *Southern Route*, p. 79.
b) Steves, *Book of Remembrance*, p. 88.

179.a) Bancroft, *Works*, Vol. XXIX, p. 19.
b) Moxley, *Southern Route*, p. 79.
c) Cornwall, *Capt. Dunbar's Co. 1846*, OHS Mss #1509, p. 35.

179.a) Bancroft, *Works*, Vol. XXIX, p. 19.
b) Moxley, *Southern Route*, p. 79.
c) Cornwall, *Capt. Dunbar's Co. 1846*, OHS Mss #1509, p. 35.

180. Cornwall, *Capt. Dunbar's Co. 1846*, OHS Mss #1509, p. 35.

181.a) Bancroft, *Works*, Vol. XXIX, p. 567.
b) Thornton, *Or. and Ca. in 1848*, Vol. 1, p. 188.

182.a) Moxley, *Southern Route*, p. 79.
b) Cornwall, *Capt. Dunbar's Co. 1846*, OHS Mss #1509, p. 35.

183. Garrison, "Reminiscences," p. 25.

184.a) Bancroft, *Works*, Vol. XXIX, p. 567.
b) Thornton, *Or. and Ca. in 1848*, Vol. 1.
c) Clark, *Eden Seekers*, p. 193.
d) Cornwall, *Capt. Dunbar's Co. 1846*, OHS Mss #1509, pp. 30, 35.

185.a) Helfrich, "Applegate Trail," (1971), Vol. 9, p. 7.
b) Scott, *Independence*, p. 138.

186.a) Carter, *Pioneer Days*, p. 83.
b) Moxley, *Southern Route*, p. 79.

187.a) Morgan, *Overland in 1846*, Vol. 1, p. 194.
b) Bancroft, *Works*, Vol. XXIX, p. 567.
c) Thornton, *Or. and Ca. in 1848*, Vol. 1, p. 198.
d) Moxley, *Southern Route*, p. 79.

188.a) Morgan, *Overland in 1846*, Vol. 1, p. 194.
b) Moxley, *Southern Route*, p. 79.

189. Steves, *Book of Remembrance*, p. 72.

190. Moxley, *Southern Route*, p. 79.

191. Steves, *Book of Remembrance*, p. 72.

192. Moxley, *Southern Route*, p. 79.

193. Steves, *Book of Remembrance*, p. 88.

194. Bancroft, *Works*, Vol. XXIX, p. 568.

195. Cornwall, *Capt. Dunbar's Co. 1846*, OHS Mss #1509, p. 35.

196.a) Bancroft, *Works*, Vol. XXIX, p. 567.
b) Helfrich, "Applegate Trail II," (1976), Vol. 14, p. 25.
c) Moxley, *Southern Route*, p. 79.

197.a) Moxley, *Southern Route*, p. 79.
b) Scott, *Independence*, p. 130.
c) Leland, "Pioneer Days." p. 2.

198. Moxley, *Southern Route*, p. 79.

199. Moxley, *Southern Route*, p. 79.

200.a) Bancroft, *Works*, Vol. XXIX, p. 567.
b) Thornton, *Or. and Ca. in 1848*, Vol. 1, p. 171.
c) Meacham, *Applegate Trail*, p. 11.
d) Moxley, *Southern Route*, p. 79.

201. Moxley, *Southern Route*, p. 79.

202. Garrison, "Reminiscences," p. 30.

203.a) Garrison, *Life and Labours*, OHS Mss #1009, p. 34.
b) Garrison, "Reminiscences," p. 30.
c) Scott, *Independence*, p. 161.
d) Moxley, *Southern Route*, p. 79.

204. Garrison, *Life and Labours*, OHS Mss #1009, p. 34.

205. Scott, *Independence*, p. 161.

206.a) Helfrich, "Applegate Trail II," (1976), Vol. 14, p. 28.
b) Scott, *Independence*, p. 209.

207.a) Helfrich, "Applegate Trail II," (1976), Vol. 14, p. 28.
b) Scott, *Independence*, p. 158.

208.a) Helfrich, "Applegate Trail II," (1976), Vol. 14, p. 28.
b) Thornton, *Or. and Ca. in 1848*, Vol. 1, p. 209.

209. Garrison, *Life and Labours*, OHS Mss #1009, p. 44.

210.a) Morgan, *Overland in 1846*, Vol. 1, pp. 186, 187.
b) Steves, *Book of Remembrance*, pp. 80, 82-84.

211. Moxley, *Southern Route*, p. 69.

212. Thornton, *Or. and Ca. in 1848*, Vol. 1, p. 234.

213. Lockley, *Pioneer Women*, p. 89.

214. Carter, *Pioneer Days*, p. 83.

215. Garrison, *Life and Labours*, OHS Mss #1009, p. 42.

216.a) Scott, *Independence*, p. 30.
b) Garrison, *Life and Labours*, OHS Mss #1009, p. 42.

217.a) Crews, *Smith Family*, OHS Mss #1188, pp. 20, 30.
b) Meacham, *Applegate Trail*, p. 21.

218. Morgan, *Overland in 1846*, Vol. 1, pp. 189-198.

219. Ibid., pp. 194, 398.

220. Ibid., p. 398.

221. Ibid., p. 193.

222. Ibid., pp. 192, 194.

223. Ibid., pp. 192, 194, 196.

224. Ibid., p. 192.

225. Ibid., pp. 192, 196.

226. Ibid., p. 192.

227. Ibid., p. 193.

228. Ibid., pp. 193, 196.

229. Ibid., p. 193.

230. Ibid., p. 194.

231. Cornwall, *Capt. Dunbar's Co. 1846*, OHS
Mss #1509, p. 39.

232. Ibid., p. 34.

APPENDIX OF
WAGONS, CAMPING EQUIPMENT, TOOLS, SUPPLIES and BELONGINGS

TERMS FOR WAGONS*
(see glossary)

puckering-string or draw-string

stakes, bolster uprights or standards

wagon bows

top, sheet or cover

wagon box or bed

bolster

axle assembly

tar bucket or grease bucket

wheel

tire

hub

Figure 1 Ox Yoke (Artifact courtesy of Southern Oregon Historical Society.)

EQUIPMENT FOR THE WAGONS* (see glossary)

roadmeter, odometer, or viameter
twenty gallon cask or wooden keg for water
wood wagon boxes
heavy ropes for holding the wagon back on steep grades
regular ropes for tying up livestock
wagon spare parts
wheel shoes
wagon jack[2]

EQUIPMENT FOR DRIVING THE TEAM* (see glossary)

whip
goad
ox yoke
ox chains
oxshoes
opodeldoc (a liniment)[3]

SPARE PARTS

pegs and shims for repairing the wheels
king bolts
nuts and bolts
linchpins
chains
axles
spokes for the wheels
six S's for chains
six open links for repairing chains
oxbows

Every six wagons should carry one spare of the following:
wagon tongue
coupling pole
king bolt and pair of hounds[4]

CAMPING EQUIPMENT

equipment
vessel to hold water
washbowl
campstool
tents, (drilled cotton) tent poles, rope and
     stakes
half-faced tent
ridge pole tent with standards
circular tent (can be put up with one pole)
lantern
candles, candle molds and tallow
tin wash tub
axes
shovel
spade with a mallet for driving picket-pins
butcher-knife, and whetstone
fish-hooks and lines
small tomahawk
spyglass (or small telescope)
bucket
iron
chamber pot[5]

bedding*
feather mattress
patchwork quilt
pillows
rubber ground cloth, oil cloth,
     gutta percha or painted
     canvas for sleeping in tents
two blankets
coverlets but not the bed
comforter[6]

private baggage
(for a three months' expedition)
comb and brush
two tooth-brushes
1 lb. castile soap
three towels
two woolen undershirts
two pair of thick cotton drawers
four pair of woolen socks
two pair of cotton socks
four colored silk handkerchiefs[7]

Figure 2 Candle Lantern owned by Applegate; Candle Mold crossed plains in 1862. (Artifacts courtesy of Southern Oregon Historical Society.)

In today's world, this list of "private baggage" might work for either gender. Although in either case, there might be a larger quantity of undergarments.

From the era this partial list of "private baggage" was taken, these items seems to be pertaining to personal effects for men. Women probably varied greatly on the amount of articles of personal effects they brought for themselves, their children and their husbands. Although I did not find a list for women, I did find a paragraph from *The Shively Guide*, by J. M. Shively, 1846 which said:

"However much help your wives and daughters have been to you at home, they can do but little for you here-herding stock, through either dew, dust, or rain, breaking brush, swimming rivers, attacking grizzly bears or savage Indians, is all out of their line of business. All they can do, is cook for camps, etceteras, &c.; nor need they have any wearing apparel, other than their ordinary clothing at home."[8]

KITCHEN COOKING UTENSILS*

coffee pot
coffee grinder
tea pot
butterchurn
two wrought-iron kettles
three-legged skillet or spider
butcher knifes
ladle
knife, fork & spoons that all fit in one handle
tin plates or pewter
cups of heavy tin with handles riveted on
mess pans (to mix bread in)
bake pan of wrought-iron (for baking bread and roasting coffee)
frying pans
dutch oven
water keg, tin or gutta percha bucket for water (Gutta-percha was
      waterproofing.)
matches[9]

Figure 3 Butter Churn, Scoop and Butter Paddle
Scoop: 1853 (Artifacts courtesy of Southern Oregon Historical Society.)

FOOD

(Main provisions and quantities per each person)

25 lbs. of bacon or pork
fresh beef driven on the hoof or dried beef
one or two milk cows (Left over milk was churned to butter by
      riding in the wagon all day.)
150 to 200 lbs. of flour
half dozen hens for laying eggs
a quantity of yeast powder for making bread
salt in double cloth sacks
pepper
saleratus (baking soda)
corn meal

hardtack
dried beans
a bushel of dried fruit
molasses
vinegar
beans and rice (They were told by some to go light on beans and
      rice because they took to long to cook and they would be
      on the move.)
tea packed in double cloth sacks
25 lbs. of sugar in double cloth sacks
15 lbs. of coffee also in double cloth sacks[10]

TOOLS FOR FIXING THINGS*

medicine cabinet	sewing box	mallets
herbs and medicines	needles and thread	a drawing knife
blue mass	pins	handsaw
quinine	scissors	auger with bits from 1/2" to 2"
opium	palm and pricker (for sewing canvas)	gimlet (a small tool for boring holes by
cathartic medicine (castor oil)	knife	hand)
bandages	ax	hammer
liniments	hatchets	spade
laudanum	awl	whetstone[12]
surgical instruments		

Supplies

ropes
whip thongs
about four pounds of assorted wrought
nails and tacks
40 lbs. of tallow
15 lbs. of black lead
tobacco
soapwhiskey
matches (corked in a bottle)
wax
bees wax
candles
twine
shoe leather
cotton cloth
buckskins for repairing harness, saddles,
bridles[11]

Figure 4 Broadaxe, Shovel and Axe Head

This shovel crossed the plaines three times. Axe Head type that helped blaze the Applegate Trail. (Artifacts courtesy of Southern Oregon Historical Society.)

GUNS

colt revolver or pistol or a pair of pistols
holster
double-barreled, percussion-lock shot gun
light rifle
old-fashioned muzzle-loading rifle
"having a percussion lock and carrying about 40 balls to the pound"
25 lbs. lead
12 lbs. best rifle powder
bullet mold
powder horn
bullet pouch
Sharps carbine
Peterson Colt
Walker Colt[13]

MUSICAL INSTRUMENTS

fiddle
banjo[14]

BELONGINGS and POSSESSIONS

farm equipment*
plow
hoe
shovel
scythe
prong-fork for pitching hay
fruit tree seedlings and garden seeds of most varieties[15]

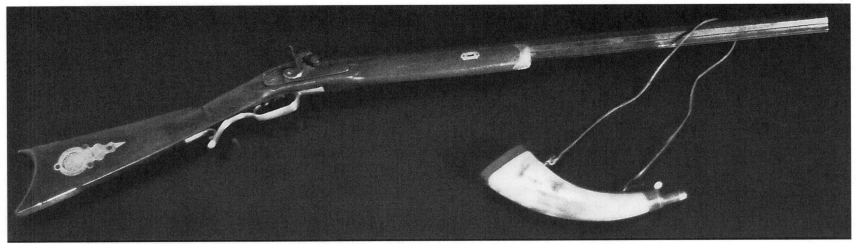

Figure 5 Long Rifle and Powder Horn
Long Rifle was brought across the plains. (Artifacts courtesy of Southern Orefgon Historical Society.)

BELONGINGS and POSSESSIONS
continued

tools for building
felling-axe for felling trees
crosscut saw
frow for splitting wood
a maul
adze for dressing the side of a
log to make it square
draw-knife for planing[16]

furniture* and heirlooms*
cookstove
rocking chair
tables
carpets[17]

furnishings*
china
silverware
fine linen
books*
plant cuttings
family album
family bible
jewelry
clothing[18]

childrens' belongings
schoolbooks
dolls[19]

clothing*
wool sack coats
rubber coats
overcoat
buckskin pants
duck trousers
woolen pantaloons (pants)
bloomers
woolen and cotton shirts
flannel shirts "open in front
with buttons"
brogans (shoes)
boots
felt hat
palm-leaf sun hat
cotton socks
sunbonnet
cotton dresses[20]

*SOME THINGS THAT WERE LEFT BEHIND
broken and abandoned wagons
dead oxen and cattle
beds and bedding
cooking utensils

tools
farm equipment
household and kitchen
furniture
carpet
books
clothing[21]

Figure 6 High Chair, Child's Shoes and Bed Coverlet
High Chair brought to Ashland, Oregon in 1853. (Artifacts courtesy of Southern Oregon Historical Society.)

1.a) Horns, *Pioneers*, p. 101.
b) George Rippey Stewart, *The California Trial: an Epic With Many Heroes* (New York, NY: McGraw-Hill, 1962), p. 110.
c) *Story of the Great American West* (Pleasantville, NY: Reader's Digest Association, 1977), p. 157.
d) Peter Watts, *A Dictionary of the Old West, 1850-1900*, (New York, NY: Alfred A. Knopf, 1977), p. 359.
e) Stewart, *California Trail*, pp. 110-112.
f) "The Oregon Trail, 1843-1993" (Special Section), *The Oregonian* (Portland, OR), March 14, 1993), p. R-29.
g) Welborn Beeson, *The Oregon & Applegate Trail Diary of Welborn Beeson in 1853* (Medford, OR: Webb Research Group, 1987), p. 26.

2.a) Frederica B. Coons, *The Trail to Oregon* (Portland, OR: Binfords & Mort, 1954), pp. 7, 39, 40.
b) Moxley, *Southern Route*, p. 26.
c) Joseph E Ware, *The Emigrants' Guide To California* (Princeton, NJ: Princeton University Press, 1932), pp. 5, 16.
d) Morgan, *Overland in 1846*, Vol. 2, p. 738.
e) Randolph B. Marcy, *The Prairie Traveler: A Handbook for Overland Expeditions* (Old Saybrook, CT: Applewood Books, no date), pp. 40, 50, 52.
f) Rounds, *Prairie Schooners*, p. 26.
g) Lambert Florin, *Western Wagon Wheels: a Pictorial Memorial to the Wheels That Won the West* (Seattle, WA: Superior Pub. Co., 1970), p. 84.
h) Horns, *Pioneers*, p. 103.
i) David Sievert Lavender, *The Overland Migrations* (Washington, D.C.: National Park Service, U.S. Department of the Interior, 1980), pp. 37, 103.
j) Stewart, *California Trail*, p. 119.
k) *Great American West*, p. 157.
l) S. H. Taylor, "Documentary Letters of S. H. Taylor to the Watertown [Wisconsin] Chronicle," *Oregon Historical Quarterly*, Vol. 22, No. 2 (Portland, OR: Oregon Historical Society, 1921), p. 139.

3.a) *Great American West*, p. 157.
b) Beeson, *Diary*, p. 25.
c) Lavender, *Overland Migrations*, p. 103.
d) Stewart, *California Trail*, p. 119.

4.a) *Great American West*, p. 156.
b) Stewart, *California Trail*, pp. 112, 119.
c) Horns, *Pioneers*, p. 103.
d) Marcy, *Prairie Traveler*, pp. 27, 40.

5.a) Ware, *Emigrants' Guide*, pp. 10, 16, 119.
b) Horns, *Pioneers*, pp. 102, 103.
c) Stewart, *California Trail*, pp. 118, 119.
d) Neil & Ting Morris, *Wagon Wheels Roll West* (New York, NY: Marshall Cavendish, 1989)
e) Florin, *Western Wagon Wheels*, p. 84.
f) Marcy, *Prairie Traveler*, pp. 40, 134.
g) Beeson, *Diary*, pp. 25, 26.
h) Garrison, "Reminiscences," p. 25.

6.a) Coons, *Trail to Oregon*, p. 7.
b) Horns, *Pioneers*, p. 102.
c) Morris & Morris, *Wagon Wheels*.
d) Ware, *Emigrants' Guide*, p. 9.
e) Marcy, *Prairie Traveler*, p. 40.
f) Lavender, *Overland Migrations*, p. 37.

7.a) Ware, *Emigrants' Guide*, p. 8.
b) Marcy, *Prairie Traveler*, p. 39.

8. Morgan, *Overland in 1846*, Vol. 4, p. 736. [This comment probably gave a lot of husbands, if they were domineering, the excuse to see that only they bought new clothes for the trip. J. M. Shively must not have met any women like Tabitha Brown.]

9.a) Coons, *Trail to Oregon*, p. 7.
b) Horns, *Pioneers*, p. 102.
c) Marcy, *Prairie Traveler*, p. 40.
d) Beeson, *Diary*, p. 25.
e) Morris & Morris, *Wagon Wheels*.
f) Morgan, *Overland in 1846*, Vol. 2, p. 735.

10.a) Bloch, *Overland to California*, p. 23.
b) Horns, *Pioneers*, p. 102.
c) Coons, *Trail to Oregon*, pp. 6, 7.
d) Marcy, *Prairie Traveler*, p. 36.
e) Lavender, *Overland Migrations*, pp. 36, 37.
f) "Oregon Trail" [*Oregonian*], p. R28.
g) Taylor, "Letters of Taylor," Vol. 22, No. 2, p. 148.
h) Stewart, *California Trail*, p. 119.

11.a) Stewart, *California Trail*, pp. 113, 119.
b) Morris & Morris, *Wagon Wheels*.
c) Marcy, *Prairie Traveler*, pp. 38, 40, 41.
d) Coons, *Trail to Oregon*, pp. 6, 7.
e) Lockley, *Pioneer Women*, p. 84.
f) Horns, *Pioneers*, p. 103.
g) Beeson, *Diary*, p. 25.
h) Florin, *Western Wagon Wheels*, p. 84.

12.a) Stewart, *California Trail*, p. 119.
b) Florin, *Western Wagon Wheels*, p. 84.
c) Coons, *Trail to Oregon*, p. 6.
d) Ware, *Emigrants' Guide*, p. 8.
e) Horns, *Pioneers*, p. 102.
f) Marcy, *Prairie Traveler*, pp. 38, 40, 41.

13.a) Beeson, *Diary*, p. 25.
b) Marcy, *Prairie Traveler*, pp. 41, 42.
c) Florin, *Western Wagon Wheels*, p. 84.
d) Ware, *Emigrants' Guide*, p. 8.
e) Horns, *Pioneers*, p. 102.
f) Morris & Morris, *Wagon Wheels*.

14. Rounds, *Prairie Schooners*, p. 89.

15.a) Horns, *Pioneers*, p. 103.
b) Chrisman, *1001 Questions*, p. 284.
c) "Oregon Trail" [*Oregonian*], p. R28.
d) Ware, *Emigrants' Guide*, p. 10.

16.a) Chrisman, *1001 Questions*, p. 284.
b) Cornwall, *Capt. Dunbar's Co. 1846*, OHS Mss #1509, p. 34.

17.a) "Oregon Trail" [*Oregonian*], p. R28.
b) Chrisman, *1001 Questions*, p. 94.

c) Horns, *Pioneers*, p. 103.
d) Rounds, *Prairie Schooners*, p. 94.
e) Thornton, *Or. and Ca. in 1848*, Vol. 1, p. 218.

18. Horns, *Pioneers*, p. 103.

19. Ibid.

20.a) Ibid.
b) Marcy, *Prairie Traveler*, p. 39.
c) Horns, *Pioneers*, p. 103.
d) "Oregon Trail" [*Oregonian*], p. R29.

21.a) Brown, "Brimfield Heroine," p. 201.
b) Carter, *Pioneer Days*, p. 79.
c) Thornton, *Or. and Ca. in 1848*, Vol. 1, pp. 218, 226.

GLOSSARY OF WAGON TERMS

There are additional terms and phases in this glossary that are not found in this book. Some descriptions have more than one phrase to express the same meaning. In the 1800's wagons and equipment were all made by hand. There were no assembly lines. There were however, wagon builders. Each wagon was still made one at a time. The person who bought the wagon usually added something to suit their specific purpose. Most wagons had their own individuality.

Axle assembly:[1] The front axle consisted of the hounds, axle, sandplate, bolster, sway bar, brail iron[2] and stakes. The front axle had a pin called a king pin that connected the axle to the rigid connecting pole or reach and allowed the front wheels and axle assembly to pivot for turning.[3] The rear axle fastened to the rear bolster, reach and hounds. The ends of the axles were lined with iron and had a hub bearing that fitted to the hub of the wheel that was also lined with iron.[4] Through the center of the wooden axle was an iron axle which extended beyond both ends of the axle. At each end was a plate and a "linchpin" to hold the wheel on.[5]

Bolster:[6] Chassis cross members that attached to the reach and the rear axle assembly. It supported the wagon box.[7]

Brail Iron: Strap iron attached to both ends of both front hounds to guide the front bolster when the axle turned.[8]

Brakes:[9] Light wagons did not have brakes;[10] prairie schooners did have brakes.[11]

Bullwhacker:[12] See teamster.

Captain:[13] On the Applegate Trail the head of the wagon train was called captain.[14] This leader was also later known as the wagon master.[15] When the head of the wagon train was known as wagon master the assistant was known as captain.[16]

Chain-locking:[17] This term referred to chaining the wheel to act as a brake[18] on typical smaller size wagons.[19]

Chocking[20] **or rough locking:**[21] If a heavy log or a large stone was used as a wheel stop for the wagon wheels, this term was called chocking or rough locking the wheels.[22] The wheels were half anchored by a heavy log to help the wagon gradually descend a grade.[23]

Conestoga Style Wagon:[24] A wagon built with similar characteristics as a Conestoga wagon. The bed usually had sloping walls at front and rear. Side walls were slightly sloped. Also known as prairie schooner.[25]

Conestoga Wagon:[26] A large freight wagon used commercially for hauling supplies primarily on the Santa Fa Trail.[27] Conestoga wagons could carry up to five tons of cargo.[28]

Connecting pole: See reach.

Coupling-pole:[29] See reach.

Dally[30] **or dolly:**[31] To wrap a rope around a tree when descending a steep grade with a wagon.[32]

Dolly:[33] See dally.

Double team:[34] To hitch two or more teams of oxen together for ascending a hill.[35]

False floor:[36] A second wooden floor of the wagon bed[37] built about 1'-0" above the wagon floor for storage.[38] Sometimes a series of wooden boxes the same height were used for the same purpose.[39]

Felloes:[40] Curved sections of the wagon wheel[41] usually made of ash.[42] See wheels.

Goad:[43] A sharp-pointed stick used to drive the oxen.[44]

Herder:[45] See stock driver.

Hounds:[46] Braces that connected from the reach or connecting pole to the bolster and axle at the rear of the wagon. They connected from the sway bar and axle to the tongue at the front of the wagon.[47]

Jockey box:[48] A tool box for the wagon and the team usually mounted on the front of the wagon[49] but sometimes mounted on the side.[50] It held grease, gloves and tools.[51]

King pin:[52] Connected the front axle assembly to the main connecting pole of the undercarriage. This allowed the wagon front wheels and axle assembly to pivot for turning.[53]

Lead Oxen:[54] Smartest and usually the smaller oxen at the front of the team to lead. The smarter of the two was usually put on the left and was the "nigh."[55]

Light Wagon:[56] Wagon commonly used by emigrants on the Oregon and Applegate Trail.[57] Most families had two or more wagons. Each wagon could carry about 3/4 ton of cargo.[58]

Odometer, roadmeter or viameter:[59] Prior to 1847,[60] emigrants used a more primitive method of measuring mileage. A cloth was tied to a wagon spoke. By measuring the diameter of the wheel and counting the wheel revolutions, they could calculate the mileage.[61]

After 1847 the roadmeter,[62] odometer or viameter[63] was an optional piece of equipment used for checking the mileage from camp to camp each day. It was a wooden gear mechanism fastened to the bed of the wagon which rotated by the revolution of the spokes on the wagon wheel. This apparatus was capable of counting up to ten miles of travel before starting over.[64]

Ox chain:[65] The ox chain was used to hook all the yoke together. The wheel oxen[66] or "wheeler"[67] yoke was hooked to a piece of iron fastened to the tongue with a pin that held it in place.[68]

Ox yoke:[69] A yoke was the harness used to hitch up two oxen at a time.[70] Each yoke mounted on top of the neck of two oxen. The back of the yoke was deeply rounded to fit the neck of the ox comfortably.[71]

Oxshoes:[72] Moon shaped iron plate used for shoeing oxen hooves. Also, moccasins of leather were worn while the feet were first tender. The hoofs could be rubbed with alcohol (or alcohol and camphor) when their feet became sore. The moccasins or oxshoes were only good to use while the feet were hardening.[73]

Ox-bow:[74] A U-shaped harness made of bent wood that went around the lower part of the neck and inside the point of the shoulder of the ox.[75] The ox bow held the ox yoke in place. It needed to be tight, but not so tight that it cut off the ox's breathing capability.[76]

Perch:[77] See reach.

Prairie Schooner:[78] A wagon built with slight boat characteristics. Walls of the bed front and rear usually sloped to make traveling across rivers easier. Prairie Schooners could carry up to one ton of cargo.[79] Conestoga wagons were a type of prairie schooner, but were too large for climbing the mountains on the emigrant trails to Oregon.[80]

Puckering-string[81] **or draw string:**[82] Draw rope used to gather the wagon top at the front and the rear of the wagon.[83]

Reach[84] **or rigid connecting pole:**[85] The main part of the undercarriage that ran the length of the wagon below the bolsters and attached to the front axle by the kingpin[86] and the rear axle between the axle and the bolster;[87] also known as coupling-pole, and perch.[88]

Rigid connecting pole:[89] See reach.

Roadmeter:[90] See odometer.

Roadometer:[91] See odometer.

Rough lock:[92] See chocking.

Running-gear[93] or undercarriage:[94] Wheels, axles, rigid connecting pole and tongue which made up the chassis.[95] Made from well-seasoned maple, poplar, hickory, ash, Osage orange, beach, elm, or oak.[96]

Sand plate: Plate between the axle and the bolster.[97]

Springs:[98] Before 1846 covered wagons were not built with springs for cushioning the ride.[99]

Stakes, bolster uprights[100] or standards:[101] Uprights that attached to the bolsters and retained the wagon box.[102]

Standards:[103] See stakes.

Stock driver[104] or herder:[105] Person who tended to and drove the herds of loose livestock at the rear of the wagon train.[106]

Subcaptain:[107] Assistant to the captain. When the head of the wagon train was known as wagon master the assistant was known as captain.[108]

Sway Bar: Connected the rear of both front hounds for stability.[109]

Tallow:[110] Fat from animals[111] that was boiled down to make candles and lubricant for the wagon axles.[112]

Tar bucket or grease bucket:[113] A covered bucket which hung on the rear axle and held a mixture of tar[114] or resin, mixed half-and-half with tallow.[115] It was used regularly for greasing the hubs and all other moving parts of the wagon. As they ran short of tar and resin, they added tallow to substitute the mixture.[116]

Team: Wagons were drawn by three[117] to eight yoke of oxen at the beginning of the Oregon Trail.[118] Three[119] or four yoke were most common,[120] but two yoke of oxen were the minimum amount required to pull a wagon.[121] By the time the emigrants with their wagons reached the Applegate Trail, they had lost one, two or as much as four yoke of oxen. They usually died from exhaustion.[122] They were faithful work animals and would sometimes fall dead from exhaustion while pulling the wagon. After they weakened, there was no hope of saving them unless they were rested.[123]

Teamster:[124] The walking driver[125] in charge of managing, driving and caring for a team of oxen.[126] This person drove the team by cracking a whip, using a goad and shouting.[127] Teamsters were also known as "bullwhacker."[128]

Tires:[129] A band of iron on the outside perimeter of the wheel to strengthen it.[130] For true strength and durability the wheel needed to fit snug against the tire.[131] When the wheels shrank up because of the dry weather, wedges made of wood were driven on both sides of the wheel between the tire and the wheel to tighten up the wheel.[132] If the wheel was to be repaired soon, the tire was temporarily tied to the wheel with a rope or a piece of raw hide.[133]

Eventually the tire would be removed and heated over a fire-pit which was made on site. The fire was made hot to shrink the tire so it would fit the wheel.[134] Under normal circumstances this would have been done at a blacksmith's shop, but there were no blacksmiths' shops on the Applegate Trail of 1846. Some wagon trains had a traveling forge on their train.[135]

Tool box: See jockey box.

Top, sheet or cover:[136] Heavy-duty canvas, muslin cotton[137] or hemp[138] used to cover the top of the wagon. It was waterproofed with paint or linseed oil.[139] The top protected the contents of the wagon from the elements. It was removed sometimes when there were strong winds[140] and pulled back for ventilation when it was hot.[141]

Undercarriage:[142] See Running-gear.

Viameter:[143] See odometer.

Wagon bed or box:[144] Wooden box that was the main body of the wagon.[145] Light wagons were approximately four or five feet wide by ten to twelve feet long[146] and two feet high[147]

Wagon bows:[148] Usually 5 or 6 made of hickory used to support the top.[149]

Wagon cover: See top

Wagon Jack:[150] Used to raise the axle of the wagon when a wheel needed to be removed. It was made of an iron-bound wood body, and had a rack-and-pinion type gear system. The vertical iron rack was raised by turning a hand crank on the side. The pinion wheel locked in place by a "pawl" which stopped the gear.[151]

Wagon sheet: See top.

Wheel shoe:[152] A curved metal shoe used as a skid plate to protect the tire from wear when the wheel was chocked or chain-locked to descend a steep grade.[153]

Wheeler:[154] Strongest oxen that were yoked to the tongue of the wagon to do more of the pulling. The one on the left was the nigh-wheeler and on the right was the off-wheeler.[155]

Wheels:[156] A wagon wheel consisted of a hub, spokes and felloes.[157] The hub was made of elm or Osage orange.[158] Spokes and felloes were made of ash.[159] The number of spokes varied from twelve to eighteen for the types of wagons used on the Applegate Trail but most were twelve, fourteen or sixteen spokes.[160] The front wheels were smaller for maneuverability in turning[161] and usually had twelve spokes.[162] The larger rear wheels allowed easier pulling[163] and usually had fourteen spokes.[164]

Whip: The whip was approximately 18 to 20 feet long and was snapped above the oxen causing a cracking sound to drive the oxen.[165]

Wooden wagon boxes:[166] Boxes of 1/2" or 3/4" pine boards[167] equal in height and built to fit together like a false floor. "...provision should be stored in half-inch pine boxes, of a uniform length, of a uniform height, and corresponding in length with the width of the wagon-bed."[168] (J.Quinn Thornton, 1848)

Yoke of oxen: (nown) A yoke was a pair of oxen. Oxen always pulled a wagon in pairs.[169] Oxen were counted in pairs called yokes.[170]

Yoke: (verb) To put a yoke on oxen.[171]

NOTES   Glossary of Wagon Terms

1. Horns, *Pioneers*, p. 101.

2. Mike Hanley, *Sagebrush and Axle Grease* (Jordon Valley, OR, 1976), p. 19.

3.a) *Great American West*, p. 157
b) Horns, Pioneers, p. 101.

4. *Great American West*, p. 157.

5. Mike Hanley, *Sagebrush and Axle Grease* (Jordon Valley, OR, 1976), p. 19.

6. Horns, *Pioneers*, p. 101.

7. Ibid.

8. *Sagebrush and Axle Grease*, p. 19.

9. Helfrich, "Applegate Trail," (1971), Vol. 9, p. 99.

10. Ibid.

11. Watts, *Dictionary*, p. 359.

12. Ibid., p. 64.

13.a) Scott, *Independence*, p. 146.
b) Rounds, *Prairie Schooners*, p. 16.
c) Ware, *Emigrants' Guide*, p. 11.
d) Marcy, *Prairie Traveler*, p. 25.

14. Scott, *Indpendence*, p. 146.

15.a) Watts, *Dictionary*, p. 75.
b) Chrisman, *1001 Questions*, p. 316.

16. Chrisman, *1001 Questions*, p. 316.

17. Watts, *Dictionary*, p. 359.

18. "The Oregon Trail & Our Valley" (Special Section), *The Medford (Oregon) Mail Tribune*, March 18, 1993), p. 8C.

19. Watts, *Dictionary*, p. 359.

20. Helfrich, *Trails West*, p. 140.

21.a) Stewart, *California Trail*, p. 112.
b) Carter, *Pioneer Days*, p. 77.

22.a) Helfrich, *Trails West*, p. 140.
b) Carter, *Pioneer Days*, p. 77.

23.a) Stewart, *California Trail*, p. 112.
b) Carter, *Pioneer Days*, p. 77.

22.a) Helfrich, *Trails West*, p. 140.
b) Carter, *Pioneer Days*, p. 77.

23.a) Watts, *Dictionary*, p. 359.
b. Helfrich, *Trails West*, p. 140.

24. Scott, *Independence*, p. 148.

25. Watts, *Dictionary*, p. 358.

26. Watts, *Dictionary*, p. 358.

27. Ibid.

28. *Great American West*, p. 156.

29. Marcy, *Prairie Traveler*, p. 26.

30. Watts, *Dictionary*, p. 359.

31. Ibid., pp. 110, 359.

32. Ibid., p. 359.

33. Ibid., pp. 110, 359.

34.a) McGlashan, *Donner Party*, p. 44.
b) Helfrich, *Trails West*, p. 140.

35. Helfrich, *Trails West*, p. 140.

36.a) Watts, *Dictionary*, p. 359.

b) Stewart, *California Trail*, p. 110.

37. Watts, *Dictionary*, p. 358.

38. Stewart, *California Trail*, p. 110.

39.a) Rounds, *Prairie Schooners*, p. 25.
b) Florin, *Western Wagon Wheels*, p. 84.

40. Frances Nankin, etd., *Cobblestone*, Vol. 2, No. 12 (December 1981)

41. *Great American West*, p. 156.

42. Nankin, ed., *Cobblestone*.

43. *Great American West*, p. 157.

44. Ibid.

45. Chrisman, *1001 Questions*, p. 316.

46. Horns, *Pioneers*, p. 101.

47.a) *Great American West*, p. 157.
b) Horns, *Pioneers*, p. 101.
c) *Sagebrush and Axle Grease*, p. 19.

48. Horns, *Pioneers*, p. 115.

49. Ibid.

50. "Oregon Trail" *[Oregonian]*, p. R29.

51. *Sagebrush and Axle Grease*, p. 20.

52. *Great American West*, p. 157.

535. Ibid.

54. Watts, *Dictionary*, p. 360.

55. Ibid.

56. Ibid., p. 359.

57. Stewart, *California Trail*, p. 108.

58. Watts, *Dictionary*, p. 359.

59.a) Coons, *Trail to Oregon*, pp. 39, 40.
b) Moxley, OHS Mss #855, p. 26.

60. Coons, *Trail to Oregon*, p. 40.

61. Moxley, OHS Mss #855, p. 26.

62. Ibid. [or roadometer (Ware, *Emigrants' Guide*, p. xxiv.)]

63. Coons, *Trail to Oregon*, pp. 39, 40.

64. Ibid.

65. Beeson, *Diary*, p. 25.

66.a) Rounds, *Prairie Schooners*, p. 47.
b) Lavender, *Overland Migrations*, p. 37.

67. Mike Hanley, Conversations with author, Jordan Valley, OR, 1996.

68.a) Watts, *Dictionary*, p. 360.
b) Mike Hanley.

69.a) Beeson, *Diary*, p. 25.
b) *Great American West*, p. 157.
c) Robert Porter, "The Fit of an Ox Yoke," *Small Farmer's Journal* (Summer, 1985), p. 26.

70. Rounds, *Prairie Schooners*, p. 47.

71. Porter, "Ox Yoke," p. 26.

72. Horns, *Pioneers*, p. 103.

73. Taylor, "Latters of Taylor," Vol. 22, No. 2, p. 139.

74.a) Watts, *Dictionary*, p. 233.
b) Horns, *Pioneers*, p. 103.

75.a) Porter, "Ox Yoke," pp. 26, 27.
b) Watts, *Dictionary*, p. 233.

76. Porter, "Ox Yoke," pp. 26, 27.

77. Marcy, *Prairie Traveler*, p. 26.

78.a) Watts, *Dictionary*, p. 358.
b) *Great American West*, p. 157.

79. "Oregon Trail" *[Oregonian]*, p. R28.

80. Watts, *Dictionary*, p. 358.

81. Stewart, *California Trail*, p. 110.

82. Horns, *Pioneers*, p. 101.

83.a) Stewart, *California Trail*, p. 110.
b) Horns, *Pioneers*, p. 110.

84. Horns, *Pioneers*, p. 101.

85. *Great American West*, p. 157.

86. *Great American West*, p. 157.

87. Horns, *Pioneers*, p. 101.

88. Marcy, *Prairie Traveler*, p. 26.

89. *Great American West*, p. 157.

90. Moxley, OHS Mss #855, p. 26.

91. Ware, *Emigrants' Guide*, p. xxiv.

92. Carter, *Pioneer Days*, p. 77.

93. Stewart, *California Trail*, p. 111.

94. Horns, *Pioneers*, p. 101.

95. Ibid.

96. Stewart, *California Trail*, p. 111.

97. *Sagebrush and Axle Grease*, p. 19.

98. Stewart, *California Trail*, p. 112.

99.a) Ibid., p. 112.
b) Mike Hanley.

100. *Great American West*, p. 157.

101. *Sagebrush and Axle Grease*, p. 19.

102. *Great American West*, p. 157.

103. *Sagebrush and Axle Grease*, p. 19.

104. Scott, *Independence*, p. 141.

105. Chrisman, *1001 Questions*, p. 316.

106.a) Watts, *Dictionary*, p. 163.
b) Carter, *Pioneer Days*, p. 89.

107. Chrisman, *1001 Questions*, p. 316.

108. Ibid.

109. *Sagebrush and Axle Grease*, p. 19.

110.a) Watts, *Dictionary*, p. 331.
b) Stewart, *California Trail*, p. 112.
c) Horns, *Pioneers*, p. 101.

111.a) Watts, *Dictionary*, pp. 331-332.
b) Stewart, *California Trail*, p. 112.

112. Watts, *Dictionary*, p. 331.

113.a) Stewart, *California Trail*, p. 112.
b) Horns, *Pioneers*, p. 101.
c) Watts, *Dictionary*, p. 359.

114. Marcy, *Prairie Traveler*, p. 40.

115.a) Stewart, *California Trail*, p. 112.
b) Horns, *Pioneers*, p. 101.

116. "Oregon Trail" *[Oregonian]*, p. R29.

117. James Hewitt, ed., *Eye-Witnesses to Wagon Trains West* (New York, NY: Charles Scribner's Sons, 1973, p. VI.

118.a) Rounds, *Prairie Schooners*, p. 17.
b) Watts, *Dictionary*, p. 359.

119. Stewart, *California Trail*, p. 115.

120. Ware, *Emigrants' Guide*, p. 8.

121. Ibid., p. 115.

122.a) Lavender, *Overland Migrations*, p. 37.
b) b) Hewitt, ed., *Eye-Witnesses*, p. 49.

124.a) Chrisman, *1001 Questions*, p. 316.
b) Garrison, *Life and Labours*, OHS Mss #1009, p. 32.

125. Watts, *Dictionary*, p. 360.

126.a) Carter, *Pioneer Days*, p. 78.
b) Garrison, *Life and Labours*, OHS Mss #1009, p. 32.

127.a) Chrisman, *1001 Questions*, p. 316.
b) *Great American West*, p. 157.

128.a) Chrisman, *1001 Questions*, pp. 316, 331.
b) Watts, *Dictionary*, p. 64.

129.a) Stewart, *California Trail*, p. 112.
b) Horns, *Pioneers*, p. 101.

130. Stewart, *California Trail*, p. 112.

131. Marcy, *Prairie Traveler*, p. 27.

132.a) Stewart, *California Trail*, p. 112.
b) Watts, *Dictionary*, p. 359.
c) Marcy, *Prairie Traveler*, p. 71.

133. Marcy, *Prairie Traveler*, p. 72.

134.a) Morris & Morris, *Wagon Wheels*, p. 112.
b) Mike Hanely.

135. Marcy, *Prairie Traveler*, p. 72.

136.a) Stewart, *California Trail*, p. 111.
b) Horns, *Pioneers*, p. 101.
c) Ware, *Emigrants' Guide*, p. 8.

d) Mike Hanley.

137.a) Stewart, *California Trail*, p. 111.
b) Horns, *Pioneers*, p. 101.

138. "Oregon Trail" *[Tribune]*, p. 8C.

139.a) Stewart, *California Trail*, p. 111.
b) "Oregon Trail" *[Tribune]* p. 8C.

140. Stewart, *California Trail*, p. 111.

141. *Great American West*, p. 156.

142. Horns, *Pioneers*, p. 101.

143. Coons, *Trail to Oregon*, pp. 39, 40.

144.a) Horns, *Pioneers*, p. 101.
b) Stewart, *California Trail*, p. 110.

145. Stewart, *California Trail*, p. 110.

146. Horns, *Pioneers*, p. 101.

147. Watts, *Dictionary*, p. 359.

148.a) Stewart, *California Trail*, p. 110.
b) Horns, *Pioneers*, p. 101.
c) Beeson, *Diary*, p. 26.

149.a) Stewart, *California Trail*, p. 110.
b) Watts, *Dictionary*, p. 359.
c) "Oregon Trail" *[Tribune]*, p. 8C
d) "Oregon Trail" *[Oregonian]*, p. R29.

150. *Great American West*, p. 157.

151. Ibid.

152. *Great American West*, p. 157.

153.a) Ibid., 157.
b) "Oregon Trail" *[Tribune]*, p. 8C

154. Watts, *Dictionary*, p. 365.

155. Ibid., p. 360.

156. Stewart, *California Trail*, p. 111.

157. *Great American West*, p. 156.

158.a) Stewart, *California Trail*, p. 111.
b) Marcy, *Prairie Traveler*, p. 26.

159.a) Nankin, ed., *Cobblestone*.
b) Stewart, *California Trail*, p. 111.

160. Leonard Everett Fisher, *The Oregon Trail* (New York, NY: Holiday House, 1990)

161. "Oregon Trail" *[Tribune]*, p. 8C.

162.a) Horns, *Pioneers*, p. 101.
b) Lavender, *Overland Migrations*, p. 39.
c) Horns, *Pioneers*, pp. 108, 198.
d) Florin, *Western Wagon Wheels*, pp. 82, 87, 101.

163. Watts, *Dictionary*, p. 359.

164.a) Horns, *Pioneers*, p. 100.
b) Lavender, *Overland Migrations*, p. 38.
c) Horns, *Pioneers*, pp. 108, 198.
d) Bill & Jan Moeller, *The Oregon Trail: a Photographic Journey* (Wilsonville, OR: Beautiful America Pub. Co., 1985), pp. 6, 51.
e) Florin, *Western Wagon Wheels*, pp. 82, 86, 101.

165. *Great American West*, p. 157.

166.a) Rounds, *Prairie Schooners*, p. 26.
b) Coons, *Trail to Oregon*, p. 7.

167.a) Morgan, *Overland in 1846*, Vol. 2, p. 734.
b) Florin, *Western Wagon Wheels*, p. 84.

168. Florin, *Western Wagon Wheels*, p. 84.

169. Rounds, *Prairie Schooners*, p. 47.

170.a) *Great American West*, p. 157.
b) Beeson, *Diary*, p. 19.

171. Mike Hanley.

COMPLETE BIBLIOGRAPHY

BOOKS

Applegate, Shannon. *Skookum: an Oregon Pioneer Family's History and Lore.* New York, NY: Beech Tree Books, 1988.

Bancroft, Hubert Howe. *The Works of Hubert Howe Bancroft*, Vol. I & II. San Francisco, CA: The History Company, Publishers, 1886.

Barken, Lavola J. *Land of the North Umpquas: Peaceful Indians of the West.* Grants Pass, OR: Te-Cum-Tom Publications, 1973.

Beeson, Welborn. *The Oregon & Applegate Trail Diary of Welborn Beeson in 1853.* Medford, OR: Webb Research Group, 1987.

Binns, Archie Fred. *Peter Skene Ogden: Fur Trader.* Portland, OR: Binfords & Mort, 1967.

Bloch Jr., Louis M., ed. *Overland to California in 1859: A Guide for Wagon Train Travelers.* Cleveland, OH: Bloch and Company, 1983.

Brown, Wilford H., ed. *This Was a Man.* North Hollywood, CA: Camas Press, 1971.

Brown, William S. *California Northeast: The Bloody Ground.* Oakland, CA: Biobooks, 1951.

Carey, Charles Henry. *A General History of Oregon Prior to 1861* (2 Vol.). Portland, OR: Metropolitan Press, 1935.

Carter, Tolbert. *Pioneer Days.* Portland, OR: Transactions of the Oregon Pioneers Association, 1906.

Chrisman, Harry E. *The 1001 Most-Asked Questions About the American West.* Chicago, IL: Shallow Press, 1982.

Clark, Malcolm. *Eden Seekers: the Settlement of Oregon, 1818-1862.* Boston, MA: Houghton Miffin Company, 1981.

Coons, Frederica B. *The Trail to Oregon.* Portland, OR: Binfords & Mort, 1954.

Corning, Howard McKinley. *Dictionary of Oregon History: Compiled From the Research Files of the Former Oregon Writer's Project with Much Added Material.* Portland, OR: Binfords & Mort, 1989.

Curran, Harold. *Fearful Crossing: The Central Overland Trail Through Nevada.* Reno, NV: Great Basin Press, 1982.

Dicken, Samuel Newton. *The Making of Oregon: a Study in Historical Geography.* Portland, OR: Oregon Historical Society, 1979.

Dye, Eva Emery. *The Soul of America: An Oregon Iliad.* New York, NY: The Press of the Pioneers, Inc., 1934.

Egan, Ferol. *Fremont: Explorer for a Restless Nation.* Garden City, NY: Doubleday & Company, Inc., 1977.

Fisher, Leonard Everett. *The Oregon Trail.* New York, NY: Holiday House, 1990.

Florin, Lambert. *Western Wagon Wheels: a Pictorial Memorial to the Wheels That Won the West.* Seattle, WA: Superior Pub. Co., 1970.

Fogdall, Alberta Brooks. *Royal Family of the Columbia: Dr. John McLoughlin and Family.* Fairfield, WA: Ye Galleon Press, 1978.

Franzwa, Gregory M. *Maps of the Oregon Trail.* Gerald, MO: The Patrice Press, 1982.

Ghent, William James. *The Road to Oregon: A Chronicle of the Great Emigrant Trail.* New York, NY: Green and Co., 1929.

Haines, Francis. *The Applegate Trail: Southern Emigrant Route.* Ashland, OR: The American Revolution Bicentennial Commission of Oregon, 1976.

Helfrich, Devere. *Emigrant Trails West: a Guide to Trail Markers Placed by Trails West, Inc. Along the California, Applegate, Lassen and Noble's Emigrant Trails in Idaho, Nevada, and California.* Reno, NV: Trails West, 1984.

Hanley, Mike. *Sagebrush and Axle Grease.* Jordon Valley, OR: (Publisher unknown), 1976.

Hewitt, James, ed. *Eye-Witnesses to Wagon Trains West.* New York, NY: Charles Scribner's Sons, 1973.

History of the Pacific Northwest, Vol. 1 & 2. Portland, OR: North Pacific History Co., 1889.

Hixon, Adrietta Applegate. *On to Oregon.* Fairfield, WA: Ye Galleon Press, 1973.

Holmes, Kenneth L. *Ewing Young Master Trapper.* Portland, OR: Binfords & Mort, for the Peter Binford Foundation, 1967.

Hoover, Mildred Brook, Hero Eugene Rensch and Ethel Grace Rensch. *Historic Spots in California.* Stanford, CA: Stanford University Press, 1966.

Horns, Hudson. *The Old West: The Pioneers.* New York, NY: Time-Life Books (no date).

Hough, Emerson. *54-40 or Fight.* New York, NY: A. L. Burt Company, 1909.

Hunt, Thomas H. *Ghost Trails to California.* American West Publishing Company, 1974.

Indians of the Rogue Valley. Medford, OR: Jackson County Extension Office of Oregon State University, 1980.

Jackson, Ronald Vern, and Gary Ronald Teeples. *Oregon 1850 Territorial Census Index.* Bountiful, UT: Accelerated Indexing Systems, Inc., 1978.

LaLande, Jeffrey M. *First Over the Siskiyous: a Commentary on Peter Skene Ogdon's 1826-1827 Journey Through the Oregon-California Borderlands.* Portland, OR: Oregon Historical Society Press, 1987.

Lavender, David Sievert. *The Overland Migrations.* Washington, D.C.: National Park Service, U.S. Dept. of the Interior, 1980.

Lawrence, Mark. *Applegate Trail Markers.* Lawrence, 1979 (Location not listed).

Lockley, Fred. *Conversations With Pioneer Women.* Eugene, OR: Rainy Day Press, 1981.

Marcy, Randolph B. *The Prairie Traveler: A Handbook for Overland Expeditions.* Old Saybrook, CT: Applewood Books, no date.

McArther, Lewis A. *Oregon Geographic Names.* Portland, OR: Oregon Historical Society Press, 1992.

McGlashan, C. F. *History of the Donner Party: a Tragedy of the Sierra.* Stanford, CA: Stanford University Press, 1947.

Meacham, Walter E. *Applegate Trail.* Portland, OR: printed by James, Kerns & Abbott, 1947.

Meeker, Ezra. *Old Emigrant Trail: Story of the Lost Trail to Oregon.* Medford, OR: Webb Research Group, 1993.

Moeller, Bill & Jan. *The Oregon Trail: a Photographic Journey.* Wilsonville, OR: Beautiful America Pub. Co., 1985.

Moore, Lucia. *The Story of Eugene.* New York, NY: Stratford House, 1949.

Morgan, Dale Lowell. *Jedediah Smith and the Opening of the West.* Indianapolis, IN: Bobbs-Merrill, 1953.

_____. *Overland in 1846: Diaries and Letters of the California-Oregon Trail*, Vol. 1 & 2. Georgetown, CA: Talisman Press, 1963.

Morris, Neil & Ting. *Wagon Wheels Roll West*. New York, NY: Marshall Cavendish, 1989.

Parrish, Philip Hammon. *Before the Covered Wagon*. Portland, OR: Binfords & Mort., c.1931.

Rickett, Harold William. *Wild Flowers of the United States*, Vol. 5. New York, NY: McGraw-Hill Book Company, 1971.

Robertson, Frank C. *Fort Hall: Gateway to the Oregon Country*. New York, NY: Hastings House, 1963.

Roske, Ralph J. *Everyman's Eden: A History of California*. New York, NY: The MacMillan Company, 1968.

Rounds, Glen. *The Prairie Schooners*. New York, NY: Holiday House, Inc., 1968.

Rucker, Maude Applegate. *The Oregon Trail and Some of it's Blazers*. New York, NY: W. Neale, 1930.

Schafer, Joseph PhD. *Jessie Applegate Pioneer and State Builder*. Eugene, OR: The University of Oregon Bulletin, 1912.

Schlesser, Norman Dennis. *Bastion of Empire, the Hudson's Bay Company's Fort Umpqua: Being a Narrative of the Early Explorations and the Fur Trade in Douglas County*. Oakland, OR: Oakland Printing Co., c.1973.

Steves, Sarah Hunt. *Book of Remembrance of Marion County, Oregon, Pioneers 1840-1860*. Portland, OR: The Berncliff Press, 1927.

Stewart, George Rippey. *The California Trial: an Epic with Many Heroes*. New York, NY: McGraw-Hill, 1962.

Story of the Great American West. Pleasantville, NY: Reader's Digest Association, 1977.

Sutton, Jack. *The Mythical State of Jefferson: a Pictorical History of Early Northern California and Southern Oregon*. Medford, OR: Josephine County Historical Society, 1973.

_____. *The Pictorial History of Southern Oregon and Northern California*. Grants Pass, OR: The Grants Pass Bulletin, 1959.

Thornton, Jessy Quinn. *Oregon and California in 1848*. New York, NY: Arno Press, 1973.

Ware, Joseph E. *The Emigrants' Guide To California*. Princeton, NJ: Princeton University Press, 1932.

Watts, Peter. *A Dictionary of the Old West, 1850-1900*. (New York, NY: Alfred A. Knopf, 1977).

Wheeler, Sessions S. *The Nevada Desert*. Caldwell, ID: The Caxton Printers, Ltd., 1971.

Zucker, Jeff. *Oregon Indians: Culture, History & Current Affairs*. Portland, OR: Western Imprints, the Press of the Oregon Historical Society, 1983.

PERIODICALS

MAGAZINES

Applegate, Lindsay. "The Applegate Trail." *Overland Journal* (Oregon-California Trails Association), Vol. 2 No. 1 (Spring, 1993).

_____. "Notes and Reminiscences of Laying Out and Establishing the Old Emigrant Road into Southern Oregon in the Year 1846." *Oregon Historical Quarterly*, Vol. 22, No. 1 (March, 1921).

"The Applegate Trail: 1846-1883 The Southern Route." *The Trail Marker*, Vol. 5 No. 1 (Summer,1994).

Atwood, Kay. "'As Long as the World Goes On': The Table Rocks and the Takelma" *Oregon Historical Quarterly*, Vol. 95, No. 4 (Winter 1994-95).

Brown, Tabitha. "A Brimfield Heroine." *Oregon Historical Quarterly*, Vol. 5, No. 2 (June, 1904).

Burchard, Mildred Baker. "Scott's and Applegate's Old South Road." *Oregon Historical Quarterly*, Vol. 41, No. 4 (December, 1942).

Elliott, T. C. "The Peter Skene Ogden Journals." *Oregon Historical Quarterly*, Vol. 11, No. 4 (December, 1923).

Garrison, A. H. "Reminiscences of Abraham Henry Garrison-Over the Oregon Trail in 1846." *Overland Journal* (Oregon-California Trails Association), Vol. 2, No. 2 (Summer, 1993).

Helfrich, Dever & Helen. "Applegate Trail." *Klamath Echoes*, Vol. 9 (Klamath Falls, OR: Klamath County Historical Society), 1971.

_____. "Applegate Trail II: 'West of the Cascades'." *Klamath Echoes*, Vol. 14 (Klamath Falls, OR: Klamath County Historical Society), 1976.

Maloney, Alice B. "Camp Sites of Jedediah Smith on the Oregon Coast." *Oregon Historical Quarterly*, Vol. 41, No. 3 (September, 1940).

_____. "Hudson's Bay Company in California." *Oregon Historical Quarterly*, Vol. 37, No. 1 (March, 1936).

Nankin, Frances, ed. *Cobblestone*, Vol. 2, No. 12 (December, 1981).

"News and Comment: Monuments and Memorials." *Oregon Historical Quarterly*, Vol. 31, No. 3 (September, 1930).

"News and Comment: Monuments and Memorials." *Oregon Historical Quarterly*, Vol. 32, No. 2 (June, 1931).

Porter, Robert. "The Fit of an Ox Yoke." *Small Farmer's Journal* (Summer, 1985).

Sargent, Alice Applegate. "A Sketch of the Rogue River Valley and Southern Oregon History." *Oregon Historical Quarterly*, Vol. 22, No. 1 (March, 1921).

Scott, Leslie M. "John Work's Journey From Vancouver to Umpqua River, and Return, in 1834." *Oregon Historical Quarterly*, Vol. 24, No. 3 (September, 1923).

Stone, Buena Cobb. "Southern Route into Oregon: Notes and a New Map." *Oregon Historical Quarterly*, Vol. 47, No. 2 (June, 1946).

Taylor, S. H. "Documentory Letters of S. H. Taylor to the Watertown [Wisconsin] Chronicle." *Oregon Historical Quarterly*, Vol. 22, No. 2 (June, 1921).

Winther, Oscar O. "Commercial Routes From 1792 to 1843 by Sea and Overland." *Oregon Historical Quarterly*, Vol. 42, No. 3 (September, 1941).

NEWSPAPERS

Applegate, Jesse. "Applegate's Way Bill." *The Oregon Spectator* (Oregon City, OR), April 6, 1848.

"The First Passenger Train." *The Ashland Daily Tidings* (Ashland, OR), May 9, 1884.

Leland, J. A. C. "Pioneer Days on Grave Creek Seen Again in Memory." *Grants Pass Daily Courier* (Grants Pass, OR), January 23, 1934.

"The Oregon Trail, 1843-1993" (Special Section). *The Oregonian* (Portland, OR), March 14, 1993.

"The Oregon Trail & Our Valley" (Special Section). *The Mail Tribune* (Medford, OR) March 18, 1993.

MANUSCRIPT COLLECTIONS

Scott, Levi. *From Independence to Independence.* Sitka, AL: unpublished
    manuscript by James Layton Collins, 1967.

Cornwall, Narcissa. *Cornwall Family, Papers: Fort Hall to Oregon, Captain
    Dunbar's Company, 1846.* Portland, OR: Oregon Historical Society
    Mss #1509, 1926.

Crews, Angeline, (Smith). *Smith (William) Family, Recollections of Angeline
    Smith Crews.* Portland, OR: Oregon Historic Society, Mss #1188,
    1886.

Garrison, A. E. *Life and Labours of Rev. A. E. Garrison.* Monmouth, OR:
    Published by the Garrison Clan, 1943.
    Portland, OR: Oregon Historical Society, Mss #1009

Moxley, W. A. *Papers, The Scott-Applegate, or Southern Route to Oregon.*
    Portland, OR: Oregon Historical Society, Mss #855, 1950.

Nichols, Claude W. *The South Road: Its Development and Significance.*
    Master's Thesis, University of Oregon, 1953.

High Rock Canyon, 27, 44, **45**, 46, 47

High Rock Lake, 27

Hill Creek, 106

Holman, Mr., 102, 126

Holt, Thomas, 112, 113, 114, 115, 116, 117, 118, 126

Hoover, Martin, 36, 40, 124

Horse Mountain, 54

Hot Creek, 25

Hot Springs Valley, 33, 34

Howell, Mr., 115, 126

Hudson, Mr., 58, 125

Hudson's Bay brigade, 11

H u d s o n ' s B a y Company, 17, 23, 118

Hudson's Bay pack trail, 10, 12, 23

Hudson's Bay Trail, 8

Humboldt, Alexander von, 13

Humboldt River, 13, 29, 33, 34, 36, 37, 40, 51

Humboldt Sink, 40

Humphrey, Mr., 96, 125

Humphrey, Mrs., 85

Hutchins, Mr., 115, 126

Idaho, 13, 15, 33, 50

Illinois, 30

I n d e p e n d e n c e, Missouri, 30

Indian trail, 69

Iowa, 30

Iron Point, 36

Jackson, President Andrew, 12

Jacobs, Mr., 125

Jenkins, Mr., 114, 117, 125, 126

Jenny Creek, 25, 65

Jenny Creek Wagon Slide, 65

Joaquin River, 11

"Joe" ("Captain's subchief"), 119

John Day River, 15, 16

Jones, Jack, 79, 126

Jones, John (or Jack), 123, 126

Jones, John, 23, 28, 29, 81

Judge Deady, 71,

Jump Off Joe Creek, 24, 78

Junction City, Oregon, 110

Kalowatset tribe, **8**, 8

Keene Creek, 25, 68

Keene Creek Diversion Dam, 68

Keene Creek Slide, 65

Keene Creek Wagon Slide, 65, 68

Kelley, Hall J., 11

Kelly, Mr., 125

Kennedy, Mr. Ezekiel, 118, 125

Kennedy, Mrs. Ezekiel, 118, 125

Keno, Oregon, 62

Kentucky, 37

Kiethly, William, 125

Kirquendall Senior, William, 125

Kirquendall, William, 34, 100, 123, 126

Klamath (Clamet) Lake, 30

Klamath Basin, 23

Klamath Echoes, 68

Klamath Junction, 69

Klamath Lake, 54, 56, 59

Klamath region, 9

Klamath River, 25, **26**, 59, 62, **62**, 63

Klamath tribes, **8**, 9

Labin, Mr., 82

LaCreole, 23

LaCreole River, 15

LaFramboise, Michel, 10

Lake Malheur, 16

Lancefield, 51

Lancefield, Robert A., 51, 65, 95, 97, 98, 105, 110, 125

Lassen Pass, 51

Lassen, Peter, 51

Latgawa tribe, **8**, 8, 9

laudanum, 42

Lease, Jacob P., 12

Lebo, Issac, 58, 105, 110

Lebo, Mr. (or Leabo), 125

Lebo, Mrs. Isaac (or Leabo), 125

Lee, Jason, 12

Lee, Wilson, 125

Leonard Hot Springs, 50

Lewis, H. C., 115

Leyland, Richard, 10

light column, 15

Lincoln, Oregon, 68

Linville, Mary, 102

Linville, Mr. Harrison (or Loveland), 33, 125

Linville, Mrs. Harrison (or Loveland), 125

Linville, Richard, 102

Lippincott, Mr. (or Lippincot), 125

"Little Mountain Pass," 47

Little Sandy, 36

Long, Mr. John, 125

Long, Mrs. John, 125

Long Prairie, 25

Long Tom "Bath," 112

Long Tom Creek tribe, **8**, 8

Long Tom River, 110, 112, 113, **113**, 114

Long Valley, 47, **47**

Lost Lake, 52

Lost River, 26, 27, 51, 53, 54, 56, 58

Lovelady, Mr. Thomas J., 37, 47, 96, 117, 125

Loveland, Mrs. Thomas J., 37, 47, 96, 117

Lovlin, Mr. and Mrs. (Lovelady or Lovelen), 125

Lower Klamath Lake, 16, 25, 26, **27**, 54, **55**, 58, 59, 62

Lower Table Rocks, 74

Lower Umpqua tribe, **8**, 8

Lowland Takelma tribe, **8**, 8

Luckiamute, River, 8, 15, 113, 114, **115**

Luckiamute tribe, 8

Mackinaw boat, 15

Malheur Mountains, 16

Malheur River, 16

Malin, Oregon, 54

Mammoth Springs, 53

Martin, William, 15

Mary's River (Oregon), 16, 110, 112, 113, 114, 115

Mary's River (Nevada), 13, 36

Mary's River tribe, 8

Massacre Lake, 47

Massacre Spring, 47

McClellan, Alexander, 15

McCloud's River, 10

McFuller, Mr., 16, 113

McGinty Point, 51

McGinty Reservoir, 51

McKay, Thomas, 9, 10, 13

McKinlay, Archibald, 15

McLeod, Alexander Roderick, 10

McLoughlin, Doctor John, 9

Medford, Oregon, 71

Meek Cut-off, 16

Meek, Joe, 12

Meek, Stephen H., 13, 16

Merlin, Oregon, 78, 82

Methodist minister, 117

Methodist Mission, 12

Middle (Alkali) Lake, 50

Middle Fork of the Willamette River, 110

Miller, Richard, 125

missionaries, 12

Missouri, 30, 113

Modoc Country, 54

Modoc Indians, 52, 54

Modoc Lake, 52

Modoc Mountains, 54

Modoc National Forest, 52

Modoc tribe, **8**, 9

Mohawk tribe, **8**, 8, 9

Molalla bands, **8**, 8

Montana, 50

Monterey, California, 11

Morin, Josiah, 47, 71, 74, 89, 90, 125

Morin, Labin, 125

Mount Hood, 16

Mount Shasta, 54

Mud Meadow, 27, 46

Muddy Creek tribe, **8**, 8

Myrtle Creek, Oregon, 95, 97, **98**

National Park, 33

Native American trade routes, 13

Native Americans (Indians), 8

Nelson, Joseph, 119

Nelson, Joshua, 126

Nesmith, J. W., 15

Nevada, 15, 36, 50, **53**, 65

Nevada desert, 16

new cut-off, 33

"new Southern Road," 122

New Year's Day, 118

Newberg, Oregon, 11

Newton Creek, 101

Newton, Mr., John, 47, 66, 68, 100, 101, 125

Newton, Mrs. John, Mrs., 100, 101, 113, 125

Newton, Thomas, 125

ERRATA

Page 15 and 23, LaCreole should be: the LaCreole

Page 8, 15, 115 and 116, Rickreall River
    should be: Rickreall Creek

Page 22, endnote 284., p. 100. should be: pp. 100, 102.

Page 112, Thomas Holt was living north of the Rickreall River
    should be: on the Santiam River

Page 124, Mr. John D. Bounds
    should be: Mr. John B. Bounds

Page 124 and 125, More emigrants who died on the trail:
    Crowley, Mrs. Calvin (and child who died at birth);
    Curtendall, James; Davidson, (son of Andrew);
    Henderson, Salita (or Lettie);
    Linville, Mrs. Mary (or Loveland);
    Smith, Louisa and Smith, William M.

Back Cover (Reference Card): VII, 112p. should be: 158 p.

ACKNOWLEDGEMENTS

The Author's Acknowledgments

This book would not have come to life so well without the help of many friends and experts in their respective fields. First and foremost, thanks go to the people that helped the most: Ethel Emerson, Oral Thompson, Barbara Holmes and William Ashworth for proofing and helping edit; and Kay Alsing and Arlie Holt for their help in contributing to the historical accuracy.

I would also like to acknowledged the following individuals, friends and their institutions for their generous support and contributions: Amy Armstrong, Gwyneth Raqosine, William Ashworth, Jennifer Cook-Sterling, Dolores Marx, Nola Hight, reference librarians and Fran Bowden, children's reference librarian of the Ashland Public Library, Ashland, Oregon; Barbara Holmes, Lincoln School librarian, Ashland, Oregon; Ruth Monick, reference librarian, Deborah A. Cook, head of circulation services, Harold Otness, reference librarian and Kelly Skogseth, reference technician, Southern Oregon State College Library, Ashland, Oregon; Peter Stark, map librarian, University of Oregon, Eugene, Oregon; Joanne Perry, map librarian, Oregon State University, Corvallis, Oregon; Terry Skibby, Ashland Heritage Committee; Susan Moulder, Talent Historical Society; Keith & Joe Arnold and Andy Hammond, Oregon California Trails Association; Carol Harbison-Samuelson, Kathy Enright, Sandra Marchese and Jacque Sundstrand, reference librarians, Janette Merriman, Curator of Collections and Mary Ames B. Sheret, collections manager, Southern Oregon Historical Society, Medford, Oregon; Garbriele Sperling and Kris White manuscripts department, Oregon Historical Society, Portland, Oregon; Teresa Fouste, reference librarian, Josephine County Library, Grants Pass, Oregon; Nickie Holden, United States Geological Survey, Denver, Colorado; Elaine Maruhn, The University of Nebraska Press of Bison Books, Lincoln, Nebraska; Marilyn Holt, Overland Journal, Oregon-California Trails Association, Independence, Missouri; Charles H. Hurst, Oregon Land Surveyor (retired); George R. Burrel, Oregon Land Surveyor; Roger Roberts, Jackson County Surveyor and Sharon Katzenbach, office supervisor, Jackson County Surveyor's Office, Medford, Oregon; Cythia Gardener, Henry Montes, Charley Tucker and John Oltman, Oregon Department of Transportation; Terry Nickerson, Wayne Rodgers, Craig Wanless and Frank Tuers, United States Department of the Interior, Bureau of Land Office; Bob Ezell, Lane County Surveyor's Office, Eugene, Oregon; Mary Janssen, AAA Oregon/Idaho; Steven M. Johnson, Public Works Director and Micky Beach, City Planner, Myrtle Creek, Oregon; and Martin Lugus, U. S. Timberland, Klamath Falls, Oregon.

I would also like to thank the following individuals and friends for their help and support: Lida Childers, Katherine and Margaret Ballard, Jeffrey M. LaLande, Kay Atwood, Darle Runnels, Betty Cox, Beverly Hilterbrand, Edmond & Cleeta Polk, Gene & Patricia Holden, Leslie & Geneva Harwood, and Donald E. Rowlett.

Last, but certainly not least I would like to thank those who have been so patient with me through the many months it took to complete this book. Special thanks to Barbara Holmes who encouraged me to begin a book; Terry Skibby for helping me get interested in Lindsay Applegate and the Applegate Trail in Ashland; and my mom, Ethel Emerson for her encouragement and faith in me.

I realize in mentioning many people who helped with this book I have not mentioned everyone involved. I appreciate and would like to thank all those involved in any way to make this book a reality.